☙ CATO ☙
SUPREME COURT
REVIEW

2024—2025

CATO SUPREME COURT REVIEW

2024—2025

ROBERT A. LEVY
CENTER FOR CONSTITUTIONAL STUDIES

INSTITUTE

Washington, D.C.

THE CATO SUPREME COURT REVIEW (ISBN 978-1-964524-79-5) is published annually at the close of each Supreme Court term by the Cato Institute, 1000 Massachusetts Ave., N.W.,Washington, D.C. 20001-5403.

CORRESPONDENCE. Correspondence regarding subscriptions, changes of address, procurement of back issues, advertising and marketing matters, and so forth, should be addressed to:

Publications Department
The Cato Institute
1000 Massachusetts Ave., N.W.
Washington, D.C. 20001

All other correspondence, including requests to quote or reproduce material, should be addressed to the editor.

CITATIONS: Citation to this volume of the Review should conform to the following style: 2024-2025 Cato Sup. Ct. Rev. (2025).

DISCLAIMER. The views expressed by the authors of the articles are their own and are not attributable to the editor, the editorial board, or the Cato Institute.

INTERNET ADDRESS. Articles from past editions are available to the general public, free of charge, at www.cato.org/pubs/scr.

978-1-964524-79-5 (print)
978-1-964524-80-1 (digital)

Printed in the United States of America.

Cato Institute
1000 Massachusetts Ave., N.W.
Washington, D.C. 20001
www.cato.org

Contents

The Government Still Knows How to Win at the Supreme Court

Thomas A. Berry*

The Cato Institute's Robert A. Levy Center for Constitutional Studies is pleased to publish this 24th volume of the *Cato Supreme Court Review*, an annual critique of the Court's most important decisions from the Term just ended plus a look at the Term ahead. We are the first such journal to be released, and the only one that approaches its task from a classical liberal, Madisonian perspective. We release this volume each year at Cato's annual Constitution Day symposium.

Like every Supreme Court Term, this past Term featured some decisions that advanced liberty and limited government and some that were setbacks from a libertarian perspective. It would have been hard for the Court to match the number of momentous decisions from last year. If anything, this Term showed that even with a Supreme Court majority that is more skeptical of government power in some respects, the government still has many advantages. In last year's Foreword I highlighted three cases from the Term that I believed classical liberals should be excited about. To counterbalance that optimism, the story of this Term was, in my opinion, several cases where the Court was all too quick to accept the government's justifications for its exercise of power. My thoughts on one of those cases, *Kennedy v. Braidwood Management,* can be found in another article in this Volume. Below are my takes on three other decisions that I found disappointing from this Term, all three of which ruled in favor of a state or federal government.

* Director, Robert A. Levy Center for Constitutional Studies, Cato Institute, and editor in chief, *Cato Supreme Court Review*.

Free Speech Coalition v. Paxton

In *Free Speech Coalition v. Paxton*,[1] the Supreme Court upheld as constitutional a Texas law mandating that websites impose age verification if those websites feature one-third or more content that is obscene for minors. In rejecting a First Amendment challenge to the law, the Supreme Court held that the law should neither be subjected to the most searching and skeptical form of judicial review (strict scrutiny) nor the most lenient and deferential (rational basis scrutiny). Rather, the Court applied the middle-ground "intermediate scrutiny."

The Court's opinion by Justice Clarence Thomas emphasized that many areas of the law distinguish based on age, including minimum age requirements to purchase guns, drive a car, or get married. And the Court reasoned that ID checks are a natural requirement for enforcing such distinctions. Prior Supreme Court cases have held that some forms of sexual content are obscene for children (meaning states can ban minors from viewing them without violating the First Amendment) but not obscene for adults. The Court concluded that if a state wants to enforce a law restricting minors' access to obscene content, ID checks are the natural means of enforcement.

On this basis, the Court concluded that only intermediate scrutiny should apply to laws establishing ID checks for access to age-restricted obscene content. The Court reasoned that the intermediate scrutiny standard is sufficient to ensure that the government is not using such ID checks as a pretext for a law aimed at limiting the access of adults to protected speech.

After determining that intermediate scrutiny applied, the Court held that the law survived intermediate scrutiny. It held so because the law advances the state's interest in shielding children from sexual content. The Court held, in addition, that requiring adults to verify their ages online before accessing such content did not impermissibly burden the speech rights of adults. Because the Court applied only intermediate (rather than strict) scrutiny, the Court did not require Texas to prove that it could achieve the state's interest in protecting children in a way that imposed less of a burden on adults.

Unfortunately, this decision upends two decades of settled understanding about adults' freedom to access legal content online without

---

[1] 145 S. Ct. 2291 (2025).

government-mandated ID checkpoints. In the case *Ashcroft v. ACLU*,[2] the Supreme Court held that strict scrutiny applied to a very similar federal law, affirming a decision blocking that law. Implausibly, the Court in *Paxton* attempted to distinguish *Ashcroft* as not binding in this case. The Court reasoned that the law in *Ashcroft* required websites to show they had verified IDs as a *defense* to a prosecution, while the Texas law requires the state to show that a website lacked the required ID verification process at an earlier stage of an enforcement proceeding.

But although the procedures and burdens of proof in the two laws differed, the upshot of both laws was the same: mandatory ID checks for accessing online adult content. In effect, the Court has now overruled *Ashcroft*'s application of strict scrutiny to laws mandating such ID checkpoints.

In addition, the Court's application of intermediate scrutiny significantly downplayed the unique risks and burdens of online ID checks for adult content. In his majority opinion, Justice Thomas wrote that "the decades-long history of some pornographic websites requiring age verification refutes any argument that the chill of verification is an insurmountable obstacle for users."[3] But the First Amendment test has never been whether a law presents an "insurmountable obstacle." As Justice Elena Kagan noted in her dissent, the "First Amendment prevents making speech hard, as well as banning it outright."[4]

Indeed, online ID checks for adult content make it harder for adults to access that speech because the risk of leaks and blackmail is significantly higher for online ID checks than for in-person ID checks. Scans and photos can all too easily be accessed for nefarious purposes. As Justice Kagan wrote in dissent, an online ID scan is not "like having to flash ID to enter a club."[5] Rather, it is "turning over information about yourself and your viewing habits—respecting speech many find repulsive—to a website operator, and then to . . . who knows? The operator might sell the information; the operator

---

[2] 542 U.S. 656 (2004).

[3] *Free Speech Coal.*, 145 S. Ct. at 2319.

[4] *Id.* at 2320 (Kagan, J., dissenting).

[5] *Id.* at 2321.

might be hacked or subpoenaed."[6] Thus, online ID checkpoints dissuade adults from accessing lawful speech and from exercising their constitutional rights. That chilling effect is far greater than any caused by ID checks for a marriage license or driver's license.

Fortunately, the Court's reasoning applies only to ID checks for content that is obscene for minors, which is the only category of speech where the Court has held that age makes a constitutional difference. The Court's reasoning in *Paxton* does not justify ID checks for online speech that is legal and constitutionally protected for people of all ages, such as social media. While the Court's decision is disappointing, it remains to be seen whether it will lead to a weakening of First Amendment protections in any area outside the context of obscenity.

TikTok v. Garland

Consider the following true scene from the U.S. Congress: One after another, members rose on the House floor to support the bill. "It is really incredible," one member said, "that we should allow an avowed and powerful enemy to be pouring poisonous propaganda into the minds of our own youth." Another member quoted an article warning of "unsolicited propaganda attacking the United States as 'imperialist,' 'war mongering,' and 'colonialist.'" The article asked rhetorically whether "a free society ha[s] to leave itself totally exposed to an unending brainwashing of foreign Communist propaganda— mostly concealed in its origin, subtle, purposeful—directed primarily at young Americans, at college students."

The impressionability of youth was a running theme of the day. The same member repeatedly emphasized that the propaganda at issue was "addressed to our youth, the teachers, and to colleges and universities, because this is a favorite trick of the Communists to get at the minds of our young people." Urging other members to support the bill, he called it "one of the most serious problems we have, to stop this Communist propaganda coming into our country. It is the technique of the Communists to work on the young minds of the various nations."

These fears might sound familiar to anyone who followed the legal controversy surrounding TikTok. But these members were not

---

[6] *Id.*

talking about TikTok. They were not talking about social media at all, because social media did not exist when they spoke. These congressional remarks were delivered not in 2024, but in 1961.[7] The members were urging support for a bill that would subject so-called "Communist political propaganda" to a regime of censorship, under which mail from abroad was opened and read by government officials. If the officials decided that a piece of mail qualified as such "propaganda," the addressee could only receive it by affirmative request.

The law mandating that TikTok "divest" or face a ban was motivated by the same flawed instinct that was on display in 1961: the belief that disfavored speech must be fought with censorship rather than with counterspeech. Members of Congress justified the TikTok law with claims that "Communist China is using TikTok as a tool to spread dangerous propaganda."[8] They described the speech available on TikTok as "bold attempts to infiltrate our country, spread propaganda."[9] And some candidly admitted that the content and viewpoint of the speech on TikTok was their primary motivation for the bill, not data privacy concerns. A co-sponsor of the bill admitted that "the greater concern is the propaganda threat" and the question of "what information America's youth gets."[10]

The rhetoric that members used to justify the two bills was strikingly similar despite being separated by 60 years. Even the metaphors echoed across the decades. In 1961: "We would not allow any other country to be shipping in dangerous drugs or disease bacteria. We would not allow anybody to pour poison into our water supply. But here is our most important possession, the minds and attitudes of our youth, and . . . we allow that enemy to pour this poisonous material day after day into the untrained and uncritical minds of

---

[7] 107 CONG. REC. 17,815 (1961) (statement of Rep. Walter Judd); *id.* at 17,818 (statement of Rep. Glenn Cunningham) (quoting Roscoe Drummond, *Propaganda War: Moscow and the Mails*, WASH. POST (July 15, 1961)); *id.* at 17,814 (statement of Rep. Glenn Cunningham).

[8] Press Release, The Select Comm. on the CCP, Gallagher, Bipartisan Coalition Introduce Legislation to Protect Americans from Foreign Adversary Controlled Applications, Including TikTok (Mar. 5, 2024), https://tinyurl.com/yshcpwew (statement of Rep. Elise Stefanik).

[9] Press Release, Rep. Beth Van Duyne, Rep. Beth Van Duyne Votes to Protect North Texans from Communist China (Mar. 13, 2024), https://tinyurl.com/3f999s7r.

[10] Jane Coaston, *What the TikTok Bill is Really About, According to a Leading Republican*, N.Y. TIMES (Apr. 1, 2024), https://tinyurl.com/rfrwhyda.

our youth."[11] In 2024: "TikTok is Communist Chinese malware that is poisoning the minds of our next generation;"[12] it is "digital fentanyl"[13] that is "poisoning the minds of our youth every day on a massive scale."[14]

In the 1960s, the Supreme Court rightly struck down the restriction on "Communist political propaganda," finding it to be "an unconstitutional abridgment of the addressee's First Amendment rights."[15] The Court described that law as being "at war with the 'uninhibited, robust, and wide-open' debate and discussion that are contemplated by the First Amendment."[16]

Unfortunately, the Court did not take the same stand for free speech in *TikTok v. Garland*.[17] The Court upheld the law, applying only intermediate scrutiny and finding that national security concerns satisfied that standard. The Court's *per curiam* opinion was explicitly cautious in its language, and the Court clearly hoped that the opinion wouldn't become a foundational precedent, given its rushed nature. In choosing to apply only intermediate scrutiny, the Court accepted the government's argument that there are speech-neutral reasons for a law to single out TikTok, despite all the evidence in the legislative record that TikTok was targeted *because of* the speech on the platform. The rushed nature of the litigation also meant that the courts did not have a sufficient evidentiary record to assure themselves that any data-privacy concerns relevant to TikTok are truly unique.

Nonetheless, one silver lining is that the Court relied only on the government's data-privacy rationale and did not accept the government's argument that it has an interest in changing the content-moderation choices on TikTok. Still, the Court was all too willing to accept the government's say-so rather than demand hard evidence that TikTok poses a unique danger. A law singling out and banning

---

[11] 107 CONG. REC. 17,815 (1961) (statement of Rep. Walter Judd).

[12] Press Release, The Select Comm. on the CCP, *supra* (statement of Rep. Elise Stefanik).

[13] Daniel Arkin, *Pence Calls TikTok 'Digital Fentanyl'*, NBC NEWS (Mar. 13, 2024), https://tinyurl.com/wkemkcka.

[14] Press Release, The Select Comm. on the CCP, *supra* (Statement of Rep. Chip Roy).

[15] *Lamont v. Postmaster General*, 381 U.S. 301, 307 (1965).

[16] *Id.* (quoting *N.Y. Times Co. v. Sullivan*, 376 U.S. 254, 270 (1964)).

[17] 145 S. Ct. 57 (2025).

a particular speaker by name requires much more judicial scrutiny and skepticism than what the Court gave it.

Lackey v. Stinnie

Suing the government is expensive work. That's why federal law authorizes the "prevailing party" in a civil rights suit against the government to request attorneys' fees.[18] But what happens if a court temporarily blocks a law as likely unconstitutional, and the legislature then repeals that law? Do the law's challengers qualify as "prevailing parties" because they got everything they wanted? Or must a court strike the final blow against a law for its challengers to qualify as "prevailing"? That is the question the Supreme Court answered in *Lackey v. Stinnie*.[19]

Unfortunately, the decision the Court reached is a setback for civil rights plaintiffs, who will now find it more difficult to muster the legal resources they need. Before *Lackey*, most appellate courts had held that a party who receives a preliminary injunction against a law is the "prevailing party" if the government then repeals the law and leaves nothing further for the court to do. That rule made sense because civil rights litigation is designed to impact the law. When people cause the law to change in their favor, they "prevail" in every sense of that concept. This principle could be easily enforced with a bright-line rule: A party that wins relief at a preliminary stage of litigation "prevails" if it then obtains a change in policy that materially alters the law in its favor.

Indeed, some of the most influential civil rights decisions in history never reached final judgment. Impact litigation is about setting precedents just as much as it is about winning a particular case. Many of the Supreme Court's most important decisions were at the preliminary injunction stage, and it would be bizarre to say that the winning side in those cases did not qualify as the "prevailing party."

But the Supreme Court in *Lackey* instead construed "prevailing party" narrowly, ruling that litigants are eligible for attorneys' fees only when courts "conclusively resolve the rights of parties on the merits."[20] That excludes suits that are mooted after a preliminary

---

[18] 42 U.S.C § 1988(b).

[19] 145 S. Ct. 659 (2025).

[20] *Id.*

injunction. As Justice Jackson noted in dissent, there is "every reason to believe that the net result of [this] decision will be less civil rights enforcement in the long run."[21] This decision will promote the "strategic mooting of cases by defendants" who see "the writing on the wall."[22]

*   *   *

It remains to be seen whether the *TiokTok* and *Free Speech Coalition* decisions will be extended to future circumstances, or whether their reasoning is unique to the particular speech at issue. And it remains to be seen whether Congress will choose to amend federal law to return to the pre-*Lackey* status quo, as Chief Justice John Roberts noted they are free to do. As always, the *Review* comes out as a first draft of the history of this Term, not a final assessment. The articles in this volume of the *Review* will give a fuller picture of the Term, both the good and the bad. We hope you enjoy the 24th volume of the *Cato Supreme Court Review*.

[21] *Id.* at 681 (Jackson, J., dissenting).
[22] *Id.* at 680.

Introduction

*Thomas A. Berry**

This is the 24th volume of the *Cato Supreme Court Review,* the nation's first in-depth assessment of the most recent Supreme Court Term, plus a look at the Term ahead. This is also my third year as editor in chief of the *Review.* It's an honor to continue to lead a publication I've long admired, and I feel a responsibility to keep the *Review* at the same high level of quality our readers expect.

While the personnel behind the *Review* may change, its core purpose and unique speed remain the same. We release the *Review* every year at our annual Constitution Day symposium, less than three months after the previous Term ends and two weeks before the next Term begins. It would be almost impossible to publish a journal any faster, and credit for that goes first and foremost to our authors, who year after year meet our unreasonable but necessary demands and deadlines.

This isn't a typical law review. We want you to read this volume, even if you're not a lawyer. We discourage authors' use of Latin phrases, page-long footnotes, and legalistic jargon. And we don't want to publish articles that are on niche topics, of interest only to the three other academics who write on the same topic. Instead, we publish digestible articles in plain English that help Americans understand the decisions of their highest court and why they matter.

And as my predecessors have regularly noted in introductions to previous volumes, we freely confess our biases. We start from first principles: We have a federal government of limited powers, those powers are divided among the several branches, and individuals have rights that act as shields against those powers. We take seriously those liberty-protective parts of the Constitution that have been too often neglected, including the affirmation of unenumerated

* Director, Robert A. Levy Center for Constitutional Studies, Cato Institute, and editor in chief, *Cato Supreme Court Review.*

rights in the Ninth Amendment and the reservation of legislative power to only the *legislature* (not the President) in Article I.

We also reject the tired dichotomy of judicial "restraint" vs. "activism." We urge judges to engage with and follow the law, which includes—most importantly—the Constitution. If that means invalidating a statute or regulation, it is the judiciary's duty to do so, without putting a "deferential" thumb on the scale in favor of the elected branches. At the same time, judges should not be outcome-oriented. Some decisions may lead to a bad *policy* outcome, but that's not an argument that the decision was *legally* wrong. Indeed, any rigorous legal philosophy must sometimes lead to policy outcomes a judge doesn't prefer, or else it is not really a *legal* methodology.

And there is another core value of the *Review*: We don't want the *Review* to be an echo chamber. We acknowledge that many cases are hard and that people of good faith can disagree on both outcomes and reasoning. We don't want the *Review* to simply repeat the "Cato position" on every case. Rather, we gather a stellar group of authors we respect and give them the freedom to write what they believe.

Lawyers applying originalism, textualism, and a presumption of liberty can reach differing conclusions on the same questions. We believe that the differing views of authors who broadly share our judicial philosophies are evidence of the strengths of these theories, not of their weakness or indeterminacy.

* * *

This year's *Review* opens, as usual, with the annual B. Kenneth Simon Lecture, delivered last year by the Honorable Judge Neomi Rao of the D.C. Circuit. Rao's topic is the Supreme Court's embrace of best meaning interpretation. As Rao explains, this approach "recognizes that law has an objectively best meaning. Judges must find that meaning by exercising independent judgment. And, importantly, best meaning interpretation is incompatible with judicial minimalism and strong forms of *stare decisis*."

Next, Larissa Whittingham writes on *FCC v. Consumers' Research*. In that case, the Supreme Court once again rejected a challenge to a statute on "nondelegation" grounds. The Court found that the law in question gave sufficient guidance to the FCC to comply with the rule against delegating legislative power to the executive. Whittingham writes that the case reveals both "the continued pattern of relying on principles of interpretation to save a statute" and "a glimpse into conceptual differences among the Justices that may divide the Court differently in future cases."

Damien Schiff and Charles Yates of the Pacific Legal Foundation cover *Seven County Infrastructure Coalition v. Eagle County*, which rejected a challenge under the National Environmental Policy Act of 1970. As they explain, the decision represents a "clear and decisive rejection of the lower courts' habit of hyper-enforcing NEPA's procedural obligations, with little deference given to agencies—all with the result of converting NEPA into a formidable substantive statute oftentimes fatal to federal projects."

Eli Nachmany of Covington & Burling writes on *Diamond Alternative Energy, LLC v. EPA*. As he explains, the decision is important not just for what it had to say about Article III standing, but also for its implications regarding the relief available under the Administrative Procedure Act. As Nachmany writes, the question remains open whether the APA allows plaintiffs to completely vacate an illegal rule. If it does not, that "would close the courthouse doors to a substantial number of plaintiffs seeking to challenge regulations that injure them."

Cato legal associate Charles Brandt and I write on *Kennedy v. Braidwood Management*, which rejected an Appointments Clause challenge to the makeup of a board exercising decision-making authority under the Affordable Care Act. We argue that the decision too generously read the interplay of several statutes to permit appointments by the HHS Secretary rather than the President. Going forward, so long as the statute might reasonably be read to require principal officer approval for the inferior appointment, the courts will deem the appointment "vested" "by law" in the sense of the Appointments Clause.

Matthew Cavedon, the new director of Cato's Project on Criminal Justice, writes on *Barnes v. Felix*. In that case, the Court held that the Fifth Circuit had taken too narrow a view of which facts are relevant to an excessive force claim against a police officer. Looking more broadly at recent cases involving the police, Cavedon writes that "safety can be endangered not just by recognizing Fourth Amendment limits but also by abandoning them. Recently, the Supreme Court has cast the Fourth Amendment only as a threat and not as a shield. Recovering a more balanced approach may bring more Americans to appreciate the Constitution, rather than dismissing it as an obstacle to normative values and urgent needs."

Patrick Jaicomo and Anya Bidwell of the Institute for Justice write on *Martin v. United States*, which they litigated up to the Supreme Court. The question in the case seems straightforward: "If federal officers raid the wrong house, causing property damage and assaulting innocent occupants, may the homeowners sue the government for damages?" But as they explain, the decision "reveals a bizarre landscape of immunities through which the Martins continue their journey in search of a remedy."

Vera Eidelman of the ACLU covers *Free Speech Coalition v. Paxton*, in which the Court upheld a Texas law mandating that websites with a given percentage of pornographic content verify the age of every visitor. Eidelman writes that the "opinion adds to the Court's expanding list of cases reflecting motivated reasoning and outcome-driven results." However, she finds some silver linings—for instance, "the Court emphasizes that strict scrutiny is really, truly strict."

Cynthia Crawford of the Americans for Prosperity Foundation writes on *Mahmoud v. Taylor*, which held that the First Amendment right to the free exercise of religion required giving parents the option to opt their kids out of certain public school reading lessons with books on gender identity themes. Crawford concludes that "*Mahmoud* presents an affirmation that parental rights to guide the religious upbringing of their children are not narrow rights that apply only where the religious community requires total, or near-total, withdrawal from the public schooling system. Rather, they extend to discrete conflicts within the public school from which the parents seek to have their children excused."

Ezra Young writes on *United States v. Skrmetti*, which upheld a Tennessee law banning gender transition surgeries for minors. Criticizing the decision, Young writes that "equal protection is an individual right that cannot be denied any person because of a label applied to her by the government. And it should make no difference whether the label is applied by voters, the political branches, or the judiciary. Nevertheless, the Supreme Court's equal protection jurisprudence allows and facilitates the judiciary meting out equal protection unequally."

Finally, John Vecchione of the New Civil Liberties Alliance authors our annual "Looking Ahead" article. Vecchione identifies several major cases to watch next Term, on topics ranging from tariffs to transgender participation in sports to redistricting and the Voting Rights Act.

* * *

This year, as always, I have had help from many other people. Most important, of course, are the authors themselves, without whose work there would be no *Review*. Our authors this year produced excellent, polished articles under tremendous time pressure and for that I sincerely thank them all. Thanks also go to my Cato Institute colleagues Clark Neily, Walter Olson, Brent Skorup, Dan Greenberg, Matthew Cavedon, and Mike Fox for help in editing the articles and for taking on a heavier load of other Cato work in August when I was buried in editing. Legal associates Christine Marsden, Harrison Prestwich, Samuel Rutzick, Caitlyn Kinard, Alexander Xenos, and Vikram Valame performed the difficult (believe me, I remember) and vital task of cite-checking and proofreading. Cato interns Caleb Krebs, Karan Gupta, Quinton Crawford, and Ben Woods also provided essential research assistance. And special thanks to Laura Bondank-Harmon, who handled all the nuts and bolts of publishing the *Review* (and assisted on edits as well). This volume couldn't have happened without her.

We hope that you enjoy this 24th volume of the *Cato Supreme Court Review*.

Best Meaning Interpretation

Hon. Neomi Rao*

It is a pleasure to be here at the Cato Institute to deliver the annual B. Kenneth Simon lecture. On this Constitution Day, Cato brings together scholars and practitioners to discuss the Supreme Court's recent work. To close out the event, my lecture will focus on what I consider to be the Supreme Court's return to a "best meaning" approach to the law. One of the clearest examples from this past Term is *Loper Bright*.[1] Not only did the Supreme Court end *Chevron* deference,[2] but the majority pronounced: "In the business of statutory interpretation, if it is not the best, it is not permissible."[3]

When said out loud, this hardly seems controversial—why would courts consider anything other than the best meaning of the law? Yet in fact there are many other approaches to constitutional and statutory interpretation that do not seek the best meaning of *the law*. Rather they emphasize the "best" policy outcome, strict adherence to precedent, judicial modesty, or deference to the political branches. We also live with the brooding omnipresence of legal realism, which casts doubt on whether law even has a meaning that judges can ascertain.

Best meaning interpretation rejects these competing understandings of the judicial power. In this lecture, I will take a closer look at the Court's embrace of best meaning interpretation. First, I will explain why best meaning interpretation marks a return to the traditional understanding of the Article III judicial power. Second, I will explain how alternative theories have competed with and, at times, eclipsed, a best meaning approach to judicial decisionmaking.

---

* Judge, United States Court of Appeals for the District of Columbia Circuit. These remarks were delivered as part of the B. Kenneth Simon Lecture hosted by the Cato Institute on September 17, 2024.

[1] Loper Bright Enters. v. Raimondo, 144 S. Ct. 2244 (2024).

[2] Chevron U.S.A., Inc. v. Nat. Res. Def. Council, Inc., 467 U.S. 837 (1984).

[3] *Loper Bright*, 144 S. Ct. at 2266.

Finally, I will elaborate on how best meaning interpretation works in practice. This approach recognizes that law has an objectively best meaning. Judges must find that meaning by exercising independent judgment. And, importantly, best meaning interpretation is incompatible with judicial minimalism and strong forms of *stare decisis*.

I. Best Meaning and the Judicial Power

Let me begin with a brief overview of how best meaning approaches are consistent with the Anglo-American legal tradition and the original meaning of the judicial power. Best meaning interpretation is one way of capturing the traditional understanding of the Article III judicial power. The courts were established to uphold the law and to protect individual rights and liberties, including from the arbitrary and unlawful actions of the government.[4]

The Article III judicial power is accompanied by a judicial duty to decide cases in *accordance with law*. Or as Chief Justice John Marshall famously said, "It is emphatically the province and duty of the judicial department to say what the law is."[5] The duty to expound and interpret the law requires ascertaining its best meaning, not creating a new meaning. As Blackstone said, the judge is "sworn to determine, not according to his own private judgement, but according to the known laws and customs of the land; not delegated to pronounce a new law, but to maintain and expound the old one."[6] Emphasizing that judges must find the best meaning of the law draws a sharp line between the law and the judge's will.[7] "The *discretion* of a Judge is the Law of Tyrants," one English judge explained, "In the best it is often times Caprice, in the worst it is every Vice, Folly, and Passion to which human Nature is liable."[8] Deciding a case in accordance with the best meaning of the law reinforces the essential separation between judgment and will.

---

[4] THE FEDERALIST NO. 78, at 405 (Alexander Hamilton) (George W. Carey & James McClellan eds., 2001).

[5] Marbury v. Madison, 5 U.S. (1 Cranch) 137, 177 (1803).

[6] 1 WILLIAM BLACKSTONE, COMMENTARIES ON THE LAWS OF ENGLAND *69 (1765).

[7] Osborn v. Bank of U.S., 22 U.S. (9 Wheat.) 738, 866 (1824) ("Judicial power, as contradistinguished from the power of the laws, has no existence. Courts are the mere instruments of the law, and can will nothing.").

[8] Doe v. Kersey (C.P. 1765), Lord Camden's Argument in Doe on the Demise of Hindson, & Ux. & al. v. Kersey, 15, 53 (London, 1766) (emphasis added), *quoted in* PHILIP HAMBURGER, LAW AND JUDICIAL DUTY 146 (2008).

Furthermore, judicial independence is linked to the duty to find the best meaning of the law. The Constitution confers independence on Article III judges by giving them life tenure and irreducible salaries.[9] That independence from political bullying and removal frees judges to decide cases in accordance with law.[10] It is unsurprising then that the Chief Justice's opinion in *Loper Bright* has more than a dozen references to judicial independence.[11] Judicial independence and judgment go hand in hand. The constitutional bedrock of judicial independence shows why *Chevron* was wrong. But more fundamentally it highlights why exercising independent judgment requires judges to find the best meaning of the law.

II. Challenges to the Best Meaning Approach

I hope that this traditional understanding of the Article III judicial power is familiar. And perhaps to this audience, a best meaning approach to interpretation is intuitive and obvious. I agree.

Best meaning interpretation is consistent with formalism and with theories of textualism and originalism that have restored a focus on the meaning of the written law. But we should not take this way of thinking for granted. The best meaning approach was eclipsed for many years by a variety of "innovative" alternatives.

Let me offer a few examples. The original progressives at the turn of the 20th Century candidly advocated for courts to step aside. Thinkers like Roscoe Pound championed "executive justice," which would allow the unfettered flourishing of expert administration.[12] The progressives openly lamented that courts relied on an archaic Constitution to protect individual rights and private property.[13] To these progressives, the best meaning of the law came at the expense of efficiency and modernity. But at least the progressives frankly

---

[9] U.S. CONST. art. III, § 1 ("The Judges, both of the supreme and inferior Courts, shall hold their Offices during good Behaviour, and shall, at stated Times, receive for their Services, a Compensation, which shall not be diminished during their Continuance in Office.").

[10] *See* Perez v. Mortg. Bankers Ass'n, 575 U.S. 92, 120–21 (2015) (Thomas, J., concurring); HAMBURGER, *supra* note 8, at 148.

[11] *See Loper Bright*, 144 S. Ct. at 2257–58, 2262–63, 2265–66, 2268–69, 2273.

[12] *See generally* Roscoe Pound, *Executive Justice*, 55 U. PA. L. REV. 137 (1907).

[13] *E.g.*, FRANK JOHNSON GOODNOW, THE AMERICAN CONCEPTION OF LIBERTY AND GOVERNMENT 12–21 (1916); JAMES M. LANDIS, THE ADMINISTRATIVE PROCESS 1–5, 96, 123–35 (1938).

acknowledged that their views were at odds with the original Constitution and the traditional understanding of the judicial power as essential for maintaining individual rights and liberties.[14]

Next we have the legal realists, who denied the possibility of an objectively best meaning of the law.[15] They believed in the radical indeterminacy of law. They considered judging a matter of personal discretion. By shrinking the realm of law, they sowed doubt about the objectivity of judges and the possibility of law as an objective and independent study.[16] Legal realism and its modern variants remain the prevailing undercurrent in the legal academy. Many law students are taught that formalism is overly simplistic and that those who think there is a best meaning of a legal text are kidding themselves.

During the Warren Court, the Supreme Court also offered interpretations of the Constitution that perhaps are most charitably characterized as aspirational, rather than faithful to the Constitution and to the limits of the Article III judicial power.[17] Justice William Brennan and Justice Thurgood Marshall, for instance, defended their decisions by reference to social justice and human dignity.[18]

---

[14] *See, e.g.,* Roscoe Pound, *Mechanical Jurisprudence,* 8 COLUM. L. REV. 605, 612 (1908) ("The law [has] become[] a body of rules. This is the condition against which sociologi[cal jurists] now protest, and protest rightly.").

[15] *See, e.g.,* Karl N. Llewellyn, *Remarks on the Theory of Appellate Decisions and the Rules or Canons About How Statutes Are to Be Construed,* 3 VAND. L. REV. 395, 396 (1950) (critiquing the "mistaken idea" that "cases themselves and in themselves, plus the correct rules on how to handle cases, provide one single correct answer to a disputed issue of law").

[16] *See, e.g.,* Oliver Wendell Holmes, *The Path of the Law,* 10 HARV. L. REV. 457, 461 (1897) ("The prophecies of what the courts will do in fact, and nothing more pretentious, are what I mean by the law."); JEROME FRANK, LAW AND THE MODERN MIND 104 (6th ed. 1930) ("Whatever produces the judge's hunches makes the law.").

[17] *See* AKHIL REED AMAR, AMERICA'S UNWRITTEN CONSTITUTION 193 (2012) (arguing the Warren Court "seemed contemptuous" of constitutional text); J. HARVIE WILKINSON III, COSMIC CONSTITUTIONAL THEORY: WHY AMERICANS ARE LOSING THEIR INALIENABLE RIGHTS TO SELF-GOVERNANCE 19 (2012) ("Perhaps more than any other cosmic constitutional theory, living constitutionalism, both in theory and in practice, has elevated judicial hubris over humility, boldness over modesty, and intervention over restraint.").

[18] *See e.g.,* Furman v. Georgia, 408 U.S. 238, 270 (1972) (Brennan, J., concurring) ("A punishment is 'cruel and unusual,' therefore, if it does not comport with human dignity."); Milliken v. Bradley, 418 U.S. 717, 782 (1974) (Marshall, J., dissenting) ("[T]his Court['s] . . . appointed task [is] making a 'living truth' of our constitutional ideal of equal justice under law.").

They looked to broader moral and political values, rather than the best meaning of the original Constitution.[19]

Or consider prominent legal theorists, such as Ronald Dworkin, who depicted his judge Hercules as one who would interpret the law consistent with particular moral and philosophical ideals.[20] Meanwhile, William Eskridge advanced a theory of dynamic statutory interpretation, according to which the meaning of the text can evolve alongside a changing social and political context.[21] And of course, the popular media is suffused with a policy-forward view of the courts. For instance, a recent *New York Times* essay grumbled that originalism prevents the courts from doing "good things."[22] Importantly, such "good things" are favored wholly apart from the best meaning *of the law*. Some law professors have called for simply abandoning the Constitution altogether.[23] I could go on, but the ideas are no doubt familiar.

Against these currents, a best meaning approach has gradually been restored. It is implicit in theories of textualism and originalism.[24] As Justice Clarence Thomas explained in his speech "Be Not Afraid" more than 20 years ago, there may be reasonable disagreement about the meaning of the law,

> [b]ut that does not mean that there is no correct answer, that there are no clear, eternal principles recognized and put into motion by our founding documents. These principles do exist. The law is not a matter of purely personal opinion. The law is a distinct, independent discipline, with certain principles and modes of analysis that yield what we can discern to be correct and incorrect answers.[25]

[19] *See* Thurgood Marshall, *The Constitution's Bicentennial: Commemorating the Wrong Document?*, 40 VAND. L. REV. 1337, 1338, 1340–41 (1987).

[20] *See generally* RONALD DWORKIN, LAW'S EMPIRE (1986).

[21] *See* William N. Eskridge, Jr., *Dynamic Statutory Interpretation*, 135 U. PA. L. REV. 1479, 1479 (1987).

[22] *See* Jennifer Szalai, *The Constitution Is Sacred. Is It Also Dangerous?*, N.Y. TIMES (Aug. 31, 2024), archived at https://perma.cc/U4ZZ-D57Q (emphasis omitted).

[23] Ryan D. Doerfler & Samuel Moyn, Opinion, *The Constitution Is Broken and Should Not Be Reclaimed*, N.Y. TIMES (Aug. 19, 2022), archived at https://perma.cc/D7SC-P8TK.

[24] *See, e.g.*, Robert H. Bork, *Neutral Principles and Some First Amendment Problems*, 47 IND. L. J. 1, 9 (1971); Antonin Scalia, *Originalism: The Lesser Evil*, 57 U. CIN. L. REV. 849, 862 (1989).

[25] Justice Clarence Thomas, Be Not Afraid, Speech at the American Enterprise Institute Annual Dinner (Feb. 13, 2001), archived at https://perma.cc/AT9T-VCMU.

When Justice Thomas joined the Supreme Court in 1991, his commitment to finding the right answer in each case was sometimes criticized as quixotic, dismissed as the voice of a lone dissent or concurrence. But now, in 2024, six Justices joined the *Loper Bright* majority, which fully embraces the traditional understanding that judges must ascertain the best meaning of the law when deciding cases.

III. Best Meaning Interpretation in Practice

Let me next turn to a practical question—how should courts go about finding the best meaning of the law? Volumes have been written on questions of statutory and constitutional interpretation. Here, I will provide an overview of best meaning interpretation at what I think of as the retail level, namely judicial decisionmaking.

Best meaning interpretation begins with positive law: the law enacted by the People and their representatives. I will not shy away from saying that best meaning interpretation *is* formalist. Justice Antonin Scalia once said that the most mindless critique of textualism is that it is "formalistic." "*Of course it is formalistic!*" he said, "The rule of law is *about* form."[26]

When interpreting a statute, for instance, a judge must first look to its text. This may require consulting dictionaries and determining whether Congress used words in a technical sense or incorporated common law principles. The meaning of a particular provision must also be understood in light of the entire statute.[27] Too often parties present bits and pieces of statutes as they have been divided up in the U.S. Code. As a judge, when faced with a question of statutory interpretation, I consider it essential to read the entire public law that Congress enacted. The meaning of each part of the statute becomes clearer on reviewing the whole scheme of the law, not to mention other similar laws.

But the inquiry does not stop there. Ascertaining the best meaning also requires a judge to consider legal background principles. These principles often include the constitutional limits on the

---

[26] Antonin Scalia, *Common Law Courts in a Civil Law System: The Role of United States Federal Courts in Interpreting the Constitution and Laws*, in A MATTER OF INTERPRETATION: FEDERAL COURTS AND THE LAW 25 (Amy Gutmann, ed., 1997) (emphasis in original).

[27] *See, e.g.*, Pennington v. Coxe, 6 U.S. (2 Cranch) 33, 52–53 (1804) (Marshall, C.J.).

federal government and the structure of separated powers. Judges must consider constitutional and other legal backdrops, such as the common law and established legal principles.[28] Meaning also derives from the context in which that law was passed—every law exists within the broader province of our legal frameworks and traditions.[29]

Although judges must work to find the best meaning of the law, they may not always agree. One example is the recent decision about whether former presidents have criminal immunity for their official acts.[30] No former president had been prosecuted for official acts— so this was an issue of first impression. Chief Justice John Roberts masterfully explained the historical understanding of the Article II executive power and the importance of its independence in the scheme of separated powers.[31] He examined the Constitution's original meaning, text, structure, and history to conclude such an immunity existed.[32] From my understanding of the issues, I think the majority had the better interpretation. But the dissenters offered a different historical understanding of the meaning of the executive power and emphasized what they viewed as the dangers of a broad presidential criminal immunity.[33] Some commentators point to such disagreement to argue that the law is indeterminate or that there is no best answer.[34] Some cases are hard. But the *difficulty* of interpretation should not be confused with the *impossibility* of finding the correct answer.

---

[28] *See* Stephen E. Sachs, *Constitutional Backdrops*, 80 Geo. Wash. L. Rev. 1813, 1831 (2012); Neomi Rao, *Textualism's Political Morality*, 73 Case W. Rsrv. L. Rev. 191, 200 (2022).

[29] *See generally* Neomi Rao, *The Province of the Law*, 46 Harv. J. L. & Pub. Pol'y 87 (2023).

[30] *See* Trump v. United States, 144 S. Ct. 2312 (2024).

[31] *See id.* at 2327–32.

[32] *See id.*

[33] *See id.* at 2357–60 (Sotomayor, J., dissenting); *id.* at 2378 (Jackson, J., dissenting).

[34] *See, e.g.*, Brian Leiter, *Constitutional Law, Moral Judgment, and the Supreme Court as Super-Legislature*, 66 Hastings L. J. 1601, 1605 (2015) ("Since federal judges do not converge on a single way of fixing constitutional meaning, it follows, on the positivist view, that in large parts of so-called 'constitutional law' there really is no law because there are no criteria of legal validity generally accepted and applied by judges.").

IV. Implications of the Best Meaning Approach

Next, I want to explore some of the implications of a best meaning approach to interpretation.

A. The literal meaning is not always the best meaning.

The best meaning approach recognizes that there is no meaning without context. Even if an interpretation appears plain, a judge must consider the broader structure, context, and history of the law to ensure that the seemingly plain meaning is in fact the best one.

I think a great example of this difference between *plain* and *best* meaning can be found in the Supreme Court's decision in *Fischer v. United States*.[35] In that case, the Court considered whether a provision of the Sarbanes-Oxley Act could be used to prosecute individuals who forcibly entered the Capitol on January 6th.[36] In brief, the statute criminalized the destruction of documents or objects for use in an official proceeding, and it also criminalized *"otherwise* obstruct[ing], influenc[ing], or imped[ing] any official proceeding."[37] In dissent, Justice Amy Coney Barrett concluded that the statute was straightforward and could be understood in just "three paragraphs" with reference to a few dictionaries and past precedents.[38] She determined that the meaning was plain and that the actions of the January 6th defendants came within that plain meaning.

But I think the majority had the better interpretation. Chief Justice Roberts concluded that the statute did not apply to the January 6th defendants. He reasoned that the best meaning of the phrase "otherwise obstructs, influences, or impedes any official proceeding" was limited by the narrower offenses listed in the preceding subsection.[39] The Chief Justice looked at the statute's text and the broader context in which Congress enacted that law, which cabined the potentially sweeping criminal liability.[40]

---

[35] 144 S. Ct. 2176 (2024).

[36] *Id.* at 2181–82.

[37] 18 U.S.C. § 1512(c)(1)–(2) (emphasis added).

[38] *Fischer*, 144 S. Ct. at 2195 (Barrett, J., dissenting).

[39] *Id.* at 2183–86 (majority opinion).

[40] *Id.* at 2186–87.

Fischer exemplifies how a supposedly "plain meaning" of a statute may not in fact be the best one once a judge has considered the statutory structure, relevant background legal principles, and the mischief the act was aimed at rectifying.

Again, the fact that the Justices disagreed does not mean that there is no right or best answer. Focusing on "best" meaning interpretation does not require a judge to turn a blind eye to legal uncertainty or the difficulty of interpretation in hard cases.[41] In fact, by emphasizing *best* meaning interpretation, the Court recognizes that there might be other plausible meanings. The best meaning approach acknowledges that deciding cases is not mechanical or always easy—the law may be uncertain on a particular question or ambiguous.[42] Nonetheless, judges must use their judgment to determine the best or most natural meaning of the law.

B. So, what about the role of stare decisis in finding the best meaning of the text?

Stare decisis has never been an inexorable command. Justices of the Supreme Court sometimes determine that a precedent is wrong or unworkable and must be overruled.[43] Stability in the law is an important principle, but it is not the only one.

Despite furious debates about *stare decisis*, its contours have never been reduced to a widely accepted formula.[44] Rather, the question

[41] *See* Gary Lawson, *Legal Indeterminacy: Its Cause and Cure*, 19 HARV. J. L. & PUB. POL'Y 411, 420–21 (1996) ("[If] all you are looking for is the best answer that you can possibly attain under the circumstances, the level of *indeterminacy* goes essentially to zero even if the level of *uncertainty* is very high.") (emphasis in original).

[42] *See* Frank H. Easterbrook, *Foreword* to ANTONIN SCALIA & BRYAN A. GARNER, READING LAW: THE INTERPRETATION OF LEGAL TEXTS, at xxiii (2012) ("Interpretation is a human enterprise, which cannot be carried out algorithmically by an expert system on a computer.").

[43] *See e.g.*, Dobbs v. Jackson Women's Health Org., 142 S. Ct. 2228, 2242 (2022) (overruling Roe v. Wade, 410 U.S. 113 (1973)); Brown v. Bd. of Educ., 347 U.S. 483, 494–95 (1954) (implicitly overruling Plessy v. Ferguson, 163 U.S. 537 (1896)); Erie R.R. Co. v. Tompkins, 304 U.S. 64, 79 (1938) (overruling Swift v. Tyson, 41 U.S. (16 Pet.) 1 (1842)); Hudson v. Guestier, 10 U.S. (6 Cranch) 281, 284 (1810) (overruling Rose v. Himely, 8 U.S. (4 Cranch) 241 (1808)).

[44] *See* Frank H. Easterbrook, *Stability and Reliability in Judicial Decisions*, 73 CORNELL L. REV. 422, 422 (1988) ("[T]here is no contest in the theory of stare decisis. Not because one candidate has swept the boards, but because no one has a principled theory to offer.").

15

of whether to follow precedent turns, as do many questions of interpretation, on judgment. As an example, consider the Supreme Court's decision in *Dobbs*, which overruled *Roe v. Wade* and returned the policy questions about abortion to the States.[45] Writing for the majority, Justice Samuel Alito explained why *Roe* and the cases that followed it were incompatible with the Fourteenth Amendment. He emphasized that "The Judicial Branch derives its legitimacy, not from following public opinion, but from deciding by its *best* lights whether [a law] comport[s] with the Constitution. The doctrine of *stare decisis* is an adjunct of this duty, and should be no more subject to the vagaries of public opinion than is the basic judicial task."[46]

By contrast, Justices Stephen Breyer, Sonia Sotomayor, and Elena Kagan's joint dissent in *Dobbs* was not really about the best meaning of the Fourteenth Amendment. They did not provide a detailed argument that *Roe* and its progeny were consistent with the Constitution. Instead, their dissent responded with the inviolability of *stare decisis*, the way "liberty" and "equality" evolve over time, and the importance of reliance interests.[47] As Justice Alito said in *Dobbs*, "We can only do our job, which is to interpret the law, *apply longstanding principles of* stare decisis, and decide this case accordingly."[48] The best meaning of the law is not always compatible with precedent.

Of course, judges must proceed with humility. In trying to determine the best meaning, a wise judge will consider the reasoning of other judges who have wrestled with difficult interpretive questions. But as Justice Neil Gorsuch explained in his *Loper Bright* concurrence, "different decisions carry different weight."[49] Well-reasoned decisions and those that are "repeatedly confirmed" may provide good evidence of best meaning.[50] On the other hand, judicial decisions that fail to engage with the best meaning of the law using traditional tools of interpretation may be less useful. Judges should give less weight to precedents that rely on policy preferences or

---

[45] *Dobbs*, 142 S. Ct. at 2242.

[46] *Id.* at 2278 (emphasis added) (quoting Planned Parenthood v. Casey, 505 U.S. 833, 963 (1992) (Rehnquist, C.J., concurring in the judgment in part and dissenting in part)).

[47] *Id.* at 2326, 2333, 2343–44 (Breyer, Sotomayor, & Kagan, JJ., dissenting).

[48] *Id.* at 2279 (majority opinion) (emphasis added).

[49] *Loper Bright*, 144 S. Ct. at 2277 (Gorsuch, J., concurring).

[50] *Id.* at 2278 (cleaned up).

values drawn from outside the law. Such decisions may tell us what some judges thought was "best," but they provide little evidence of the best meaning of the *law*.

But even a clearly reasoned decision is not *automatically* the best meaning of the law simply because it was decided first. This basic truth runs through our legal tradition from Blackstone and Chief Justice Marshall through to the present.[51] This respectful, but not deferential, attitude to judicial precedent applies equally to the longstanding practices of the political branches. Particularly in cases of first impression where there might be a long-settled practice outside the courts, judges should consider the views of the political branches in understanding their respective constitutional powers.[52] But such arrangements cannot trump the court's independent judgment.[53] As the Chief Justice explained in *Loper Bright*, there is a long tradition of courts affording *respect* to executive branch interpretations, but respect is a far cry from deference.[54]

At bottom, the independent duty of the courts to say what the law is means that they must ascertain the best meaning of the law. If that best meaning conflicts with precedent, the judges must say so.

C. Next, how should we think about judicial minimalism and a best meaning approach?

A best meaning mode of interpretation is incompatible with judicial minimalism. Judicial minimalism is often touted as a "passive virtue."[55] This often means a supposedly prudential choice not to

---

[51] *See id.* at 2276; *see also* Gamble v. United States, 139 S. Ct. 1960, 1983 (2019) (Thomas, J., concurring) ("[J]udges *should* disregard precedent that articulates a rule incorrectly when necessary to vindicate the old rule from misrepresentation." (cleaned up)); *see also* 1 BLACKSTONE, *supra* note 6, at *71 ("[T]he law, and the opinion of the judge are not always convertible terms, or one and the same thing; since it sometimes may happen that the judge may *mistake* the law.") (emphasis in original).

[52] Youngstown Sheet & Tube Co. v. Sawyer, 343 U.S. 579, 610 (1952) (Frankfurter, J., concurring) ("Deeply embedded traditional ways of conducting government cannot supplant the Constitution or legislation, but they give meaning to the words of a text or supply them."); NLRB v. Noel Canning, 573 U.S. 513, 525 (2014) (same).

[53] *See Noel Canning*, 573 U.S. at 525.

[54] *Loper Bright*, 144 S. Ct. at 2257–58 ("'Respect,' though, was just that. The views of the Executive Branch could inform the judgment of the Judiciary, but did not supersede it.").

[55] *See* Alexander M. Bickel, *Foreword: The Passive Virtues*, 75 HARV. L. REV. 40, 79 (1961).

decide legal questions even when they are properly before the court. Of course, courts should not be willful or strain to resolve questions not properly presented in a case. Party presentation limits the issues before the court, even if not the range of possible legal arguments.[56] But minimalism is emphatically not a claim about the best meaning of the law.[57] Rather, it is a claim about the judge's role—that the judge should duck questions presented by a case, deciding as little as possible. Restraint and minimalism have few guideposts—and leave much to the judge's discretion. Deciding not to decide a difficult or controversial question presented in a case may be as much an act of *will* as deciding a question not properly presented.

The Constitution establishes a delicate balance between the three departments of the federal government, vesting each with particular powers and providing limits on their exercise. For ambition to counteract ambition, each department must exercise its powers fully.[58] For instance, the Court has often invalidated the attempts of Congress or the Executive to give up their powers. The Court has struck down innovations like the one-house legislative veto or the line-item veto.[59] And there is good reason for this. The Constitution carefully limits and separates power in order to preserve individual liberty.[60] It is perhaps easier to appreciate the threats from a branch that overreaches its powers. But individual liberty is also threatened when one of the branches *abdicates* its powers.[61]

---

[56] N.Y. State Rifle & Pistol Ass'n v. Bruen, 142 S. Ct. 2111, 2130 n.6 (2022) ("The job of judges is not to resolve historical questions in the abstract; it is to resolve *legal* questions presented in particular cases or controversies.") (emphasis in original).

[57] *See* Diane S. Sykes, *Minimalism and Its Limits*, 2014–2015 CATO SUP. CT. REV. 17, 22 (2015) ("[A]lthough minimalism is an approach to judging, it's *not* a theory of constitutional interpretation. Unlike originalism, it's not a method for determining the meaning, scope, and application of the Constitution.") (emphasis in original).

[58] *See* THE FEDERALIST No. 51, *supra* note 4, at 268 (James Madison).

[59] INS v. Chadha, 462 U.S. 919, 959 (1983) (striking down the legislative veto); Clinton v. City of New York, 524 U.S. 417, 448–49 (1998) (striking down the line-item veto).

[60] *See* Metro. Wash. Airports Auth. v. Citizens for the Abatement of Aircraft Noise, Inc., 501 U.S. 252, 272 (1991) ("The ultimate purpose of this separation of powers is to protect the liberty and security of the governed."); Morrison v. Olson, 487 U.S. 654, 710–11 (1988) (Scalia, J., dissenting) ("While the separation of powers may prevent us from righting every wrong, it does so in order to ensure that we do not lose liberty.").

[61] *See* Neomi Rao, *Administrative Collusion: How Delegation Diminishes the Collective Congress*, 90 N.Y.U. L. REV. 1463, 1465 n.7 (2015).

Judges should stay within their constitutional limits. But within those limits, judges should not cower from deciding issues properly presented in a case. And for the Supreme Court, this means granting review in the cases that need to be decided. As I have often heard Justice Thomas say, it is the "J-O-B *job*" of a judge to decide cases. By determining the best meaning of the law and applying it to the case before them, courts fulfill their duty to uphold the law and protect individual rights and liberties.

V. The Importance of *Judgment*

There is much more to be said about these topics. But for tonight, I would like to conclude on the importance of retaining faith in the possibility of reasoned and independent judgment by our courts.

Aiming to find the best meaning of the law requires judgment. Ideally judges have this requisite judgment because, as Hamilton hoped, they would be learned in the law, legal precedents, and the legal backdrops of common law and political theory.[62] Maintaining the rule of law requires having faith in both the objective meaning of law and the possibility of reasoned judgment by courts. Yet both are under severe strain. Consider Justice Kagan's dissent in *Loper Bright*. She accuses the majority of "judicial hubris" in overruling *Chevron*.[63] She emphasizes that the law is often ambiguous and uncertain, and that statutes "run out."[64] If the law often runs out, then most judicial interpretations are just policy choices.

Yet uncertainty in the law is nothing new. And ambiguity has never been a warrant for abdicating the judicial power.[65] Our Founders and the theorists they looked to recognized the problem of ambiguity and the difficulty of interpretation in hard cases.[66]

---

[62] The Federalist No. 78, *supra* note 4, at 407 (Alexander Hamilton).

[63] *Loper Bright*, 144 S. Ct. at 2294 (Kagan, J., dissenting).

[64] *Id.*

[65] *Gamble*, 139 S. Ct. at 1987 (Thomas, J., concurring) ("Although the law may be, on rare occasion, truly ambiguous—meaning susceptible to multiple, equally correct legal meanings—the law never 'runs out.'").

[66] The Federalist No. 37, *supra* note 4, at 183 (James Madison) ("The experience of ages, with the continued and combined labours of the most enlightened legislators and jurists, have been equally unsuccessful in delineating the several objects and limits of different codes of laws . . . .[N]o language is so copious as to supply words and phrases for every complex idea, or so correct as not to include many, equivocally denoting different ideas."); 1 Blackstone, *supra* note 6, at *59–61 (surveying methods used to "interpret the will of the legislator" when the "words are dubious").

They believed, however, that judges could rely on their learning, experience, and judgment to render a decision according to law.[67]

An emphasis on uncertainty and indeterminacy has long been the seemingly sophisticated posture to take. But it has the dangerous consequence of shrinking the province of the law, and therefore the province of the courts. If the law frequently runs out, courts have nothing to do other than decide cases by deferring to the political branches.

A weakening of the courts is not just a problem for the institutional power of the courts. The traditional purview of the courts is to adjudicate the rights and obligations of individuals—to settle both private rights as well as public rights against the government. But if a good deal of law is simply indeterminate, individuals will have less recourse to protect their rights. Shrinking the realm of law in order to promote judicial modesty or humility does not promote the rule of law. Nor does it protect individuals raising legal claims and rights against the leviathan that is our federal government.

This is why courts have an obligation to exercise their independent judgment to decide cases in accordance with the best meaning of the law. Applying the traditional tools of interpretation and reasoned judgment to deciding hard cases is not "hubris." It is our sworn duty.

---

[67] *See, e.g.*, THE FEDERALIST No. 78, *supra* note 4, at 407 (Alexander Hamilton); *see also* John O. McGinnis, *The Duty of Clarity*, 84 GEO. WASH. L. REV. 843, 871–72 (2016) ("[For] [j]udges at the time of the Framing . . . law was not only a science but a demanding one. It required the application of a great deal of knowledge of various relevant considerations. But it was precisely the application of legal science that reflected the view of many in the founding generation that the meaning of law could be discovered, not made . . . . Even if the text of the Constitution taken on its own is susceptible to different interpretations, the science of law at the time creates a sophisticated technology of interpretation that is thought to reduce uncertainty.").

Vindicating the Nondelegation Doctrine: *FCC v. Consumers' Research's* Four Perspectives on a "Principle Universally Recognized"

*Larissa M. Whittingham**

That Congress cannot delegate legislative power to the President is a principle universally recognized as vital to the integrity and maintenance of the system of government ordained by the Constitution.

Field v. Clark, 143 U.S. 649, 692 (1892)

I. Overview

The nondelegation doctrine sits within the U.S. Supreme Court's separation of powers jurisprudence. It is a principle sourced from the structure, rather than the text, of the Constitution. Throughout the nearly 250 years of American history, the Supreme Court has repeatedly affirmed the validity of the doctrine in American law and embraced the Court's role in reviewing constitutional challenges arising from it. Although proponents of a vigorous nondelegation doctrine may complain that the Court has not wielded it to strike down a law more frequently, none of the Court's nondelegation precedents foreclose such a result in a future case. A close examination of the 2025 nondelegation decision, *FCC v. Consumers' Research*, reveals (1) the continued pattern of relying on principles of interpretation to save a statute, and (2) a glimpse into conceptual differences among the Justices that may divide the Court differently in future cases.

* Alumna, Retail Litigation Center and Husch Blackwell.

A. The Nondelegation Doctrine—A Unifying Idea with Polarizing Implementation

What we now know as the "nondelegation doctrine" traces back at least as early as John Locke's 1690 "Second Treatise of Government."[1] The concept was important enough to Locke that he included it as one of only four explanatory points in Chapter XI: "Of the Extent of the Legislative Power."[2] Locke says, "The legislative cannot transfer the power of making laws to any other hands: for it being but a delegated power from the people, they who have it cannot pass it over to others."[3]

Chief Justice John Marshall canonized this concept in American law within an 1825 Supreme Court decision, *Wayman v. Southard*: "It will not be contended that Congress can delegate to the courts or to any other tribunals powers which are strictly and exclusively legislative."[4] Two hundred years later, in *FCC v. Consumers' Research*, the Court described the doctrine this way:

> Article I of the Constitution provides that '[a]ll legislative Powers herein granted shall be vested in a Congress of the United States.' §1. Accompanying that assignment of power to Congress is a bar on its further delegation: Legislative power, we have held, belongs to the legislative branch, and to no other.[5]

---

[1] JOHN LOCKE, SECOND TREATISE OF GOVERNMENT ch. XI (The Project Gutenberg eBook 2003). The Latin maxim *delegatus non potest delegare* may trace back even earlier. *See* Patrick W. Duff and Horace E. Whiteside, *Delegata Potestas Non Potest Delegari: A Maxim of American Constitutional Law*, 14 CORNELL L. REV. 168, 171 (1929). The Supreme Court cited the maxim in a seminal nondelegation case, though noting it has its roots in agency law. J.W. Hampton, Jr. & Co. v. United States, 276 U.S. 394, 405–06 (1928) ("The well known maxim '*Delegata potestas non potest delegari*' applicable to the law of agency in the general and common law, is well understood, and has had wider application in the construction of our federal and state constitutions than it has in private law.").

[2] LOCKE, SECOND TREATISE ch. XI.

[3] *Id.* at § 141. Locke's explanation of what this article calls "nondelegation" explicitly roots itself in the idea of "subdelegation." That is, Congress itself received a delegation from the people in the Constitution and cannot further delegate its powers without consent from the original source of Congress's own authority. Gary Lawson has explored this framework extensively—and helpfully—and says the "nondelegation doctrine" is better phrased as the "non-subdelegation" principle. *See* Gary Lawson, *Mr. Gorsuch, Meet Mr. Marshall: A Private-Law Framework for the Public-Law Puzzle of Subdelegation*, No. 20-16 B.U. SCH. L. PUB. L. & LEGAL THEORY PAPER (2020).

[4] Wayman v. Southard, 23 U.S. (10 Wheat.) 1, 43 (1825).

[5] FCC v. Consumers' Rsch., 145 S. Ct. 2482, 2496 (2025).

Indeed, it still holds true that "in every case in which the question has been raised, the Court has recognized that there are limits of delegation which there is no constitutional authority to transcend."[6]

Despite centuries of agreement that the U.S. Constitution prohibits Congress from delegating "powers which are strictly and exclusively legislative"[7] to other branches, the Supreme Court has been cautious about enforcing the doctrine. It has used this principle to strike down federal statutes only twice (both of those in 1935). Courts recognize that identifying which instructions within a statute (i.e., challenged "delegations") are permissible or impermissible is difficult.[8] The problem is one of line drawing, recognized in the 1825 decision rooting the nondelegation doctrine in American constitutional law. Chief Justice Marshall there acknowledged:

> The line has not been exactly drawn which separates those important subjects which must be entirely regulated by the legislature itself from those of less interest in which a general provision may be made and power given to those who are to act under such general provisions to fill up the details.[9]

"Fill[ing] up the details" reflects a "practical understanding that, in our increasingly complex society, replete with ever-changing and more technical problems, Congress simply cannot do its job absent an ability to delegate power under broad general directives."[10] Said differently, Congress may "seek[] assistance from another

---

[6] Pan. Refin. Co. v. Ryan, 293 U.S. 388, 430 (1935).

[7] *Wayman*, 23 U.S. at 42.

[8] Justice Antonin Scalia's dissent in *Mistretta v. United States* expresses deep concern for courts' ability to police the nondelegation guarantee: "But while the doctrine of unconstitutional delegation is unquestionably a fundamental element of our constitutional system, it is not an element readily enforceable by the courts." 488 U.S. 361, 415 (1989) (Scalia, J., dissenting). He conceded that "no statute can be entirely precise" and, as a result, some level of policy judgments must inure to the executive branch implementing the statute. *Id.* He concluded that the "debate over unconstitutional delegation becomes a debate not over a point of principle, but over a question of degree" and opined that the "scope of delegation is largely uncontrollable by the court[s]." *Id.* at 415–16. That said, this discussion is in a footnote because neither a majority of the Court at any time, nor any Justice in the current Court, has blessed a notion that the nondelegation doctrine may be nonjusticiable.

[9] *Wayman*, 23 U.S. at 43.

[10] *Mistretta*, 488 U.S. at 372 (majority op.).

branch[,]"[11] including in areas that require "judgment on matters of policy."[12]

Whether a particular statute merely grants authority to "fill up the details"[13] of congressional intent or to actually "transfer the power of making laws"[14] has been the subject of frequent constitutional challenges throughout our nation's history. The spirited Supreme Court opinions resulting from those challenges—opinions of the Court, concurrences, and dissents—offer varied perspectives on *how* to ensure the "principle universally recognized as vital to the integrity and maintenance of the system of government ordained by the Constitution"[15] is applied.

One decision stood out in its analysis of the line-drawing problem. In 1928, Chief Justice William Howard Taft authored the opinion of the Court in *J.W. Hampton, Jr. & Co. v. United States*.[16] The Court said, "If Congress shall lay down by legislative act an intelligible principle to which the person or body authorized to [act] is directed to conform, such legislative action is not a forbidden delegation of legislative power."[17] Thus, the "intelligible principle" standard was born. Whether the Court intended to create a "test"[18] in *J.W. Hampton* is unclear, but the phrase "intelligible principle" has developed a legacy shaping the implementation of the nondelegation doctrine.

B. Recent Background of Nondelegation Doctrine Cases

In 2017, Keith Whittington and Jason Luliano identified a "predictable pattern" of nondelegation doctrine cases at the U.S.

---

[11] *J.W. Hampton, Jr. & Co.*, 276 U.S. at 406.

[12] *Mistretta*, 488 U.S. at 377 (majority op.).

[13] *Wayman*, 23 U.S. at 43.

[14] Locke, Second Treatise ch. XI, § 141.

[15] *Field*, 143 U.S. at 692.

[16] 276 U.S. 394.

[17] *Id.* at 408–09.

[18] *Mistretta*, 488 U.S. at 409 ("Applying this 'intelligible principle' test to congressional delegations, our jurisprudence has been driven by a practical understanding that, in our increasingly complex society, replete with ever-changing and more technical problems, Congress simply cannot do its job absent an ability to delegate power under broad general directives.").

Supreme Court.[19] "Every few years," they said, a court of appeals invalidates a federal statute on the doctrine's basis, then the Supreme Court takes the case and "overturns the appellate decision, holding that the statute is a constitutional delegation of legislative authority."[20] Since that writing, the Court has issued two more nondelegation decisions, in 2019 and again in the 2024-2025 term, both times sanctioning the doctrine's importance while holding that the challenged statute does not run afoul of the separation of powers.[21] In both cases, the majority and dissents preliminarily diverged not on the validity or importance of the nondelegation doctrine, but on the scope of the power conferred because of differing interpretations of the challenged statute.

The concurring and dissenting opinions accompanying the Court's 2019 nondelegation decision, *Gundy v. United States,* hinted at changes to the Court's approach toward the nondelegation doctrine. The Court split 5–3,[22] and Justice Samuel Alito concurred, saying he would "support [the] effort" to reconsider the intelligible principle approach in a case where the majority of the Court was likewise willing.[23] As Gary Lawson put it that year, it was "very hard to read *Gundy* and not count to five under your breath."[24] Fast forward to July 2, 2024, and Justice Clarence Thomas similarly observed in a dissent from denial of certiorari in a nondelegation challenge that "[a]t least five Justices have already expressed an interest in reconsidering this Court's approach to Congress's delegations of legislative power."[25]

Consequently, court watchers were justified in eagerly awaiting a decision in *FCC v. Consumers' Research,* an appeal from the *en banc* Fifth Circuit's ruling that the Federal Communication Commission's funding mechanism of programs to fulfill a statutory mandate for "universal services" violated the Constitution's separation of powers.

---

[19] Keith E. Whittington & Jason Luliano, *The Myth of the Nondelegation Doctrine,* 165 U. Pa. L. Rev. 379, 380 (2017).

[20] *Id.*

[21] Gundy v. United States, 588 U.S. 128, 132 (2019); *Consumers' Rsch.,* 145 S. Ct. at 2492.

[22] The newly confirmed Justice Brett Kavanaugh did not participate in the decision.

[23] *Gundy,* 588 U.S. at 149 (Alito, J., concurring in the judgment).

[24] Gary Lawson, *"I'm Leavin' It (All) Up to You":* Gundy *and the (Sort-of) Resurrection of the Subdelegation Doctrine,* 2018–2019 Cato Sup. Ct. Rev. 31 (2019).

[25] Allstates Refractory Contractors, LLC v. Su, 603 U.S. ___, slip op. at 3 (2024) (Thomas, J., dissenting).

C. Consumers' Research Challenge of the Universal Services Funding Mechanism

The case leading to the 2025 nondelegation buzz arose over the funding structure for the Universal Service Fund (the "fund"). The fund is mandated by a 1996 amendment to the Communications Act of 1934. The original act created the Federal Communications Commission (FCC), and the 1996 amendment (the "Telecommunications Act") established a "new framework" for a longstanding requirement that the FCC ensure that "basic communications services extend across the country" ("universal services").[26] In pursuit of universal services, the FCC must provide communication assistance to rural hospitals, schools, and libraries; expand communications access for consumers in rural or other high-cost areas; and pay subsidies for designated populations in need of better communication services.[27]

Achieving the guarantee of universal services costs money, of course, and Congress embedded a plan to fund the requirement in the Telecommunications Act. The statute requires qualifying telecommunication carriers to contribute to the fund and allows those carriers to pass on the costs to consumers (check your phone bill for a universal services line item!). There is no pre-established rate for contribution or a cap on the amount that carriers will be required to contribute.[28] Instead, the FCC developed a formula to decide who pays how much: the amount is determined by multiplying a participating carrier's own projected revenue by a fraction (expressed as a percentage) that changes quarterly. The numerator of the fraction is the projected expenses for providing universal services for the upcoming quarter (both the actual services and administrative expenses of maintaining the program), and the denominator is the total projected revenue of all "contributing carriers" during the same period.[29]

Shortly after the act's amendment, the FCC appointed the Universal Service Administrative Company (the "administrator") to maintain the fund. Relevant to the nondelegation challenge, the administrator

[26] *Consumers' Rsch.*, 145 S. Ct. at 2493.

[27] *Id.*

[28] *Id.* at 2626 (Gorsuch, J., dissenting).

[29] *Id.* at 2494 (majority op.).

calculates the fund's projected expenses and the total projected revenue of the contributing carriers and supplies that information to the FCC for approval when establishing each new quarter's contribution rate. Since the administrator began operating the fund (two years after the Telecommunications Act was enacted, redefining universal services), the rate that carriers have paid has gone from 4 percent to 37 percent of their revenue from interstate and international telecommunications.[30] (Notably, the percentage of total carrier revenue attributable to these services has decreased in the same period, so the increase in percentage of total is not completely attributable to rate increases.) Thus, the payment has gone from $2.29 billion to about $8.59 billion.[31] Relevant to the legal challenge of the fund, the government was willing to assume for purposes of this case that the required contributions constituted a tax on the carriers.[32]

Consumers' Research[33] challenged the constitutionality of the universal services funding mechanism on two relevant grounds: (1) Congress's failure to specify a rate or a cap on the amount of revenue the FCC could require from contributing carriers was an unconstitutional delegation of legislative power, and (2) the FCC's involvement of a private organization (the administrator) in calculating the rate of contribution and collecting the funds was an impermissible delegation of authority to a private party (the "private nondelegation doctrine").

A three-judge panel of the Fifth Circuit rejected Consumers' Research's claims, holding that no unconstitutional delegation occurred either from Congress to the FCC or from the FCC to the administrator. Three months after the decision, the *en banc* Fifth Circuit agreed to reconsider the challenge. The full Fifth Circuit ruled in Consumers' Research's favor on the grounds that the "combination of delegations" between Congress to the FCC and the FCC to the administrator violated the Constitution.

---

[30] *Id.* at 2526 (Gorsuch, J., dissenting).

[31] *Id.* at 2523; *but see id.* at 2504 n.8 (claiming that the dates used did not represent a fair benchmark year) (majority op.).

[32] Oral Argument Transcript at 53, FCC v. Consumers' Rsch., No. 24-354 (U.S. Mar. 26, 2025).

[33] Consumers' Research was joined by a group of petitioners. The litigants challenging the statute are collectively referred to herein as "Consumers' Research."

The Supreme Court granted certiorari on the following questions presented:

1. Whether Congress violated the nondelegation doctrine by authorizing the Commission to determine, within the limits set forth in Section 254, the amount that providers must contribute to the Fund.

2. Whether the Commission violated the nondelegation doctrine by using the Administrator's financial projections in computing universal service contribution rates.

3. Whether the combination of Congress's conferral of authority on the Commission and the Commission's delegation of administrative responsibilities to the Administrator violates the nondelegation doctrine.[34]

II. The Four Opinions of *FCC v. Consumers' Research*

The Supreme Court's *FCC v. Consumers' Research* decision was one of five cases resolved on the last decision day of the 2024-2025 term. Despite the prospect of change teased in the 2019 *Gundy* dissent and subsequent writings, the Court soundly affirmed (6–3) the longstanding "intelligible principle" test for the constitutionality of a congressional delegation and rejected attempts to articulate a unique standard for delegations related to revenue-raising. It also rejected the "private nondelegation doctrine" claims in this case because the administrator's role "is broadly subordinate to the Commission."[35] Thus, no delegation occurred that needed to be scrutinized.[36]

The case yielded four opinions: the opinion of the Court (authored by Justice Elena Kagan and joined by Chief Justice John Roberts and Justices Kavanaugh, Sonia Sotomayor, Amy Coney Barrett, and Ketanji Brown Jackson), a concurrence by Justice Jackson, a concurrence by Justice Kavanaugh, and a dissent authored by

---

[34] Petition for a Writ of Certiorari, FCC v. Consumers' Rsch., No. 24-354 (U.S. Sept. 30, 2024). The grant of certiorari identified the following additional question: "Whether this case is moot in light of the challenger's failure to seek preliminary relief before the Fifth Circuit." The Court resolved this question in a footnote, noting that the parties agree that the case is not moot, as does the Court, and noting that the Court's decisions "have never hinted" at a requirement to seek preliminary relief "in order to avail itself of the capable-of-repetition rule." *Consumers' Rsch.*, 145 S. Ct. at 2496 n.1.

[35] *Consumers' Rsch.*, 145 S. Ct. at 2508.

[36] *Id.*

Justice Neil Gorsuch and joined by Justices Thomas and Alito. Court watchers who think back to the 2019 *Gundy* decision may be surprised at which side of the "v" Chief Justice Roberts appeared on. In *Gundy,* Chief Justice Roberts joined Justice Gorsuch's dissenting opinion which said, among other things, that the intelligible principle test came from "divorcing a passing comment from its context, ignoring all that came before and after, and treating an isolated phrase as if it were controlling."[37] In *Consumers' Research,* Chief Justice Roberts joined, without any noted hesitation, the majority opinion, stating that the Court "set out the 'intelligible principle' standard as the universal method for assessing delegations" and blessing its continued use.[38] The other Justice that proponents of a revitalized nondelegation doctrine were closely watching was Justice Kavanaugh. Justice Kavanaugh did not participate in the *Gundy* decision but authored a "statement" respecting the denial of certiorari in a later, similar case, noting "Justice Gorsuch's scholarly analysis of the Constitution's nondelegation doctrine in his *Gundy* dissent may warrant further consideration in future cases."[39] Defying the expectations of some, Chief Justice Roberts and Justice Kavanaugh both supported the application of the longstanding intelligible principle standard and refused to apply it more stringently to a revenue raising statute.

Regardless, the majority and dissenters were united both in recognizing the nondelegation doctrine as a necessary part of the Court's constitutional jurisprudence and in acknowledging the difficulty of drawing the line in close cases. As the dueling opinions wrestled with potential consequences of the opposing perspective, they preached the justification of their own. One line stood out from the opinion of the Court when grappling with the dissent and the argument of the respondent. The Court said, "the Consumers' Research approach does nothing to vindicate the nondelegation doctrine or, more broadly, the separation of powers."[40]

What would "vindicate the nondelegation doctrine"? Journey with me through the four opinions of *FCC v. Consumers' Research* to explore the diversity of perspectives on nondelegation: the "principle

---

[37] *Gundy,* 588 U.S. at 163 (Gorsuch, J., dissenting).

[38] *Consumers' Rsch.,* 145 S. Ct. at 2501.

[39] Paul v. United States, 140 S. Ct. 342, 342 (2019).

[40] *Consumers' Rsch.,* 145 S. Ct. at 2501.

universally recognized as vital to the integrity and maintenance of the system of government ordained by the Constitution."[41]

A. The Opinion of the Court

Justice Kagan wrote for the majority and was joined by Chief Justice Roberts and Justices Sotomayor, Barrett, Jackson, and Kavanaugh. To the majority, reviewing the Universal Services Fund was business as usual for a nondelegation case. First, as noted above, the Court comfortably blessed the longstanding principle that bars the delegation of legislative power.[42] Nevertheless, the Court echoed the familiar refrain in nondelegation cases that Congress may "seek[] assistance" from coordinate branches, often by vesting "discretion" in agencies to "fill up the details" of how to implement a particular law.[43]

Thus, the question in most nondelegation challenges is merely where to draw the line between permissible and impermissible grants of authority to another branch. The "standard" or "test" for determining the line is "whether Congress has set out an 'intelligible principle' to guide what it has given an agency to do."[44] This test depends on context, allowing courts to consider the scope of the powers the agency can wield based on Congress's instructions (i.e., the grant of authority) when evaluating the level of detail needed for those instructions to meet constitutional muster.[45] To pass the intelligible principle test, Congress must have identified a "general policy" animating the instructions and provided some "boundaries" of what the agency (or other recipient of the grant of authority) can do to further that policy. Relatedly, the instructions must be clear enough to allow "'the courts and the public [to] ascertain whether the agency' has followed the law."[46]

If Congress has followed those steps, the Court "will not disturb its grant of authority."[47] Indeed, in nearly 250 years, the Supreme

---

[41] Field v. Clark, 143 U.S. 649, 692 (1892).

[42] Consumers' Rsch., 145 S. Ct. at 2496.

[43] Id. at 2496–97.

[44] Id. at 2497 (quoting J.W. Hampton, Jr. & Co., 276 U.S. at 409).

[45] Id.

[46] Id. (quoting OPP Cotton Mills, Inc. v. Adm'r of Wage & Hour Div., 312 U.S. 126, 144 (1941)).

[47] Id.

Court has only invalidated a statutory provision based on the non-delegation doctrine twice, both in 1935.[48]

What Consumers' Research claimed was special in this case is the delegation of a revenue-raising function without a precise rate or a numerical limit on the amount of money the agency could require companies to pay. Consumers' Research argued that "Congress must set a 'definite' or 'objective limit' on how much money an agency can collect—a numeric cap, a fixed rate, or the equivalent."[49] The Court made swift work of this argument, both rejecting a "special nondelegation rule for revenue-raising legislation" and saying that the current standard is "trained on intelligible principles, not on numeric caps and 'mathematical formula[s].'"[50]

The Court looked to two prior nondelegation decisions in declining to treat revenue-raising statutes differently: *J.W. Hampton* (the 1928 decision establishing the intelligible principle test) and *Skinner v. Mid-America Pipeline Co.* (a 1989 decision). In *J.W. Hampton*, the Court evaluated the constitutionality of a provision that allowed the president to increase certain tariff rates upon factual findings related to the cost of growth or production of goods in competing countries.[51] While the Court was not presented with the exact question of a need for a precise rate or cap, it proceeded with analysis that created the test now known as the "intelligible principle" standard without specifying that judicial review would differ in cases not involving revenue. Sixty years later, in *Skinner*, the Court applied the language of "intelligible principle" from *J.W. Hampton* to the evaluation of a statute that allowed an executive department to set fee rates, and specifically rejected applying a "two-tiered theory of nondelegation" to differentiate between taxation and nontaxation cases (though the statute evaluated in that case did include a cap).[52] In the Court's view, these precedents foreclosed the ability to specially review grants of authority involving

---

[48] *See* Panama Refin. Co. v. Ryan, 293 U.S. 388 (1935); A.L.A. Schechter Poultry Corp. v. United States, 295 U.S. 495 (1935).

[49] *Consumers' Rsch.*, 145 S. Ct. at 2497 (quoting Brief for Respondents, FCC v. Consumers' Rsch., No. 24-354 (Feb. 11, 2025)).

[50] *Id.* at 2498.

[51] *See* J.W. Hampton, Jr. & Co. v. United States, 276 U.S. 394 (1928).

[52] *See* Skinner v. Mid-Am. Pipeline Co., 490 U.S. 212 (1989).

revenue raising, including setting numeric caps if a sufficient non-numeric boundary exists in the statute.

The Court opined that this outcome was preferable as a policy matter because, it claimed, accepting Consumers' Research's and the dissent's proposed cap or rate-setting requirement would "throw a host of federal statutes into doubt."[53] Indeed, the government identified a list of statutes—from FDIC insurance to postage rates—that contain revenue raising provisions to be set by the executive branch that do not contain set rates or revenue caps.[54] These statutes drew much discussion at oral argument, including whether there should be a distinction in constitutional analysis between revenue raisers that constitute a fee versus a tax. According to the majority, applying the same nondelegation analysis to revenue-raising grants of authority as to any other type of alleged delegation would have the benefit of avoiding the "morass"[55] of determining whether a required payment was a fee or a tax.

With that conclusion made, the Court was able to move on to the fact-bound determination of whether the particular grant of authority to the FCC to collect revenue to fund universal services was an impermissible delegation of legislative power.

First, the Court recognized a limiting principle in the word "sufficient." The statute "directs the FCC to collect the amount that is 'sufficient' to support the universal-service programs Congress has told it to implement."[56] "[I]n fact," the Court said, "the word 'sufficient' sets a floor and a ceiling" in the amount of money the FCC is allowed to raise.[57] If the FCC raises much above or below the amount necessary, "it violates the statute."[58] This limitation is more meaningful than a mere cap on the total amount, according to the Court.

Second, the Court said Congress satisfactorily set boundaries on the "nature and content of universal services," so the FCC is limited

---

[53] *Consumers' Rsch.*, 145 S. Ct. at 2498.

[54] Reply Brief for the Federal Petitioners at 8, FCC v. Consumers' Rsch. (Nos. 24-354, 24-422) (Mar. 13, 2025).

[55] *Consumers' Rsch.*, 145 S. Ct. at 2499.

[56] *Id.* at 2501.

[57] *Id.* at 2502.

[58] *Id.*

in what kinds of things it can "sufficiently" fund.[59] In this portion of the analysis, the majority and dissent differed in their statutory interpretation of exactly what authority Congress granted to the FCC. The Court viewed the principles guiding universal services as required limitations on what can be a part of the universal services program.[60] Moreover, it was unconcerned by the inclusion of a provision "enabling the FCC to articulate '[a]dditional principles'" beyond the ones delineated in guiding the development of universal services because, in its view, any new principles must be "consistent with" the remainder of the statute.[61] Notably (or, tellingly, according to Justice Gorsuch's dissent), the Court included a footnote in its analysis of this component, referencing three sections of the Telecommunications Act. It clarified that it based its holding on an analysis of only Section 254, which governs the basic universal services funding model, adding, "[w]e have no occasion to address any nondelegation issues raised by" two other sections that allow for the funding of "advanced" or "additional" services.[62]

It is worth pausing here to dwell on the importance of the prior two conclusions. Using its statutory interpretation muscles, the Court identified "meaningful guideposts for the FCC to follow when carrying out its delegated function of collecting and spending contributions from carriers."[63] The Court acknowledged that giving the FCC license to raise an unlimited amount of money would likely pose "constitutional problem[s]"[64] but disagreed with the *interpretive* claim that the word "sufficient" had only a downward limit. Next, the Court's interpretation of the role of certain "principles" for the FCC to consider varied sharply from Consumers' Research's and the dissent's view, saying that "we view the statutory criteria—which, contra the dissent, . . . define universal service—as

---

[59] *Id.*

[60] *Id.*

[61] *Id.* at 2506. Indeed, the Supreme Court has upheld broad statutory grants of discretion, such as decisions promoting the "public interest" because the phrase is deemed to "take meaning from the purposes of the regulatory legislation." *Id.* at 2507 (quoting *NAACP v. FPC*, 425 U.S. 662, 669 (1976)).

[62] *Id.* at 2505 n.9.

[63] *Id.* at 2501.

[64] *Id.* at 2502.

separately mandatory."[65] The Court took pains to distinguish its interpretation of the scope of authority actually granted in the statute from what was posited by Consumers' Research:

> At every turn, [Consumers' Research] read[s] Section 254 extravagantly, the better to create a constitutional problem. . . . All in all, the arguments do not show statutory construction at its best. Nor, relatedly, do they show proper respect for a coordinate branch of Government. Statutes (including regulatory statutes) should be read, if possible, to comport with the Constitution, not to contradict it. That disposition nowhere appears in the efforts Consumers' Research and the dissent make to force Section 254 past the Constitution's breaking point.[66]

To focus on a point of agreement among the Justices: there is a breaking point! The outcome in *FCC v. Consumers' Research* is similar to the 2019 *Gundy* nondelegation decision. There, the opinion of the Court and the dissent were working from different sets of "facts." Or, more precisely, were working from different interpretations of what responsibilities the statute actually gave the executive branch. Although Justice Gorsuch claimed that this was done disingenuously in both cases (in *Gundy*, claiming the Court "reimagines the term[s] of the statute,"[67] and in this case saying, "the Court eventually resorts to rewriting the statute"[68]), the different perspectives are essential to recognize when contemplating the Court's greater nondelegation jurisprudence. Everyone agrees the nondelegation principle is operative and requires an assessment of the scope of authority conveyed in determining the line between permissible and impermissible. In recent cases, the Court and the dissent have been applying the intelligible principle test to *different scopes of authority* because of disagreeing interpretations of the grant of authority. More on this later.

Finally, the Court quickly rejects the theory that the FCC impermissibly delegated authority to the administrator or that, in turn, the combination of authority granted to the FCC and the administrator

---

[65] *Id.* at 2506 (emphasis added).

[66] *Id.* at 2507 (internal citations omitted).

[67] *Gundy*, 588 U.S. at 149 (Gorsuch, J., dissenting).

[68] *Consumers' Rsch.*, 145 S. Ct. at 2529 (Gorsuch, J., dissenting).

together yielded an unconstitutional delegation. Dispositively, the FCC did not actually give the administrator authority for the Court to analyze in the nondelegation lens.[69] Rather, "the Administrator is broadly subordinate to the Commission."[70] In the Court's view, the administrator does not make policy or set rules but rather merely collects numbers, offers recommendations, and provides documents to the FCC. The FCC, then, is the final authority in all processes anticipated in the statute. As for the "combination" theory the Fifth Circuit adopted, the Court easily summed up: "a meritless public nondelegation challenge plus a meritless private nondelegation challenge cannot equal a meritorious 'combination' claim."[71]

B. Justice Kavanaugh's Concurrence

Despite joining the majority opinion in full, Justice Kavanaugh wrote separately for two stated purposes: (1) to "outline" the "background and rationale behind the intelligible principle test," and (2) to explain his view that delegations to independent agencies raise enhanced constitutional concerns that may require different treatment.[72] Perhaps the first point was necessary because of a belief that the Court's history with the nondelegation doctrine was in need of vindicating?

1. The intelligible principle test—Kavanaugh style

Justice Kavanaugh leads his reflection on the intelligible principle test with an emphasis on permissible "delegations," citing early examples of Congress instructing the president or executive branch officials to issue regulations or decide details of implementation of various statutes.[73] While he blesses the notion that "the Court has not said that 'anything goes' with respect to those delegations[,]" Justice Kavanaugh draws a slightly different analytical line to divide permissible and impermissible delegations.

---

[69] *Id.* at 2508 (majority op.).

[70] *Id.*

[71] *Id.* at 2511.

[72] *Id.* at 2511–12 (Kavanaugh, J., concurring).

[73] *Id.* at 2512.

Conceptually, to Justice Kavanaugh, a permissible delegation is merely guidance for the president in fulfilling his *executive* role of ensuring the laws are faithfully executed. Thus, no separation of powers problem would exist because the "delegation" is not even a limited grant of an Article I power, but an instruction for fulfilling an Article II power in the context of the relevant statute. As he described the Court's prior holdings, "any congressional grant of authority must supply some guidance to the President—*otherwise the President would no longer be exercising 'executive Power' when implementing legislation.*"[74] He thus frames the intelligible principle test as a means to "ensure that the President is exercising executive power when implementing legislation[.]"[75]

Justice Kavanaugh's formulation of what occurs during a contested delegation is an extension of Justice Scalia's framework as described in his dissent in *Mistretta v. United States:*[76]

> The whole theory of *lawful* congressional "delegation" is not that Congress is sometimes too busy or too divided, and can therefore assign its responsibility of making law to someone else, but rather that a certain degree of discretion, and thus of lawmaking, **inheres in most executive or judicial action,** and it is up to Congress, by the relative specificity or generality of its statutory commands, **to determine—up to a point—how small or how large that degree shall be.** . . . [T]he Executive could be given the power to adopt policies and rules specifying in detail what radio and television licenses will be in the 'public interest, convenience or necessity,' **because that was ancillary to the exercise of its executive powers** in granting and policing licenses[.][77]

---

[74] *Id.* at 2513 (emphasis added).

[75] *Id.* at 2514. Notably, this formulation may not mesh with Justice Robert H. Jackson's conception of the separation of powers articulated in his concurrence in *Youngstown.* Youngstown Sheet & Tube Co. v. Sawyer, 343 U.S. 579 (1952) (Jackson, J., concurring). Jackson said, "When the President acts pursuant to an express or implied authorization of Congress, his authority is at its maximum, for it includes all that he possesses in his own right *plus* all that Congress can delegate." *Id.* at 635 (emphasis added). Justice Jackson appears to acknowledge that some amount of legislative power may be truly shared with the executive branch but, other than a footnote extensively quoting *United States v. Curtiss-Wright,* does not offer significant insight into the nondelegation doctrine. *Id.* at 635 n.2.

[76] 488 U.S. 361, 417 (1989) (Scalia, J., dissenting).

[77] *Id.* at 418 (bold emphasis added).

Justice Scalia emphasized the point by saying that "[s]trictly speaking, there is *no* acceptable delegation of power[,]" and went on to quote John Locke's *Second Treatise of Government* in support of the statement.[78] Instead, he said:

> The focus of controversy, in the long line of our so-called excessive delegation cases, has been whether the *degree* of generality contained in the authorization for exercise of executive or judicial powers in a particular field is so unacceptably high as to *amount* to a delegation of legislative powers.[79]

Clarifying this conceptual formulation may have been an important part of why Justice Kavanaugh chose to write separately. Regardless of any differences in perspective on what occurs on either side of the line of permissible and impermissible delegation, Justice Kavanaugh and the rest of the majority are comfortable using the same test to figure out where the line is drawn: the intelligible principle standard. Justice Kavanaugh blesses the test, saying it is "not toothless" and "has had staying power[.]"[80] He rejects the opportunity to "try to spell out a definitive guide for applying the intelligible principle test" but still went on to "emphasize three points" before transitioning to his perspective on grants of authority to independent agencies.

First, he simply echoes a common thread between the majority opinion and Justice Gorsuch's dissent. Both agree that the scope of power embedded in a delegation is relevant to determining whether the delegation is permissible.[81] While he elaborates on his final two points, this two-sentence paragraph appears to offer a noncontroversial olive branch noting that all members of the Court may have skepticism over an extremely powerful delegation and would use "common sense" to assess future challenges. This point is extremely relevant in outcomes like *Gundy* and this case, where the majority and the dissent are operating under different

---

[78] *Id.* at 419 (emphasis in original).

[79] *Id.* (emphasis in original).

[80] *Consumers' Rsch.*, 145 S. Ct. at 2515 (Kavanaugh, J., concurring).

[81] *Id.*

interpretations of the relevant statutory grant. While Chief Justice Roberts did not write separately in either case, this point may very well be why he landed on "opposite" sides in those cases—perhaps disagreeing with the Court's statutory interpretation in *Gundy* while agreeing with it here.

Second, Justice Kavanaugh pivots from strict constitutional analysis to policy considerations. He claims that "many of the broader structural concerns about expansive delegations have been substantially mitigated by this Court's recent case law[.]"[82] While a strict constitutionalist[83] may not care whether the policy aims of a particular doctrine are met elsewhere when considering when and how to apply that doctrine, Justice Kavanaugh appears to be comforted that limitations on executive power related to congressional action are possible based on two other lines of Supreme Court precedents: (1) the elimination of *Chevron* deference, and (2) the growth of the major questions canon of interpretation.[84]

Citing *Loper Bright Enterprises v. Raimondo*,[85] Justice Kavanaugh notes that the "President's actions when implementing legislation *are* constrained . . . by the scope of Congress's authorization and by any restrictions set forth in that statutory text."[86] Indeed, while he does not say so explicitly, that is exactly what happened here: the Court interpreted the statutory provision on its own and articulated a more limited scope of authority than the litigant claimed or the dissent

---

[82] *Id.*

[83] *See* Lawson, *supra* note 24, at 64 ("But if one is less a constitutionalist than a *conservative*, one might worry a great deal about the 'appropriate' judicial role, public perceptions of the Court, the dangers of judicial 'activism,' and a host of other policy-laden considerations that are not grounded in constitutional meaning.").

[84] *Consumers' Rsch.*, 145 S. Ct. at 2515–16 (Kavanaugh, J., concurring) ("Second, many of the broader structural concerns about expansive delegations have been substantially mitigated by this Court's recent case law in related areas—in particular (i) the Court's rejection of so-called *Chevron* deference and (ii) the Court's application of the major questions canon of statutory interpretation.").

[85] 603 U.S. 369, 394–406 (2024). In *Loper Bright*, the Supreme Court overruled *Chevron U.S.A. Inc. v. Nat. Res. Def. Council, Inc.*, 467 U.S. 837 (1984), which held that courts should defer to permissible agency interpretations of statutes.

[86] *Consumers' Rsch.*, 145 S. Ct. at 2515 (Kavanaugh, J., concurring) (emphasis in original).

believed existed.[87] Additionally, in a sense, the constitutional under-pinnings of *Loper Bright*[88] are its own flavor of the nondelegation doctrine. In that context, neither Congress (by statute) nor the courts (by a judicially created doctrine of deference) can delegate the Article III responsibility for interpreting the law to Article II executive agencies. While Justice Kavanaugh does not use the language of nondelegation in respect to *Loper Bright's* overruling of *Chevron* deference, he is reassured by the ability of the judiciary to independently recognize limits to congressionally granted delegations within a statute's text.[89]

Justice Kavanaugh goes on to point out that the major questions canon of construction may result in similar policy outcomes as a robust application of the nondelegation doctrine. He says that canon "reflects both the background separation of powers understandings and the commonsense interpretive maxim that Congress does not usually 'hide elephants in mouseholes' when granting authority to the President."[90] Notably, he retreats from the idea he floated in a statement respecting the denial of certiorari in a separate case of a "nondelegation principle for major questions."[91] Instead, he embraces major questions merely as a canon of construction, rather than a constitutional principle to apply with (or instead of) the intelligible principle standard.

Third, Justice Kavanaugh's final point arguably strays even farther afield of the actual constitutional question at hand. He declares that the nondelegation doctrine plays an "even more limited

---

[87] Indeed, Consumers' Research asserted at oral argument that the FCC itself interpreted the statute in a more expansive manner than the Court eventually held. Oral Argument Transcript at 115, FCC v. Consumers' Rsch., No. 24-354 (March 26, 2025) ("[T]he principles in 254(b) are ones that the FCC does not have to substantively comply with. This is not some extreme, unusual reading as they try to make it sound. That's been their uniform interpretation for 25 years."). Regardless, the Court cited *Loper Bright* in defense of reading the statute independently to determine "what power Congress has conferred." *Consumers' Rsch.*, 145 S. Ct. at 2506.

[88] The Court in *Loper Bright* based its holdings on the statutory text of the Administrative Procedure Act, rather than constitutional requirements. However, the Court noted the statute "incorporates the traditional understanding of the judicial function" and repeatedly invoked constitutionally sourced concepts in justifying its holding. *See* Loper Bright Enter. v. Raimondo, 603 U.S. 369, 386–390, 394, 403 (2024).

[89] Notably, any statute that does not contain limitations that the judiciary can examine may be at risk under the intelligible principle test.

[90] *Consumers' Rsch.*, 145 S. Ct. at 2516 (Kavanaugh, J., concurring).

[91] Paul v. United States, 140 S. Ct. 342, 342 (2019) (statement of Kavanaugh, J.).

role" in national security and foreign policy matters "in light of the President's constitutional responsibilities *and independent Article II authority.*"[92] The latter part of his sentence gives away the disconnect with the nondelegation doctrine. The nondelegation doctrine—as the Supreme Court has defined it without fail—deals with the ability of one branch (typically, Congress) to delegate some or any of *that branch's* authority. A court interpreting a congressional delegation to the executive branch in a subject where both branches have overlapping powers will be faced with a different set of questions than another case interpreting a delegation of a "strictly and exclusively legislature power" (such as the power to tax).[93]

Indeed, judicial review of a congressional grant of authority in a subject matter that involves independent Article II or Article III powers (such as national security and foreign policy) must include an analysis of the extent of the *independent* powers of the branch that is receiving the delegation. To the extent the two branches powers *truly overlap*, then Congress's "delegation" of part of its nonexclusive legislative authority in that context (such as foreign policy) may actually transform into a "regulation" of executive or judicial powers. Indeed, the authority Justice Kavanaugh relies on to support his third point anticipates regulation (i.e., restriction or limitation) of authority, rather than delegation.[94] This would certainly be a

---

[92] *Consumers' Rsch.*, 145 S. Ct. at 2516 (Kavanaugh, J., concurring) (emphasis added).

[93] *Wayman*, 23 U.S. at 42. The Court has previously implied a more stringent nondelegation test in foreign affairs matters but did not elaborate on whether such an analysis would only apply *after* analyzing independent authority for the relevant conduct and finding it lacking as to the specific foreign affairs issue challenged under the nondelegation doctrine. *See United States v. Curtiss-Wright Exp. Corp.*, 299 U.S. 304, 321–22 (1936). There, the difference in analysis was justified by prudential reasons, rather than a strict separation of powers review. *Id.* ("When the President is to be authorized by legislation to act in respect of a matter intended to affect a situation in foreign territory, the legislator properly bears in mind the important consideration that the form of the President's actions—or, indeed, whether he shall act at all—may well depend, among other things, upon the nature of the confidential information which he has or may thereafter receive, or upon the effect which his action may have upon our foreign relations. This consideration, in connection with what we have already said on the subject, discloses the unwisdom of requiring Congress in this field of governmental power to lay down narrowly definite standards by which the President is to be governed.").

[94] *See, e.g., Consumers' Rsch.*, 145 S. Ct. at 2516 (Kavanaugh, J., concurring) (noting that the president must often be accorded freedom "from statutory restriction") (quoting Indus. Union Dept., AFL-CIO v. Am. Petroleum Inst., 448 U.S. 607, 684 (1980)).

separation of powers question, but not necessarily a nondelegation one, in the sense it has been applied historically.[95]

Alternatively, the congressional grant of authority may apply to a different aspect of the subject matter not wrapped up in the independent executive or judicial authority. In that case, the traditional nondelegation test would apply. A timely (as of the time of this writing) example of a connected but not overlapping topic is tariff authority. Multiple challenges are making their way through the courts of appeals on whether Congress delegated authority to the executive branch to enact tariffs through the International Economic Emergency Powers Act. And, more importantly for our purposes, if Congress did so, does the Constitution allow the delegation of that power in the manner it has been used (i.e., application of the nondelegation doctrine)?[96] Justice Kavanaugh's third point shows he is hesitant to apply the nondelegation doctrine in cases involving foreign policy and national security, but his concurrence fails to recognize that such large fields may involve separate—and *potentially nonoverlapping*—executive and legislative independent powers.

Although Justice Kavanaugh claims the nondelegation doctrine and major questions canon (which he incorporates into point three after also invoking it in point two) do "not translate" to the national security or foreign policy contexts, the underlying questions in those contexts may involve Article II powers distinct from the Article I powers that would trigger a nondelegation analysis.

---

[95] As an example, *Trump v. United States*, 603 U.S. 593 (2024) (the executive "immunity" decision), could be read as establishing a "non*regulation*" doctrine. There, the Supreme Court held that Congress cannot legislatively regulate (in that case, by generally applicable criminal laws applied to the president) areas within the "conclusive and preclusive" authority the Constitution grants to the executive branch. *Id*. Notably, *Youngstown Sheet & Tube Co. v. Sawyer* may have envisioned some congressional ability to regulate even independent executive authority: "When the President takes measures incompatible with the expressed or implied will of Congress, his power is at its lowest ebb, for then he can rely only upon his own constitutional powers *minus any constitutional powers of Congress over the matter*." 343 U.S. 579, 638 (1952) (emphasis added).

[96] *See* Petition for a Writ of Certiorari Before Judgment, *Learning Res., Inc. v. Trump*, No. 24-1287 (June 17, 2025); Notice for Oral Argument Proceedings in *V.O.S. Selections, Inc. v. Trump*, V.O.S. Selections, Inc. v. Trump, No. 25-1813 (Fed. Cir. July 15, 2025).

2. Independent agencies

Justice Kavanaugh's perspective on delegation to independent agencies flows naturally from his view on permissible grants of authority from Congress to another branch. If a permissible grant is merely an instruction for how the president is to perform his Article II responsibility (in the Congress-to-executive context) to see that the law is faithfully executed, then the same nondelegation analysis could not apply to a recipient of congressional delegation that has no independent constitutional authority (i.e., an agency that is truly independent from the executive branch).[97]

Instead of dwelling on the analytical difference, however, Justice Kavanaugh returns once again to a policy point. He stresses the problem of lack of accountability of independent agencies with rule-making power:

> [W]hen Congress delegates authority to an independent agency, no democratically elected official is accountable. Whom do the people blame and hold responsible for a bad decision or policy adopted by an independent agency? Such a system of disembodied independent agencies with enormous power over the American people and American economy operates in substantial tension with the principle of democratic accountability incorporated into the Constitution's text and structure, as well as historical practice and foundational Article II precedents.[98]

Because Justice Kavanaugh views the lack of statutory for-cause removal protections for the FCC as rendering the FCC fully within the purview of the executive branch (and, thus, not an independent agency), he does not define exactly how a different standard for nondelegation review in the independent agency context should play out. He does say that "[i]n an appropriate case, [the] Court should address that problem."[99]

---

[97] Indeed, this is the basis of Justice Scalia's dissent in *Mistretta*, despite his agreement with the Court's intelligible principle analysis that upheld the United States Sentencing Commission. Mistretta v. United States, 488 U.S. 361, 420–27 (1989) (Scalia, J., dissenting).

[98] *Consumers' Rsch.*, 145 S. Ct. at 2518 (Kavanaugh, J., concurring).

[99] *Id.*

C. Justice Jackson's Concurrence

Justice Jackson authored a solo two-page concurrence to express her "skepticism that the private nondelegation doctrine—which purports to bar the Government from delegating authority to private actors—is a viable and independent doctrine in the first place" because "[n]othing in the text of the Constitution appears to support a *per se* rule barring private delegations."[100] She cautions that "we should not lightly assume that Article III implicitly directs the Judiciary to find" a limit to another branch's power.[101]

Assuming her brief comments indicate a willingness to entertain some grants of authority to a private party, this understanding of the nondelegation doctrine immediately clashes with Justice Kavanaugh's formulation of the nondelegation doctrine. If permissible delegations are mere instructions to another branch on how to fulfill that branch's constitutional duties, then it is entirely possible that a future Court could interpret the Constitution to prohibit, per se, delegations to groups without any independent constitutional authority—be they independent agencies or private actors. Justice Jackson rightly recognizes the lack of constitutional text differentiating recipients of grants of constitutional authority but does not grapple with the structural, separation of powers considerations animating the doctrine in her short concurrence. She will likely have a chance in a future case, which will shine additional light on the varied perspectives of delegation.

D. The Dissent

Justice Gorsuch, joined by Justices Thomas and Alito, calls the universal services funding mechanism a "delegation beyond anything yet seen in the U.S. Reports[.]"[102] In his view, the case "begins and ends" with the first question presented. He formulated the question[103]

---

[100] *Id.* at 2518 (Jackson., J., concurring).

[101] *Id.* (quoting Consumer Fin. Prot. Bureau v. Cmty. Fin. Servs. Ass'n of Am., Ltd., 601 U.S. 416, 446 (2024) (Jackson, J., concurring)).

[102] *Consumers' Rsch.*, 145 S. Ct. at 2519 (Gorsuch, J., dissenting).

[103] Though later conceding the universal services fund may be a tax, the government's cert petition avoided the word in its phrasing of the first question presented, putting it this way: "Whether Congress violated the nondelegation doctrine by authorizing the Commission to determine, within the limits set forth in Section 254, the amount that providers must contribute to the Fund." Petition for a Writ of Certiorari, FCC v. Consumers' Rsch., No. 24-354 (Sept. 30, 2024).

as follows: "did Congress violate the Constitution by delegating to the FCC the power to tax?"[104]

The emphasis on taxation is apparent from the starting lines of the dissent, which opens with the observation that "[w]ithin the federal government, Congress 'alone has access to the pockets of the people.' The Constitution affords only our elected representatives the power to decide which taxes the government can collect and at what rates." [105]

Without advocating for overturning precedent, Justice Gorsuch was forced to work within the same intelligible principle test for grants of authority related to taxes as delegations for anything else.[106] In 1989, the Supreme Court considered a challenge to a delegation to the Secretary of Transportation to "establish a system of user fees to cover the costs of administering certain federal pipeline safety programs[.]"[107] There, the Court paid homage to the taxing power but said that Congress, "when enacting tax legislation, has varied the degree of specificity and the consequent degree of discretionary authority delegated to the Executive in such enactments"[108] and largely applied the typical intelligible principle standard.

Staying within that framework, Justice Gorsuch stresses the oft-repeated adage that the "intelligible principle test is context dependent"[109] and describes the historical and textual importance of the taxing power. He claims, "the Constitution does not require Congress to make every decision, [but] there are some choices that belong to Congress alone—including setting a tax's rate or, at least, capping receipts."[110] Like Justice Kavanaugh's discussion of the non-delegation doctrine in the context of independent agencies, Justice Gorsuch highlights the policy results of requiring Congress to set a tax rate or, at a minimum, a numeric cap on the amounts an individual or body other than Congress could require, saying that if Congress were to enact a ridiculously high cap that an executive

---

[104] *Consumers' Rsch.*, 145 S. Ct. at 2524 (Gorsuch, J., dissenting).

[105] *Id.* at 2519 (internal citation omitted) (quoting THE FEDERALIST No. 48 at 334 (J. Cooke ed. 1961) (James Madison)).

[106] *See* Skinner v. Mid-Am. Pipeline Co., 490 U.S. 212, 212 (1989).

[107] *Id.* at 214.

[108] *Id.* at 221.

[109] *Consumers' Rsch.*, 145 S. Ct. at 2535 (Gorsuch, J., dissenting).

[110] *Id.* at 2532.

agency could charge up to, "the American people would at least know whom to thank when the corresponding charges showed up on their phone bills."[111]

Near the end of his dissent, Justice Gorsuch points out that "[i]n so many other arenas, this Court vigorously polices the Constitution's allocation of power."[112] This accountability has applied to both delegations of the giving branch's power and regulations of a neighboring branch's power. "Yet there is one exception[,]" he says:

> When Congress has willingly surrendered its power to the Executive Branch, this Court's responses can only be described as feeble. . . . What happens when Congress, weary of the hard business of legislating and facing strong incentives to pass the buck, cedes its lawmaking power, clearly and unmistakably, to an executive that craves it? No canon of construction can bar the way.[113]

Such an admonition not only rejects the ability for statutory interpretation, generally, to save the day (indeed, this is where he claims the majority's interpretation in this case was not in good faith but, instead, was itself a "usurp[ing] of legislative power"[114]). It also rebuts Justice Kavanaugh's comfort in the major questions canon.

Despite Justice Gorsuch's hostility to the Court's statutory interpretation of Section 254, he embraces the majority's footnote 9, which peels off from its analysis two broader statutory sections, saying that even the Court cannot "bring itself to bless such a lavish delegation of taxing authority."[115] Whether a reader joins Justice Gorsuch's perspective that the Court is engineering a statutory interpretation of Section 254 to avoid applying the nondelegation doctrine or trusts the good faith interpretation of the majority of the Court, the result is the same: the scope of the power delegated matters to the full Court. None of the opinions of *FCC v. Consumers' Research* embraces an ability of Congress to delegate unlimited revenue-raising powers to the executive branch. Closing with a

---

[111] *Id.* at 2537.
[112] *Id.* at 2538.
[113] *Id.*
[114] *Id.*
[115] *Id.* at 2531.

restatement of a principle all members of the Court appear to agree with, Justice Gorsuch reminds us:

> The Constitution promises that our elected representatives in Congress, and they alone, will make the laws that bind us. . . . When it comes to other aspects of the separation of powers, we have found manageable ways to honor the Constitution's design. This one requires no less of us.[116]

III. Putting It All Together: The Future of the Principle Universally Recognized

FCC v. Consumers' Research is one of those cases in which what the Court *didn't* do is bigger news than what the Court *did* do. On the one hand, the Court didn't "reconsider the approach"[117] of how to analyze nondelegation challenges (i.e., the intelligible principle test), and it didn't adopt a heightened or different standard for reviewing revenue-raising grants of authority. On the other hand, it *also* didn't question the longstanding doctrine that the Constitution bars Congress from delegating legislative authority, or that courts must examine the scope of power conferred by Congress in determining whether the grant of authority is a permissible or impermissible "delegation."

So—yet again—we can say that "in every case in which the question has been raised, the Court has recognized that there are limits of delegation which there is no constitutional authority to transcend."[118] Indeed, this "principle universally recognized" is so unanimous among the members of the Court that the majority condemns the approach of the dissent as failing to "vindicate the nondelegation doctrine or, more broadly, the separation of powers."[119] Instead of weakening the doctrine, the dueling opinions justify their conflicting conclusions with different interpretations of the statute: both the majority and the dissent imply that if their counterpart read the statute to confer the same scope of power as they did, all would be on the same side.

---

[116] *Id.* at 2539.

[117] In the words of Justice Alito's concurrence in *Gundy v. United States,* 588 U.S. 128, 149 (2019).

[118] *Pan. Refin. Co. v. Ryan,* 293 U.S. 388, 430 (1935).

[119] *Consumers' Rsch.,* 145 S. Ct. at 2501 (majority op.).

Thus, the first takeaway from a close look at the four opinions of *FCC v. Consumers' Research* is the vital importance of tools of statutory interpretation. Mundane? Maybe. Dispositive even in nondelegation cases? Absolutely.

Next, the concurrences in *FCC v. Consumers' Research* preview a conceptual difference in what is happening on either side of the line of permissible versus impermissible grants of authority. This difference is likely to splinter the Court along different lines in the future. In Justice Kavanaugh's view, grants of authority to the executive branch are mere instructions for exercising independent executive branch authority in implementing that law. In this view, because the validity of assignments relies on another branch's independent powers, grants of authority to independent agencies or private parties will almost certainly fall on the impermissible line. Justice Jackson's caution over "limit[ing]" another branch's authority indicates a different view on permissible grants of power, untethered to an independent source of power held by the recipient of such a grant. If the view revealed in the short concurrence reflects her conception of delegations, then she will likely apply the same intelligible principle analysis to private parties and to the mine run of executive grant cases. And though Justice Kavanaugh spoke only for himself, his views on the nondelegation doctrine in the context of national security and foreign policy are likely to play a pivotal role in future cases.

Thus, the second takeaway is that litigants advancing nondelegation arguments, and scholars analyzing them, should consider carefully how each justice views what is actually taking place when Congress embeds within a statute duties for another branch or body (public or private) to perform. Is the validity of the assignment reliant on independent authority of the recipient (i.e., Article II or Article III powers) or wholly dependent on the statute's grant? The several justices who have not separately written in recent nondelegation cases may be willing to adopt unexpected outcomes if convinced to adopt one formulation or the other of what occurs during a permissible "delegation."

Ultimately, the Court still has not contested the 1892 Supreme Court declaration that the statement, "Congress cannot delegate legislative power to the President[,]" remains a "principle universally recognized as vital to the integrity and maintenance of the system of government ordained by the Constitution."[120] Rather, *FCC v. Consumers' Research* demonstrates that conflicting outcomes of non-delegation challenges are vindicated by the use of ordinary tools of statutory interpretation to limit the scope of power conferred and provides insights into the differing conceptual frameworks of what Congress is achieving through those contested "delegations" that will likely shape the outcomes of future nondelegation challenges.

[120] Field v. Clark, 143 U.S. 649, 692 (1892).

Seven County Infrastructure Coalition v. Eagle County: A New Era in Federal Environmental Law

Damien M. Schiff* and Charles T. Yates**

Introduction

"One can say, without exaggeration, that the 'modern era' of environmental law began with the signing of [the National Environmental Policy Act (NEPA)] by President [Richard] Nixon on New Year's Day 1970."[1] One could equally say, without exaggeration, that the modern era of environmental law ended, at least with respect to NEPA, in *Seven County Infrastructure Coalition v. Eagle County.*[2] NEPA requires federal agencies to assess the environmental impact of proposed major federal projects and to consider environmentally less-damaging alternatives. Over the decades following NEPA's enactment, certain lower federal courts transmogrified NEPA's purely procedural obligation into a powerful tool to defeat major infrastructure projects. It is this anti-development contortion of the law that, one hopes, has ended with *Seven County.*

At one level, the decision really does nothing new. The Supreme Court has never ruled in favor of a NEPA challenge, and the NEPA challengers lost again in *Seven County.* What is new is the decision's clear, decisive and definitive rejection of the lower courts' practice of hyper-enforcing NEPA's procedural obligations, with little deference given to agencies—all with the result of converting NEPA into a formidable substantive statute oftentimes fatal to federal projects. What is also remarkable is how *Seven County* achieves this course correction: Justice Brett Kavanaugh's majority opinion repeatedly cites common

* Senior Attorney, Pacific Legal Foundation.

** Attorney, Pacific Legal Foundation.

[1] William L. Andreen, *In Pursuit of NEPA's Promise: The Role of Executive Oversight in the Implementation of Environmental Policy,* 64 IND. L.J. 205, 205 n.2 (1989).

[2] 145 S. Ct. 1497 (2025).

sense and the economic drag of an over-inflated NEPA as leading reasons for rejecting the lower courts' excessively zealous enforcement.

We begin this article with a brief review of the legislative process that produced NEPA, as well as of the quick-to-emerge and too-long-enduring divergence between the Supreme Court and lower courts over how to apply NEPA. We next analyze the *Seven County* majority as well as Justice Sonia Sotomayor's concurrence. We then conclude with a few broader observations about *Seven County*'s impact on environmental and administrative law, as well as the decision's relationship to recent political efforts to reinvigorate American infrastructure and natural resource development.

I. Environmental Law's Modern Era Begins: NEPA in Congress

The 1960s was a time of shifting view among Americans about the environment: what started in the 18th century as a fear of wilderness and matured in the 19th century as an attitude of confident mastery had devolved by the mid-20th century into a timidity born of perceived overuse and self-poisoning.[3] This was the age of Rachel Carson,[4] Stuart Udall,[5] and Paul Ehrlich.[6] A general fear and malaise beset America by the end of the decade.[7] *Time* named 1969 the "Year of Ecology" and labeled ecologists the "New Jeremiahs."[8] Even the

---

[3] *See* Subcomm. on Sci., Rsch. & Dev. of the H. Comm. on Sci. & Astronautics, 90th Cong., Managing the Env't 13–15 (Comm. Print 1968).

[4] *See* Richard A. Epstein, *The Many Sins of NEPA*, 6 Tex. A&M L. Rev. 1, 4 (2018) ("Congress passed NEPA at the dawn of the environmental movement as part of the vast public appeal of Rachel Carson's *Silent Spring*. . . .").

[5] *See* Ved P. Nanda, *The Environment, Climate Change, and Human Rights: The Significance of the Human Right to Environment*, 50 Denv. J. Int'l L. & Pol'y 89, 91 (2022) (noting the significance of Udall's *Quiet Crisis* in "spurring," among other things, NEPA).

[6] Erik Podhora, *Lessons for Climate Change Reform from Environmental History: 19th Century Wildlife Protection and the 20th Century Environmental Movement*, 30 J. Envtl. L. & Litig. 1, 28 (2015) ("Widely read books like . . . Paul Ehrlich's *The Population Bomb* highlighted the scope of problems caused by pollution and the need to take immediate action.").

[7] *See* A. Dan Tarlock, *The Story of* Calvert Cliffs: *A Court Construes the National Environmental Policy Act to Create a Powerful Cause of Action*, in Environmental Law Stories 77, 80–81 (Richard J. Lazarus & Oliver A. Houck eds. 2005).

[8] Sam Kalen, *Ecology Comes of Age: NEPA's Lost Mandate*, 21 Duke Envtl. L. & Pol'y F. 113, 124 (2010).

U.S. Chamber of Commerce that year published a pamphlet entitled "The Need: To Manage Our Environment."[9]

This environmental alarmism[10] was not without some warrant. The Santa Barbara oil spill,[11] the New York City smog event of Thanksgiving 1966,[12] and the burning of the Cuyahoga River[13] put people on edge. Many believed that the Earth would soon become overpopulated, with no food left to eat and no air left to breath.[14] Others were beset by a Luddite-inspired concern that technology had become too effective, and too destructive, in harnessing natural resources.[15] A national legislative response was thought to be needed.[16]

The first bill for federal environmental coordination had been submitted back in 1959[17] and, about the same time, the Eisenhower Administration considered the establishment of a Department of

[9] *See National Environmental Policy: Hearing on S. 1075, S. 237, and S. 1752 Before the S. Comm. on Interior and Insular Affs.*, 91st Cong. 31 (1969) [hereinafter *Hearing*].

[10] *See, e.g.*, S. COMM. ON INTERIOR AND INSULAR AFFS., 90TH CONG., A NAT'L POL'Y FOR THE ENV'T 1 (Comm. Print 1968) [hereinafter NAT'L POL'Y] ("But there is, nevertheless, general consensus throughout most walks of life that a serious state of affairs exists . . . .").

[11] *See* Epstein, *supra* note 4, at 4 (noting "the extensive public outrage that stemmed from the . . . massive oil leaks into Santa Barbara waters in 1969").

[12] Barry Friedman, *What Is Public Safety?*, 102 B.U. L. REV. 725, 743 (2022) ("[D]uring Thanksgiving weekend of 1966, ground-level smog in New York City caused an estimated 168 deaths and health problems for some 10% of city residents.").

[13] *See* Jonathan H. Adler, *Fables of the Cuyahoga: Reconstructing a History of Environmental Protection*, 14 FORDHAM ENVTL. L.J. 89, 94 (2002) ("The June 22, 1969, fire on the Cuyahoga is the 'seminal' event in the history of water pollution control in America. . . .").

[14] S. COMM. ON INTERIOR AND INSULAR AFFS. & H. COMM. ON SCI. AND AERONAUTICS, 90TH CONG., WHITE PAPER ON A NAT'L POL'Y FOR THE ENV'T 3 (Comm. Print 1968) [hereinafter White Paper] ("It is clear that all segments of the world—all soils, waters, woods, mountains, plains, oceans, and ice-covered continents—will be occupied and used by man. . . . Everything between soil and sky will be moved about, redistributed and degraded as man continues to exploit the surface of the planet."), https://ceq.doe.gov/docs/laws-regulations/Congress-White-Paper.pdf.

[15] *See, e.g.*, NAT'L POL'Y, *supra* note 10, at 5 ("In summary, within the present generation the pressures of man and technology have exploded into the environment with unprecedented speed and unforeseen destructiveness.").

[16] S. REP. NO. 91-296, at 5 (1969) ("In spite of the growing public recognition of the urgency of many environmental problems and the need to reorder national goals and priorities to deal with these problems, there is still no comprehensive national policy on environmental management.").

[17] John R. Sandler, Note, *The National Environmental Policy Act: A Sheep in Wolf's Clothing?*, 37 BROOK. L. REV. 139, 140 (1970).

Natural Resources. But at this stage the problem was perceived largely as one of insufficient coordination among agencies.[18]

Soon, however, interest in legislation accelerated, in part because of the publication of two influential congressional committee reports[19] and the convening of a congressional "colloquium" on a national environmental policy.[20] Thereafter, legislative interest deepened, from seeking to require mere heightened coordination among federal agencies to establishing a substantive federal environmental policy informed by the developing science of ecology.[21] As Professor Dan Tarlock observes, "NEPA was enacted just as the idea of environmental protection was making the transition from a public policy problem identified and defined by elites to a mass political issue that demanded swift Congressional and Executive response."[22]

Senator Henry Jackson of Washington and Representative John Dingell of Michigan became the leaders of that congressional response.[23] Senator Jackson's initial legislative proposal envisioned simply a federal environmental entrepot—an agency that would research how government programs affect the environment and distribute that information throughout the federal bureaucracy.[24] The Dingell bill did the same but went further than the original Jackson bill in articulating a national environmental policy.[25]

The Nixon administration was not opposed in principle to these proposals.[26] Its preference, though, was for legislation limited to the establishment of an environmental clearinghouse within the Executive Office of the President.[27]

---

[18] Daniel A. Dreyfus & Helen M. Ingram, *The National Environmental Policy Act: A View of Intent and Practice*, 16 NAT. RES. J. 243, 245 (1976).

[19] Andreen, *supra* note 1, at 212–13.

[20] Kalen, *supra* note 8, at 136–38.

[21] Dreyfus & Ingram, *supra* note 18, at 245–46.

[22] Tarlock, *supra* note 7, at 84.

[23] Kalen, *supra* note 8, at 135–39.

[24] *Hearing, supra* note 9, at 1–3, 35. *See also* NAT'L POL'Y, *supra* note 10, at 20.

[25] Andreen, *supra* note 1, at 218–19.

[26] *Hearing, supra* note 9, at 69 ("The present administration is delighted with the interest of this committee and with the Congress generally in this environmental problem.") (statement of Dr. Lee A. DuBridge, President's Science Adviser).

[27] Sandler, *supra* note 17, at 140–41.

Only later in the legislative process did the idea surface of adding a requirement that all federal agencies analyze the environmental impact of their activities.[28] That was likely the direct result of hearing testimony given by Professor Lynton K. Caldwell, [29] author of the influential *National Policy on the Environment* committee print, under the instruction of professional commitee staff members Van Ness and Daniel Dreyfus. He testified that Senator Jackson's bill needed "action-forcing or operation measures."[30] After the hearing, Senator Jackson conferred with his staff and then produced the embryo of the environmental impact statement (EIS) requirement as we know it today. As explained by his staffers, the requirement that the agency decisionmaker issue a "finding" that the environmental impacts of the proposed action had been studied and considered, and any unavoidable adverse impacts justified, was conceived to overcome the Nixon administration's perceived hostility to the environmental policy preferred by Congress.[31] The full Senate approved the committee bill through unanimous consent.[32]

In the House, the Dingell bill sailed through,[33] although it was moderated somewhat by a last-minute amendment from Representative Wayne Aspinall, to the effect that "nothing in this Act shall increase, decrease or change any responsibility or authority of any Federal official or agency created by other provision of law."[34] Shortly thereafter, the House requested a conference with the Senate. But a "curious thing then occurred before the Senate agreed to the conference: It amended the bill."[35]

---

[28] Andreen, *supra* note 1, at 215–17.

[29] *See* Kalen, *supra* note 8, at 141 (observing that Senator Jackson had already recognized the need for an action-forcing mechanism and that the senator's and the committee's staff had "effectively scripted" Caldwell's testimony).

[30] *Hearing, supra* note 9, at 116.

[31] Dreyfus & Ingram, *supra* note 18, at 251. Nixon was "the most protective president of the environment since President Theodore Roosevelt." Denis Binder, *NEPA at 50: Standing Tall*, 23 CHAP. L. REV. 1, 3 (2019). But the environmentalism that Nixon advanced is much more of the "housekeeping" than the "commissars" variety. *See generally* RICHARD NEUHAUS, IN DEFENSE OF PEOPLE: ECOLOGY AND THE SEDUCTION OF RADICALISM 276–78 (1971).

[32] Andreen, *supra* note 1, at 218.

[33] *Id.* at 218–19.

[34] *See* H.R. REP. NO. 91-765, at 9 (1969) (Conf. Rep.); Kalen, *supra* note 8, at 147.

[35] Andreen, *supra* note 1, at 219.

This amendment would become known as the Muskie-Jackson Compromise. Senator Edmund Muskie of Maine[36] chaired the Public Works Committee and had been somewhat turned off by what he viewed as Senator Jackson's attack on the jurisdiction of the former's committee.[37] Publicly, Muskie stated that he was concerned that merely requiring federal agencies to make a factual "finding" regarding environmental impacts was not enough. He proposed changing the requirement of a "finding" to a "detailed statement" for which input would first have to be sought from outside agencies.[38] Muskie, very concerned about supposedly blinkered single-mission federal agencies, believed that the change was necessary to ensure that these agencies would faithfully implement the EIS requirement.[39] The finding-to-statement change, arising from the "protracted and bitter" negotiations between the senators and their staff,[40] would prove momentous: it would convert the EIS process from one primarily intended to be internal to the agency to one that would create a forum for "public participatory policymaking."[41] It would also, as we shall see, enable litigants to obtain a more demanding level of judicial scrutiny because courts could more easily characterize their review of an agency's NEPA document as procedural rather than substantive.

The bill that emerged from conference largely preserved the Jackson bill as amended by the Jackson-Muskie compromise. The most significant change was the deletion of language from the Jackson bill that would have recognized that "each person has a fundamental and inalienable right to a healthful environment."[42] This is particularly notable because Senator Jackson and others thought that such language was necessary to make NEPA actionable by citizen-plaintiffs.[43] Another significant change was the deletion of the Aspinall

[36] Senator Muskie's environmentalism was sufficiently zealous to earn him the moniker "Mr. Clean." *See* Heream Yang, Note, *NEPA's Environmental Vision: Close, But Not Quite*, 42 VA. ENVTL. L.J. 120, 154 (2024).

[37] Kalen, *supra* note 8, at 144.

[38] Andreen, *supra* note 1, at 220–21; 115 CONG. REC. 29051 (1969).

[39] Dreyfus & Ingram, *supra* note 18, at 253.

[40] The dispute was caused in part "by the desire of both Senators to gain reputations as 'good' environmentalists, especially since the presidential primary season was in the offing." Andreen, *supra* note 1, at 220 n.107.

[41] Dreyfus & Ingram, *supra* note 18, at 258.

[42] H.R. REP. NO. 91-765, at 8 (Conf. Rep.).

[43] Kalen, *supra* note 8, at 155.

amendment to the House bill, which explicitly affirmed that NEPA did not affect existing agency authorities to regulate or to protect the environment. This might suggest that the conference intended the bill to have a substantive component, yet the conference report conceded that agencies must comply with NEPA "unless the existing law applicable to such agency's operations expressly prohibits or makes full compliance with one of the directives impossible."[44] Such was also the view of Senator Jackson's staff.[45]

Little debate occurred over the conference report, perhaps because of the fast-approaching Christmas recess, and the amended bill was swiftly approved by both Houses.[46] At the western White House, President Nixon signed the bill on New Year's Day 1970.

NEPA as enacted has three main sections in two titles. The first establishes the national policy on the environment and directs all federal agencies to use their authorities to further that policy as follows:

(1) fulfill the responsibilities of each generation as trustee of the environment for succeeding generations;

(2) assure for all Americans safe, healthful, productive, and esthetically and culturally pleasing surroundings;

(3) attain the widest range of beneficial uses of the environment without degradation, risk to health or safety, or other undesirable and unintended consequences;

(4) preserve important historic, cultural, and natural aspects of our national heritage, and maintain, wherever possible, an environment which supports diversity and variety of individual choice;

(5) achieve a balance between population and resource use which will permit high standards of living and a wide sharing of life's amenities; and

(6) enhance the quality of renewable resources and approach the maximum attainable recycling of depletable resources.[47]

The statute's second main part establishes the EIS obligation, directing that, for all "major Federal actions significantly affecting the

---

[44] H.R. Rep. No. 91-765, at 9 (Conf. Rep.).

[45] Kalen, *supra* note 8, at 154.

[46] Andreen, *supra* note 1, at 223.

[47] 42 U.S.C. § 4331(b).

quality of the human environment," the responsible agency prepare a "detailed statement" on the following:

(i) reasonably foreseeable environmental effects of the proposed agency action;

(ii) any reasonably foreseeable adverse environmental effects which cannot be avoided should the proposal be implemented;

(iii) a reasonable range of alternatives to the proposed agency action, including an analysis of any negative environmental impacts of not implementing the proposed agency action in the case of a no action alternative, that are technically and economically feasible, and meet the purpose and need of the proposal;

(iv) the relationship between local short-term uses of man's environment and the maintenance and enhancement of long-term productivity; and

(v) any irreversible and irretrievable commitments of Federal resources which would be involved in the proposed agency action should it be implemented.[48]

The statute's third main section establishes the Council on Environmental Quality (CEQ) in the Executive Office of the President.[49] CEQ's duties are principally to advise the president on environmental issues, relay agencies' compliance with NEPA, and act as a repository of environmental data for the executive branch.[50]

II. A Federal Environmental "Common Law": NEPA in the Courts prior to *Seven County*

A. Calvert Cliffs: *Environmentalism Ascends to the Courts*

The role of the courts in policing agency compliance with NEPA was initially unclear.[51] Nevertheless, judicial review under the new statute began in earnest in 1971, when Judge Skelly Wright of the

[48] *Id.* § 4332(C).

[49] *Id.* § 4342. The template for CEQ was the Council of Economic Advisers. Dreyfus & Ingram, *supra* note 18, at 248.

[50] *See* 42 U.S.C. § 4344. Note that, as discussed further below, CEQ's 1978 decision to promulgate detailed regulations—ostensibly governing *all* agencies' compliance with NEPA—significantly expanded CEQ's role in NEPA's administration.

[51] *See* Richard Lazarus, *The National Environmental Policy Act in the U.S. Supreme Court: A Reappraisal and a Peek Behind the Curtains*, 100 Geo. L.J. 1507, 1515 (2012) ("NEPA's drafters . . . apparently believed that the primary enforcement mechanism of NEPA's EIS requirement would not be lawsuits. . . ." (citing Tarlock, *supra* note 7, at 87–88)).

District of Columbia Circuit issued his opinion in *Calvert Cliffs' Coordinating Committee, Inc. v. United States Atomic Energy Commission*.[52] In *Calvert Cliffs* a group of environmentalist plaintiffs challenged rules recently adopted by the Atomic Energy Commission (since abolished and reconstituted as the Nuclear Regulatory Commission[53]). These rules established procedures to govern the consideration of environmental impacts in the approval of new nuclear power facilities.[54] The D.C. Circuit determined that the commission's rules did "not comply with the congressional policy" set forth in NEPA and remanded them for further rulemaking.[55]

The lasting significance of *Calvert Cliffs* is less in its specific controversy—which was grounded in the unique socio-political debate surrounding nuclear technology prevalent in the middle of the 20th century[56]—and more in the court's broad statements regarding the judicial role in policing agency environmental compliance under NEPA. Judge Wright began his opinion by announcing that "[t]hese cases are only the beginning of what promises to become a flood of new litigation—litigation seeking judicial assistance in protecting our natural environment."[57] This announcement was driven by Judge Wright's discerning "the commitment of the Government to control, at long last, the destructive engine of material 'progress,'" and his view that it is the "duty" of the courts "to see that [such] important legislative purposes, heralded in the halls of Congress, are not lost or misdirected in the vast hallways of the federal bureaucracy."[58] Judge Wright then announced a framework for NEPA review that drew a "sharp distinction between what he described as NEPA's 'general substantive policy,' outlined in Section 102(1), and its 'procedural' mandate, set forth in Section 102(2)."[59] In Judge Wright's view, while NEPA's "general substantive policy" might be a "flexible one," its

---

[52] 449 F.2d 1109 (D.C. Cir. 1971).

[53] *See Our History*, U.S. Nuclear Reg. Comm'n (Feb. 20, 2025), https://www.nrc.gov/about-nrc/history.html.

[54] *See Calvert Cliffs*, 449 F.2d at 1111–12.

[55] *Id.* at 1112.

[56] *See generally* Tarlock, *supra* note 7, at 79–82.

[57] *Calvert Cliffs*, 449 F.2d at 1111. As Professor Lazarus notes, perhaps the most striking aspect of the opinion "is how Wright took the notion of a 'flood' and turned it from a negative into a positive." Lazarus, *supra* note 51, at 1516.

[58] *Calvert Cliffs*, 449 F.2d at 1111.

[59] Lazarus, *supra* note 51, at 1516-17 (quoting *Calvert Cliffs*, 449 F.2d at 1112).

procedural requirements "establish a strict standard of compliance" to be "rigorously enforced."[60]

Calvert Cliffs was subsequently pared back by the Supreme Court.[61] Nevertheless, as we will discuss further below, the specter of Judge Wright's expansive view of NEPA never fully dissipated.[62]

B. NEPA at the Supreme Court: Narrow Review of a Purely Procedural Statute

The first NEPA case to reach the Supreme Court on the merits came two years after *Calvert Cliffs*: the Supreme Court ruled against a group of environmental plaintiffs in *United States v. Students Challenging Regulatory Agency Procedures (SCRAP I)*.[63] Following *SCRAP I*, environmental plaintiffs then lost 16 cases in a row at the high court[64]—in most instances unanimously.[65]

The Supreme Court's NEPA decisions were generally quite technical and often dictated by the cases' factual or statutory peculiarities.[66] One discernable throughline in the Court's NEPA opinions, however, is the "procedural-substantive" distinction first announced by Judge Wright. In stark contrast to Judge Wright's vision, the Supreme Court applied NEPA's procedural-substantive distinction time and time again, to emphasize the narrow scope of judicial review. In the Court's view, as a statute that "imposes only procedural requirements,"[67]

---

[60] *Calvert Cliffs*, 449 F.2d at 1112, 1114. *See also* Lazarus, *supra* note 51, at 1517.

[61] *See* Tarlock, *supra* note 7, at 104.

[62] *See* Lazarus, *supra* note 51, at 1516 (describing *Calvert Cliffs* as "a harbinger of what followed").

[63] 412 U.S. 669 (1973).

[64] *See* Aberdeen & Rockfish R.R. Co. v. Students Challenging Regul. Agency Procs., 422 U.S. 289 (1975) (*SCRAP II*); Hint Ridge Dev. Co. v. Scenic Rivers Ass'n of Okla., 426 U.S. 776 (1976); Kleppe v. Sierra Club, 427 U.S. 390 (1976); Vt. Yankee Nuclear Power Corp. v. Nat. Res. Def. Council, Inc., 435 U.S. 519 (1978); Andrus v. Sierra Club, 442 U.S. 347 (1979); Strycker's Bay Neighborhood Council, Inc. v. Karlen, 444 U.S. 223 (1980); Weinberger v. Catholic Action of Haw./Peace Educ. Project, 454 U.S. 139 (1981); Metro. Edison Co. v. People Against Nuclear Energy, 460 U.S. 766 (1983); Balt. Gas & Elec. Co. v. Nat. Res. Def. Council, Inc., 462 U.S. 87 (1983); Robertson v. Methow Valley Citizens Council, 490 U.S. 332 (1989); Marsh v. Or. Nat. Res. Council, 490 U.S. 360 (1989); Robertson v. Seattle Audubon Soc'y, 503 U.S. 429 (1992); U.S. Dep't of Transp. v. Pub. Citizen, 541 U.S. 752 (2004); Norton v. S. Utah Wilderness All., 542 U.S. 55 (2004); Winter v. Nat. Res. Def. Council, Inc., 555 U.S. 7 (2008); Monsanto Co. v. Geertson Seed Farms, 561 U.S. 139 (2010).

[65] *See* Lazarus, *supra* note 51, at 1536–65 (surveying the cases).

[66] *Cf. id.* (summarizing the cases).

[67] *Winter*, 555 U.S. at 23.

NEPA "does not mandate particular results, but simply prescribes the necessary process" for an agency's environmental review of a proposed action.[68] In the Court's telling, because "NEPA merely prohibits uninformed—rather than unwise—agency action," an "agency is not constrained" in its substantive discretion to "decid[e] that other values outweigh the environmental costs."[69] The role of the courts is merely to police the outer bounds of agency environmental decision-making by ensuring "that the agency has taken a 'hard look' at environmental consequences," while declining to "interject itself within the area of discretion of the executive as to the choice of the action to be taken."[70]

C. NEPA in the Lower Courts: A Quasi-substantive Environmental "Common Law"

Despite the Supreme Court's consistently—and again, often unanimously—narrow view of the judicial role in NEPA review, Judge Wright's vision lived on in the lower courts. Since *Calvert Cliffs*, a virtual "'common law' of impact assessment with substantial consequences for agency noncompliance" has arisen in the lower courts.[71] This "common law" has primarily developed in the D.C. and Ninth Circuits—which hear the vast majority of NEPA disputes.[72]

The framework for NEPA review that has arisen in the Ninth Circuit is especially out of step with the deferential orientation of the Supreme Court's NEPA pronouncements. For example, the Ninth Circuit has added four additional NEPA-specific factors for reviewing agency action.[73] It has "substantially enlarged the universe of

---

[68] *Methow Valley Citizens Council*, 490 U.S. at 350.

[69] *Id.*

[70] *Sierra Club*, 427 U.S. at 410 n.21 (quoting Nat. Res. Def. Council v. Morton, 458 F.2d 827, 838 (D.C. Cir. 1972)).

[71] Tarlock, *supra* note 7, at 102. *See also* Lazarus, *supra* note 51, at 1518 ("The courts created, in effect, a virtual 'common law' of detailed NEPA procedural requirements. . . .").

[72] *See* David E. Adelman & Robert L. Glicksman, *Presidential and Judicial Politics in Environmental Litigation*, 50 ARIZ. ST. L.J. 3, 33 (2018) (finding that courts in the Ninth Circuit hear roughly half of all NEPA cases, with the D.C. Circuit hearing roughly 10 percent).

[73] *See* Mark C. Rutzick, *A Long and Winding Road: How the National Environmental Policy Act Has Become the Most Expensive and Least Effective Environmental Law in the History of the United States, and How to Fix It*, FEDERALIST SOC'Y: REGUL. TRANSPARENCY PROJECT 7–8 (Oct. 16, 2018), (collecting cases), https://regproject.org/wp-content/uploads/RTP-Energy-Environment-Working-Group-Paper-National-Environmental-Policy-Act.pdf.

agency decisions requiring an EIS,"[74] by holding "that an agency must also prepare an EIS if a plaintiff does no more than present 'substantial questions whether a project *may* have a significant effect.'"[75] And it has provided for the issuance of near-"automatic" injunctions in NEPA cases,[76] by prioritizing NEPA-derived environmental concerns in its equitable balancing of the injunction factors.[77] Applying this framework, courts within the Ninth Circuit have ruled in favor of environmental NEPA plaintiffs at staggering rates.[78]

The development of this demanding common law of NEPA was further abetted by CEQ's 1978 promulgation[79] of "a comprehensive set" of NEPA regulations.[80] These regulations are credited as lying "at the heart of NEPA's unexpected impact."[81] In an interesting (although not unexpected) turn, these regulations were recently vacated by the D.C. Circuit on the grounds that CEQ never had the authority to issue them[82]—a fact that does little to remedy the legal framework they helped establish.

D. Two-track Judicial Review and Its Negative Consequences

The key takeaway is that over time, a two-track approach to NEPA review emerged. The lower courts—throughout the course of thousands of NEPA decisions[83]—developed a federal common law that broadly imposed quasi-substantive duties. The Supreme Court

---

[74] *Id.* at 8.

[75] *Id.* (quoting Idaho Sporting Cong. v. Thomas, 137 F.3d 1146, 1150 (9th Cir. 1998)) (emphasis added).

[76] *Id.*

[77] Save Our Ecosystems v. Clark, 747 F.2d 1240, 1250 (9th Cir. 1984) ("[T]he policies underlying NEPA 'weight the scales in favor of those seeking the suspension of all action until the Act's requirements are met. . . .'" (quoting Alpine Lake Prot. Soc'y v. Schlapfer, 518 F.2d 1089, 1090 (9th Cir. 1975)).

[78] *See* Adelman & Glicksman, *supra* note 72, at 39 n.152 ("Plaintiffs in the Ninth Circuit during the Bush Administration prevailed in 42 percent of the NEPA cases versus 15 percent in all other circuits collectively. . . ."); *see also* Rutzick, *supra* note 73, at 7.

[79] *See National Environmental Policy Act—Implementation of Procedural Provisions,* 43 Fed. Reg. 55978 (Nov. 29, 1978) (codified at 40 C.F.R. pt. 1500 et. seq.).

[80] Lazarus, *supra* note 51, at 1518.

[81] Rutzick, *supra* note 73, at 5.

[82] Marin Audubon Soc'y v. Fed. Aviation Admin., 121 F.4th 902, 914 (D.C. Cir. 2024).

[83] *See* Rutzick, *supra* note 73, at 11 ("[E]nvironmental advocates have filed at least 4,000 federal lawsuits alleging violations of NEPA and the CEQ regulations.").

periodically intervened in a small number of cases to announce "decisions which vary between indifference and hostility toward NEPA,"[84] and which narrowly imposed purely procedural duties. Two negative practical consequences of this phenomenon are worthy of emphasis.

First, on the litigation side, the lower courts' treatment of NEPA "created an unparalleled opportunity for environmental advocates to use NEPA litigation to block proposals that require a federal permit or approval, or use federal funds."[85] As one judge recently observed, the "unyielding decline" that has occurred in "productivity growth in the construction industry" since 1970 can be confidently attributed to environmentalist NEPA litigation.[86]

Second, on the agency side, the development of NEPA in the lower courts resulted in the advent of so-called "defensive NEPA"[87]— whereby "the length, preparation time and cost of" NEPA documents increased over time as a result of "federal agencies' understandable inclination to seek to avoid litigation by addressing every imaginable environmental issue in detail."[88] In other words, as environmentalist-driven litigation became more perilous for agencies, the burdens of the NEPA process very quickly overwhelmed the federal government.

Taken together these negative consequences have imposed nothing short of a straitjacket on the American economy,[89] a well-documented problem that in recent years has become the object of increasingly bipartisan public ire.[90]

---

[84] Tarlock, *supra* note 7, at 104.

[85] Rutzick, *supra* note 73, at 10.

[86] Appalachian Voices v. Fed. Energy Reg. Comm'n, 139 F.4th 903, 916 (D.C. Cir. 2025) (Henderson, J., concurring).

[87] *See* Michael J. Mortimer et al., *Environmental and Social Risks: Defensive National Environmental Policy Act in the US Forest Service*, 109 J. FORESTRY 27, 27 (2011).

[88] Rutzick, *supra* note 73, at 11 n.52.

[89] *See Appalachian Voices*, 139 F.4th at 925 (Henderson, J., concurring) ("Because of judicial tinkering with NEPA's original design, litigation became a fixed feature of agencies'—and developers'—efforts to undertake any new action. . . .").

[90] NEPA is perhaps the most singularly important issue animating the newfound bipartisan "Abundance" movement. *See* Andres Picon, *Bipartisan "Abundance" Caucus Sets Sights on NEPA*, E&E NEWS (July 8, 2025), https://www.eenews.net/articles/bipartisan-abundance-caucus-sets-sights-on-nepa/.

III. The Supreme Court Unanimously Sets the Record Straight: The *Seven County* Decision

A. Litigation History and Background

Seven County began with a rather parochial dispute over the U.S. Surface Transportation Board's decision to approve the construction of an approximately 88-mile-long railroad line in the Uinta Basin of northeastern Utah.

The Interstate Commerce Commission Termination Act (ICTA) dictates that the construction of new railroads must first be approved by the Surface Transportation Board.[91] After receiving an application for approval, the board must issue a public notice and initiate an administrative proceeding—which may be streamlined.[92] In addition to complying with ICTA's requirements, the board must follow NEPA's requirements—including the preparation of an EIS, should a proposed railroad project be "major."[93]

The Uinta Basin is a sparsely populated region of the Mountain West, rich in crude oil. Due to its geographical remoteness, it is not served by existing railroad infrastructure, and as a result, crude oil extracted in the Basin must be carried out via trucks, navigating perilous mountain roads. To rectify this problem, in early 2020, Petitioner the Seven County Infrastructure Coalition—a group of seven Utah counties—sought approval from the board to construct a railroad line connecting the basin to the interstate rail network.[94]

In response to the coalition's request, the board initiated the statutory proceeding required by ICTA; conducted the environmental review required by NEPA; and in December 2021, approved the project.[95] In doing so, the board concluded that the substantial economic and transportation benefits of the project "outweighed the environmental impacts identified" in its EIS.[96]

---

[91] *See* Seven Cnty. Infrastructure Coal. v. Eagle Cnty., 145 S. Ct. 1497, 1508 (2025) (citing 49 U.S.C. § 10901).

[92] *See id.* (citing 49 U.S.C. §§ 10101, 10502, 10901).

[93] *See id.*

[94] *Id.*

[95] *Id.* at 1508–09.

[96] *Id.*

The board's NEPA review was of the "standard"[97] variety—burdensome and lengthy. The board first prepared a draft EIS and invited public comment. It held six public meetings. And it then collected more than 1,900 public comments. In August 2021, the board then published a whopping 3,600-page final EIS.[98] In its EIS the board analyzed at length a number of potentially significant environmental consequences, including "disruptions to local wetlands, land use, and recreation."[99] The board also thoroughly addressed several "minor impacts," which included air pollution and disruptions to wildlife.[100]

The EIS additionally acknowledged the potential environmental impact of increased oil drilling "upstream" of the railroad and increased "downstream" processing of crude oil.[101] Its analysis of these issues, however, was necessarily more limited given their speculative nature—and because many of these activities are outside the board's control. As for "upstream oil drilling," such activity remains unplanned, and in any event, the board possesses no "authority or control" over such development, which is instead subject to permitting by other governmental agencies.[102] As for "downstream" impacts, the board acknowledged that crude oil transported along the proposed railroad would reach markets in Louisiana and Texas, increasing environmental impacts associated with industrial oil refining.[103] However, the board had no reliable data predicting which specific destinations would receive the oil. And again, as an agency with statutory authority limited to the construction and operation of railroads, the board would be powerless to regulate (and thus alleviate) impacts associated with oil refining.[104]

After the railroad's final approval, there followed the now customary next step: NEPA litigation to block the project. In early 2022, a

---

[97] *Id.* at 1508.
[98] *Id.*
[99] *Id.*
[100] *Id.*
[101] *Id.* at 1508–09.
[102] *Id.* at 1509.
[103] *Id.*
[104] *Id.*

Colorado county and several national environmental organizations sued the board by filing petitions for review in the D.C. Circuit.[105] The D.C. Circuit ultimately vacated the board's approval order and EIS on the grounds that the board had violated NEPA by limiting its analysis of the railroad's "upstream" and "downstream" effects.[106]

The Supreme Court then granted certiorari,[107] and unanimously reversed the D.C. Circuit. Justice Kavanaugh wrote the majority opinion, joined by Chief Justice John Roberts, and Justices Clarence Thomas, Samuel Alito, and Amy Coney Barrett. And Justice Sotomayor wrote an opinion concurring in the judgment, joined by Justices Elena Kagan and Ketanji Brown Jackson.[108]

B. The Majority Opinion

Justice Kavanaugh's majority opinion can be summarized in two parts. First, the majority clarified the deferential standard of review applicable in NEPA litigation. Second, the majority resolved the specific question at issue—the extent to which attenuated upstream and downstream impacts must be analyzed under NEPA.

1. Deference: The touchstone of NEPA review

In clarifying and restating the standard of review applicable to NEPA litigation, the majority began and ended its analysis by stating that "the central principle of judicial review in NEPA cases is deference."[109] The majority deemed it necessary to restate this principle on account of the "aggressive role in policing agency compliance

---

[105] *Id.*

[106] *Id.* (citing Eagle Cnty. v. U.S. Surface Transp. Bd., 82 F.4th 1152, 1175–80 (D.C. Cir. 2023)). The D.C. Circuit also voided the project's approval for failure to comply with several additional statutory requirements, such as those imposed by the Endangered Species Act. *See Eagle Cnty.*, 82 F.4th at 1186–96. These additional grounds for vacatur were not at issue in the Supreme Court. They do, however, serve as an important illustration of how the many layers of environmental review imposed upon federal agencies can work in tandem to frustrate development. *See* Jonathan Adler, *Permitting the Future*, 75 CASE W. RES. L. REV. 1, 7–9 (2024).

[107] *See* Seven Cnty. Infrastructure Coal. v. Eagle Cnty., 144 S. Ct. 2680 (2024).

[108] *See Seven Cnty.*, 145 S. Ct at 1504. Justice Neil Gorsuch took no part in the consideration or decision of the case.

[109] *Id.* at 1511. *See also id.* at 1515.

with NEPA" assumed by certain lower courts.[110] The majority recognized how the judicial role assumed by the lower courts has resulted in "litigation-averse agencies . . . tak[ing] ever more time . . . to prepare ever longer EISs for future projects."[111] And it recognized how this shift has "transformed" NEPA from "a modest procedural requirement into a blunt and haphazard tool employed by project opponents . . . to try to stop or at least slow down new infrastructure and construction projects."[112] In other words, the majority's decision to restate and clarify the NEPA standard of review was borne out of its express recognition of the two primary negative consequences of the lower courts ignoring the Court's prior NEPA pronouncements— "defensive" NEPA and obstructionist litigation. In the majority's view, these consequences have become so dire[113] that a "course correction of sorts is appropriate to bring judicial review under NEPA back in line with the statutory text and common sense."[114]

And correct course the Supreme Court did. The majority made clear that NEPA decisionmaking must be reviewed under the deferential arbitrary-and-capricious standard of the Administrative Procedure Act (APA).[115] Under this standard, "a court asks not whether it agrees with the agency decision, but rather only whether the agency action was reasonable and reasonably explained."[116] This standard is commonly known as the *State Farm* standard, named for the first Supreme Court decision in which it was explicated.[117] Under *State Farm*, an agency decision is reasonable—and must be deferred to—provided the agency has identified a "rational connection between the facts found and the choice made,"[118]

---

[110] *Id.* at 1511.

[111] *Id.*

[112] *Id.*

[113] *See id.* at 1514 ("A 1970 legislative acorn has grown over the years into a judicial oak that has hindered infrastructure development 'under the guise' of just a little more process.") (quoting *Vermont Yankee*, 435 U.S. at 558).

[114] *Id.*

[115] *Id.* at 1511.

[116] *Id.*

[117] *See* Mot. Vehicle Mfrs. Ass'n v. State Farm Mut. Auto. Ins. Co., 463 U.S. 29 (1983).

[118] *State Farm*, 463 U.S. at 43 (quoting Burlington Truck Lines v. United States, 371 U.S. 156, 168 (1962)).

and has not otherwise "failed to consider an important aspect of the problem[.]"[119] The majority also recognized the application of a subprinciple to *State Farm*: where agency decisionmaking involves "speculative assessments or predictive or scientific judgments"—as it often the case in the NEPA context—"a court must be at its 'most deferential.'"[120] This subprinciple is commonly known as *Baltimore Gas and Electric* deference—named for the first Supreme Court decision in which *it* was explicated.

Importantly, the majority explained that when applying these deference doctrines, courts "must account for the fact that NEPA is a *purely procedural statute*."[121] NEPA imposes no "substantive constraints" on the agency's ultimate decision and thus "'the only role for a court' is to confirm that the agency has addressed environmental consequences and feasible alternatives as to the relevant project."[122] As for the choices made in addressing environmental consequences and alternatives, a court must accept those choices provided "they fall within a broad zone of reasonableness."[123]

Even more importantly, the majority made clear that because "an EIS is only one input into an agency's decision," the focus of judicial review must be the agency's *final* decision (not simply the EIS itself)—that is, in *Seven County*, the board's ultimate decision to approve the railroad.[124] And as a corollary, even if the EIS "falls short in some respects," any such deficiency does not necessarily require

---

[119] *Id.* at 29. This variety of "deference" is distinct from that which the reader may be most familiar with: so-called *Chevron* deference, under which courts were required to defer to agency *legal* interpretations of statutes which they administered. *See* Jack M. Beermann, *Chevron Deference Is Dead, Long Live Deference*, in 2023–2024 CATO SUP. CT. REV. 31 (2024) (discussing *Chevron* deference and its demise). *State Farm* deference comes into play at a separate phase of the decisional process: all agreeing that a statute confers unambiguous legal authority on an agency to exercise discretion, the agency has leeway in which to make rational factual and policy choices in exercising that discretion. *See Seven Cnty.*, 145 S. Ct. at 1511. While *Chevron* deference has given way to *de novo* review on statutory interpretation questions, deferential review of reasoned agency decisionmaking under *State Farm* lives on. *See* Loper Bright Enters. v. Raimondo, 603 U.S. 369, 395 (2024).

[120] *Seven Cnty.*, 145 S. Ct. at 1512 (quoting *Balt. Gas & Elec.*, 462 U.S. at 103).

[121] *Id.* at 1511.

[122] *Id.* (quoting *Strycker's Bay Neighborhood Council, Inc.*, 444 U.S. at 227).

[123] *Id.* at 1513.

[124] *Id.* at 1511.

vacatur of the final decision.[125] A party seeking vacatur on NEPA grounds must demonstrate that the agency might actually reverse course should it add the overlooked information.[126]

All in all, an EIS is not to be reviewed as if its adequacy were an end in itself, but rather to determine whether some choice made in an agency's analysis of environmental consequences is so patently unreasonable as to call into question the agency's ultimate decision to approve a project—a decision which will generally involve weighing many factors beyond the environment. In assessing the gravity of a purportedly unreasonable NEPA choice vis-à-vis the ultimate decision, courts must give significant leeway to the agency under the deferential *State Farm* standard—supplemented with the even more deferential *Baltimore Gas and Electric* principle where an agency's choice involves predictive or scientific judgment. And prior to vacating an agency decision on NEPA grounds, a court must find that the NEPA deficiency—if rectified—might change the ultimate outcome.[127]

2. Upstream and downstream effects: Limiting the scope of NEPA to the direct effects of the project at hand

Applying these principles, the majority easily concluded that the D.C. Circuit had erred. As the majority explained, under the Court's longstanding precedents, "the textually mandated focus of NEPA" is "the project at hand."[128] Future projects or geographically separated projects that might result from the immediate project are simply beyond NEPA's scope. Even though such projects—and their environmental effects—might be "factually foreseeable," that does not make them relevant.[129] In reaching this conclusion, the court invoked the legal concept of "proximate causation"[130]—the "causal chain" between the project at hand and a geographically or temporally separate project is simply "too attenuated."[131] However, this invocation

125 *Id.* at 1514.

126 *Id.*

127 *See generally id.* at 1511–15.

128 *Id.*

129 *Id.*

130 *Id.* at 1516.

131 *Id.* (quoting *Metro. Edison Co.*, 460 U.S. at 774).

of proximate causation is better understood as being illustrative—as opposed to an affirmative "proximate causation *rule*" for NEPA. We believe it is more accurate to understand the operative rule in the negative: a "mere but for causal relationship" between the immediate project and some future project "is insufficient to make an agency responsible for a particular effect."[132] And under no circumstances may a court "invoke" such a causal relationship to order agency review of far flung projects.[133]

The majority further emphasized that where an agency "possess[es] no regulatory authority" over a geographically or temporally separate project, the causal chain will be definitively broken, and the agency presumptively need not consider the effects of that project.[134] Direct regulatory control is the key.

To be sure, the majority recognized that there may be difficult and close cases—there might often be a "gray area" in defining whether two projects are one or distinct.[135] But here is where the majority's earlier deference pronouncements become important. Under such uncertainty the only relevant question for a reviewing court is whether "the agency drew a reasonable and manageable line."[136]

In any event, to the majority, the relationship between the Uinta Basin railroad and the "upstream" and "downstream" effects identified by the D.C. Circuit was not a close question. The board properly explained "that the environmental consequences of future oil drilling in the Basin are distinct from construction and operation of the railroad line."[137] Likewise, it correctly explained that oil refining along the Gulf Coast is "well outside" its scope.[138] NEPA requires nothing more. Making the question even easier was the fact that the board possesses no regulatory authority over oil drilling and refining.[139]

---

[132] *Id.* at 1517 (quoting *Pub. Citizen*, 541 U.S. at 767) (cleaned up).

[133] *Id.*

[134] *Id.* at 1516.

[135] *Id.*

[136] *Id.* (quoting *Pub. Citizen*, 541 U.S. at 767) (cleaned up).

[137] *Id.* at 1518.

[138] *Id.*

[139] *Id.* at 1516.

C. The Concurrence

In the concurring Justices' view, the majority had "unnecessarily ground[ed] its analysis . . . in matters of policy," because resolution of the case "follows inexorably" from the Court's NEPA precedents.[140]

The concurring Justices viewed two precedents as most pertinent: *Public Citizen*[141] and *Metropolitan Edison Company*.[142] In the concurrence's view, taken together, these cases set forth "dual limitations" on an agency's duty to consider environmental information under NEPA, which in turn give rise to a "two-step analysis" to guide judicial review.[143] First, a court must inquire into whether an agency is precluded under its organic statute from considering a particular issue—because it is powerless to modify or mitigate the effects of that issue. Where such inability to act exists, a court cannot demand that the agency consider that issue.[144] This rule follows from *Public Citizen*.[145] Second, where an agency decides not to review a particular impact because of its causal attenuation from the project at hand, a reviewing court's only role is to ask whether the agency's decision not to consider such impacts was arbitrary. This second step follows from *Metropolitan Edison* and the general principles of deference governing a court's review of agency decisionmaking.[146]

In the concurring Justices' estimation, *Seven County* was an open-and-shut case to be resolved at the first (*Public Citizen*) step: the board has no statutory authority to reject a railway application because of how products transported along that railway might be used by third parties.[147] The agency stated as much in its EIS, and NEPA requires nothing more. An agency simply need not consider environmental consequences it is powerless to prevent.[148]

The reasoning and conclusion of the concurrence are not so very different from the majority—save for the majority's broader

---

[140] *Id.* at 1519 (Sotomayor, J., concurring).

[141] 541 U.S. at 752.

[142] 460 U.S. at 766.

[143] *Seven Cnty.*, 145 S. Ct. at 1523 (Sotomayor, J., concurring).

[144] *Id.*

[145] *See id.* (citing *Public Citizen*, 541 U.S. at 766–67).

[146] *See id.* (citing *Metro. Edison Co.*, 460 at 774–76).

[147] *Id.* at 1523–24.

[148] *See id.*

pronouncements regarding the ill effects of NEPA's historical misapplication. The concurrence substantially agreed with the majority's statement of the deferential standard of review applicable in NEPA litigation. And it agreed that the board's being statutorily precluded from mitigating the environmental consequences of potential upstream and downstream projects clearly excused the board from considering such consequences.[149]

IV. A New Era: *Seven County*'s Significant Implications for Federal Environmental Law

A. NEPA Overtaken by State Farm

Seven County represents a reforming of NEPA into principally an information-distributing and accountability-assigning statute. The decision flatly rejects the lower courts' contortion of the statute into a quasi-substantive control of agency decisionmaking. Of course, even after *Seven County*, NEPA will still require agencies to research and assess the impact of their "major" actions; agencies will still need to solicit public comment; they will still need to publicize their analysis and take public responsibility for their proposals. These aspects of NEPA, which certainly were intended by its framers,[150] will perdure.[151] But what will end after *Seven County* is the practice of NEPA regulating the substance of agency decisionmaking by stopping projects because an agency's "detailed statement" of a project's effects on the human environment is suboptimal.

This consequence comes from *Seven County*'s reaffirmation of three points: (1) NEPA is a purely procedural statute, (2) even in NEPA cases the focal point of judicial review is the reasonableness of the *ultimate* agency decision, and (3) vacatur should not issue as a matter of course for NEPA violations but rather only where the error is so significant that compliance might well lead the agency to a different *overall* result.[152]

---

[149] *See id.*

[150] *See, e.g.,* S. REP. No. 91-296, at 19–21 (1969) (discussing the statute's EIS requirement).

[151] *Accord Seven County,* 145 S. Ct. at 1510 (majority opinion) ("Properly applied, NEPA helps agencies to make better decisions and to ensure good project management.").

[152] *Seven County,* 145 S. Ct. at 1511–12.

In other words, the quasi-substantive component of NEPA developed over the decades in the lower courts has been largely overtaken by the equally quasi-substantive *State Farm* standard for agency decisionmaking under the APA: for agency action to survive judicial review, the agency must identify a "rational connection between the facts found and the choice made."[153] To be sure, NEPA undoubtedly strengthens that review: it's a lot easier for a court to determine whether, for example, an agency has failed entirely to consider a major (environmental) aspect of the problem, or has selected a course of action decidedly against the weight of the (ecological) evidence, when the court has before it an environmental impact statement addressing (or purporting to address) those issues. But whether the agency action will be affirmed or vacated will depend, after *Seven County*, on the reasonableness of the decision itself, not the legal or factual sufficiency of the NEPA documentation in isolation.

This does not mean the many years of environmentalist litigation and favorable lower court NEPA rulings have been for nought. The subsuming of NEPA into *State Farm* is at least partly the result of the lower court case law developing so-called "hard look" review for informal agency rulemaking and adjudication in NEPA cases in the decade or so between the statute's passage and the Court's 1983 ruling in *State Farm*. Moreover, it's fair to say that NEPA as written and NEPA as interpreted by the lower courts have helped to color federal administrative common law "green."[154] Just as with costs, the environment has become a background consideration for virtually all agency action. Moreover, as another decision from this term suggests, for an agency truly to "consider" an aspect of the problem before it, the agency cannot merely acknowledge the problem but instead must explain how the problem will be resolved or why resolution is not possible or advisable.[155] Thus, even after *Seven County*, one should expect lower courts to continue to require agencies to take environmental considerations into

---

[153] *State Farm*, 463 U.S. at 43 (quoting *Burlington Truck Lines*, 371 U.S. at 168).

[154] *See* Tarlock, *supra* note 7, at 78 (observing that "advance environmental impact assessment" is now "one of the foundational principles" of environmental law).

[155] *See* FCC v. Consumers' Rsch., 145 S. Ct. 2482, 2505 (2025).

account.[156] Indeed, environmental considerations are perhaps even more legally justified as part of APA review than costs, precisely because the former have an explicit statutory warrant in NEPA.

Still, without doubt, *Seven County* represents a major loss for environmental litigants, especially those dozen or so organizations that bring the significant majority of NEPA cases.[157] Going forward, those organizations will likely have little reason to advance a NEPA claim because the (very few, given the Court's deference discussion) NEPA errors that might require vacatur of the decision could just as easily be reformulated as violations of the APA's arbitrary and capricious standard, under *State Farm*. Moreover without vacatur, and the delay that comes with such relief, NEPA's potency for strategic litigants will be much reduced.[158]

This result comes from *Seven County's* definitive rejection of NEPA as, ironically enough, a hyper-procedural statute. What made NEPA so formidable was the lower courts' demand that its complex and often confusing requirements, as articulated by CEQ regulations and lower court rulings, be punctiliously observed—on pain of the project approval's vacatur and the project's relegation to the start of the administrative process. Lower courts felt authorized to take such drastic action because they were, after all, only enforcing procedure, not dictating substance.[159] Now, in *Seven County*, the Court has made clear that violation of NEPA's procedure does not necessarily mean the agency's decision was unreasonable or was inadequately explained—which is the only basis for vacatur.[160]

---

[156] There is arguably in the Supreme Court a countervailing trend as well, namely, requiring agencies as a default rule to take economic impacts into account. *See, e.g.,* Michigan v. U.S. Envtl. Prot. Agency, 576 U.S. 743, 752–53 (2015).

[157] *Cf.* Br. Amicus Curiae of the Prop. & Env't Rsch. Ctr. in Support of Petitioners at 19, Seven Cnty. Infrastructure Coal. v. Eagle Cnty., 145 S. Ct. 1497 (2025) (No. 23-975) ("Indeed, more than a third of NEPA cases litigated before appellate courts in the last decade were brought by just ten organizations. . . .")

[158] *See* Binder, *supra* note 31, at 43–44.

[159] *Cf.* Bennett v. Spear, 520 U.S. 154, 172 (1997) ("It is rudimentary administrative law that discretion as to the substance of the ultimate decision does not confer discretion to ignore the required procedures of decisionmaking. Since it is the omission of these required procedures that petitioners complain of, their . . . claim is reviewable. . . .") (quotation modified).

[160] *Seven County*, 145 S. Ct. at 1514.

B. Seven County *as Abundance Policy Statement*

The Justices comprising the majority in *Seven County* surely believed they were simply interpreting NEPA as written. Nevertheless, it is hard to come away from the opinion without thinking that their statutory interpretation was affected by NEPA's reputation as a powerful litigation tool of NIMBYs (green and otherwise) to defeat lawful projects. That policy concern is, after all, the object of the only component of the concurrence critical of the majority.[161] And the language of Justice Kavanaugh's majority opinion gives significant grounds to support that interpretation.

For example, Justice Kavanaugh writes that the "goal of the law is to inform agency decisionmaking, not to paralyze it."[162] He notes, "NEPA has transformed from a modest procedural requirement into a blunt and haphazard tool employed by project opponents (who may not always be entirely motivated by concern for the environment) to try to stop or at least slow down new infrastructure and construction projects."[163] He laments that the judicially transformed NEPA "means fewer and more expensive" infrastructure projects, as well as "fewer jobs."[164] He therefore concludes that a "course correction of sorts is appropriate to bring judicial review under NEPA back in line with the statutory text and common sense," given that "Congress did not design NEPA for *judges* to hamstring new infrastructure and construction projects."[165]

Given these statements of the majority opinion, we tentatively assert that the Court is developing a new statutory canon, akin to the major questions doctrine,[166] triggered by economic impact: courts should interpret statutory language to bolster rather than hinder the American economy. Indeed, Justice Kavanaugh concludes his opinion explicitly on these lines: "In deciding cases involving the American economy, courts should strive, where possible, for clarity

---

[161] *Id.* at 1519 (Sotomayor, J., concurring in the judgment).

[162] *Id.* at 1507 (majority opinion).

[163] *Id.* at 1513.

[164] *Id.* at 1514.

[165] *Id. Accord* Dreyfus & Ingram, *supra* note 18, at 256 ("It is certainly true, however, that the conferees never contemplated anything so extravagant as the multiple volume dissertations which now are commonly produced.").

[166] *See* Luke Wake & Damien Schiff, *Practical Applications of the Major Questions Doctrine*, 2024 Harv. J.L. & Pub. Pol'y Per Curiam 20, 20.

and predictability."[167] One might detect here the influence of the second Trump administration's neo-Rooseveltian public lands policies[168] as well as that of the Abundance Agenda,[169] particularly the latter's critique of environmental and land-use regulation in depressing the production of housing.[170]

Is the majority guilty of the concurrence's claim that the former's analysis is based mainly on policy? The foregoing quotes certainly establish that the majority was acutely aware of the negative policy effects of the lower courts' interpretation of NEPA. But the majority's legal analysis appears to be founded principally on text and deference to agency fact-finding, not pure policymaking. As for text, the Court's conclusion as to "upstream" and "downstream" effects is based on "the textually mandated focus of NEPA [being] the 'proposed action.'"[171] And the Court's strong affirmance of judicial deference to an agency's NEPA decisionmaking is based on decades of the Court's case law interpreting the APA's indulgent "arbitrary or capricious" standard of review.[172]

It is true that the majority supports its analysis in part by reference to "common sense." But contrary to the concurrence, this analytical defense injects policymaking into legal analysis no more than any of a number of established canons of interpretation.[173] In any event, perhaps the Court's use of "common sense" to reform NEPA finds

---

[167] *Seven County*, 145 S. Ct. at 1518.

[168] As expounded by Gifford Pinchot, Theodore Roosevelt's principal "environmental" deputy:

> The first duty of the human race on the material side is to control the use of the earth and all that therein is. . . . Conservation is the foresighted utilization, preservation, and/or renewal of forests, waters, lands, and minerals, for the greatest good of the greatest number for the longest time.

GIFFORD PINCHOT, BREAKING NEW GROUND 505 (Island Press 1974) (1947).

[169] *See* Kevin Frazier, *Abundance Constitutionalism: Heralding an Age of Liberty by Learning from the Nation's Foundational Legal Documents*, 100 NOTRE DAME L. REV. 197, 201 (2025) ("What the Abundance Agenda aims to correct is a government prone to inaction or, worse, to frustrate or delay societally-beneficial action.").

[170] *See* Alexander D. Lewis, *Fix Housing to Fix America: Unlocking Housing Abundance with Land-Use Reform*, 50 J. CORP. L. 775, 795–98 (2025).

[171] *Seven County*, 145 S. Ct. at 1515 (quoting 42 U.S.C. § 4332(C)(i)).

[172] *Id.* at 1511–12.

[173] *See* Amy Coney Barrett, *Substantive Canons and Faithful Agency*, 90 B.U. L. REV. 109, 110 (2010) ("[I]t is generally recognized that substantive canons advance policies independent of those expressed in the statute.").

a parallel in another Justice Kavanaugh opinion from this term—*Diamond Alternative Energy, LLC v. EPA*.[174] There, writing for the majority, Justice Kavanaugh again employed "common sense," as applied to market economics, to reject the government's attack on the industry petitioner's standing.[175]

Conclusion

"Just as NEPA is not a green Magna Carta, federal judges are not the barons at Runnymede."[176] The Supreme Court in *Seven County* fully adopted that circumspect view of lower courts' longstanding over-enforcement of NEPA. To be sure, the Supreme Court has always been antithetical to NEPA enforcement, and *Seven County* continues that trend. But where *Seven County* breaks new ground is to reject lower courts' practice of demanding strict compliance with NEPA on pain of the rejection of an entire project. Now, courts must defer to agencies' NEPA decisionmaking just as they must with other administrative actions. Now, agencies do not need to review environmental effects that are far removed in time or place from the proposed project, or that are not subject to the agencies' direct regulatory review. Now, a project approval should be vacated only if the agency's decision is unreasonable or inadequately explained, a conclusion that doesn't necessarily follow from NEPA noncompliance.

But not all has changed—or better, some part of the old regime persists. Most importantly, the "hard look" review of *State Farm* will still govern project approvals both within and outside of NEPA; and that review is something that arises as much from the lower courts' mis-enforcement of NEPA as it does from any statute authorizing judicial review. What also persists is the Supreme Court's notable lack of interest in environmental law as a special discipline, as something requiring special expertise or solicitude over and above any other component of the modern federal regulatory apparatus, and—in counterbalance with the foregoing—a growing sympathy with the regulated public which must bear the oftentimes excessive burdens, occasionally judicially abetted, imposed by the administrative state.

---

[174] 145 S. Ct. 2121 (2025).

[175] *See id.* at 2137.

[176] Citizens Against Burlington, Inc. v. Busey, 938 F.2d 190, 194 (D.C. Cir. 1991) (Thomas, J.).

Vacatur as Complete Relief

Eli Nachmany*

Remedies are the next frontier in administrative law. One question vexes jurists and scholars in particular: What does the Administrative Procedure Act (APA) mean when it instructs courts to "set aside" agency action? On one reading, "set aside" means "vacate"—the court wipes the agency action off the books entirely. On another reading, however, "set aside" has a more circumscribed meaning: disregard the regulation in individual cases (i.e., enforcement actions). The debate is one of statutory interpretation, and this essay does not seek to resolve it. Rather, this essay points out a potential follow-on consequence of the debate's resolution: If "set aside" means only "disregard," then unregulated third parties may not be able to challenge agency action that has a predictable, adverse effect on them.

The Supreme Court's opinion in *Diamond Alternative Energy, LLC v. EPA*—the subject of this essay—is illustrative. Formally, the case was about the Article III standing doctrine. A consortium of fuel producers sued the Environmental Protection Agency (EPA), seeking to invalidate (i.e., "vacate") a waiver that the EPA had granted, rescinded, and granted again to California so that the Golden State could establish its own (strict) emissions standards for car manufacturers. The California law did not regulate the fuel producers directly; rather, the fuel producers' theory of their injury was that the regulations would have an impact on the design of cars and thereby decrease the market demand for the producers' fuel. The Court held that this injury could be redressed—for purposes of Article III standing—by invalidating the EPA's reinstatement of the waiver, as the fuel producers sought to do.

---

* Harvard Law School, JD 2022. The views expressed in this article do not reflect those of the author's employer or its clients.

The Court appeared to assume that vacatur of the reinstated EPA waiver was an available remedy. But it was also a necessary remedy to provide complete relief to the fuel producers. The case—or, more accurately, the underlying theory of the case—is an example of how the resolution of the vacatur debate could foreclose some plaintiffs from meaningful relief in regulatory litigation. The fuel producers would never have an opportunity to ask a court to disregard the EPA waiver (under the alternative understanding of "set aside"). If invalidation of the EPA waiver was not a possibility, then the fuel producers would not have a redressable injury. Under prevailing theories of statutory interpretation, that policy consequence is largely irrelevant to the task of determining what "set aside" means in the Administrative Procedure Act. Nevertheless, this reality raises the stakes of the debate; one potential interpretation of the APA would close the courthouse doors to a substantial number of plaintiffs seeking to challenge regulations that injure them.

This essay proceeds in two parts. Part I takes a close look at *Diamond Alternative Energy*. This part surveys the lead-up to the case and recounts the Court's holding that unregulated third-party plaintiffs had Article III standing to challenge an agency action that adversely impacted their interests. But, as Part I lays out, the Court's Article III holding depended on a key assumption: the plaintiffs could get a court to invalidate the agency action in question. Part II zooms out and explains why *Diamond Alternative Energy* is illustrative of a kind of lawsuit that could not go forward if "set aside" means disregard as opposed to vacate. This part begins by providing background on the debate about the meaning of "set aside." Then, this part situates the lawsuit at issue in *Diamond Alternative Energy* as an example of how the "set aside" debate could materially affect the regulatory litigation pipeline. Part II concludes with some considerations for Congress.

I. The Path to *Diamond Alternative Energy, LLC v. EPA*

In *Diamond Alternative Energy*, the Supreme Court ruled that fuel producers had Article III standing to sue the EPA about a waiver that the agency had granted to the State of California. The waiver allowed California to impose stringent fuel emissions standards on cars, which would have injured the fuel producers by causing reduced demand for their product. Justice Brett Kavanaugh authored the opinion of the Court for a seven-Justice majority, holding that this injury was redressable by invalidation of the waiver. This part reviews both the case and the fundamental assumption upon which the majority's opinion rested.

A. The Theory of the Case

The lawsuit underlying *Diamond Alternative Energy* involved an EPA waiver to the State of California which allowed California to establish its own emissions standards for automobiles. Because California's stringent standards would push the automobile industry to make cars that consumed less gasoline, fuel producers worried that the California regulations would reduce demand for their product. So, the fuel producers sued the EPA, seeking to invalidate the waiver. California intervened in the lawsuit and challenged the fuel producers' standing to sue. The D.C. Circuit accepted California's argument and dismissed the case, but the Supreme Court reversed. The Court's opinion held that invalidation of the waiver would redress the fuel producers' injury.

In general, the Clean Air Act preempts state promulgation of fuel emissions standards for automobiles. Yet the statute—enacted in 1967—allows the EPA to exempt California, in particular, from the law's preemptive effects. California was "the only state that had adopted standards (other than crankcase emission standards) for the control of emissions from new motor vehicles or new motor vehicle engines as of March 30, 1966"; and Section 209(a) of the law established certain circumstances under which the EPA could waive preemption as to California.[1] The law requires, among other things, that California "need[s] such . . . standards to meet compelling and extraordinary conditions."[2] And time and again, California has obtained EPA waivers to promulgate tailored "emissions standards to combat local California air-quality problems like smog."[3]

---

[1] Ohio v. EPA, 98 F.4th 288, 294 (D.C. Cir. 2024) (discussing 42 U.S.C. § 7543(a)), *rev'd sub nom.* Diamond Alt. Energy, LLC v. EPA, 145 S. Ct. 2121 (2025). At the time, "California's southern coastal cities faced an acute smog problem that national vehicle emission standards were unlikely to resolve." Initial Brief for Private Petitioners at 2, Ohio v. EPA, No. 22-1081 (and consolidated cases) (D.C. Cir. Oct. 24, 2022) [hereinafter Petitioners' Initial D.C. Circuit Brief].

[2] 42 U.S.C. § 7543(b)(1)(B).

[3] Diamond Alt. Energy, LLC v. EPA, 145 S. Ct. 2121, 2130 (2025).

79

Yet "[b]eginning in 2005, California also attempted to use its unique preemption exemption . . . to address global climate change."[4] The George W. Bush Administration's EPA rejected these efforts in 2008, but the Obama Administration's EPA granted such a waiver in connection with a 2012 request for permission to enact California-specific regulations involving automobiles for model years 2017 to 2025.[5] The Trump Administration's EPA rescinded its approval in 2019, and the Biden Administration's EPA reinstated the waiver in 2022.[6] Pursuant to the waiver, California imposed regulations that "generally require automakers (i) to limit average greenhouse-gas emissions across their fleets of new motor vehicles sold in the State and (ii) to manufacture a certain percentage of electric vehicles as part of their vehicle fleets."[7] In practice, that would mean less automobile demand for such fuels as gasoline, diesel, and ethanol.

Fuel producers—among others—sued the EPA in 2022 to invalidate the waiver. Under a special statutory review provision, the fuel producers' lawsuit went directly to the D.C. Circuit.[8] The fuel producers asserted that "climate change is not an 'extraordinary' condition within the meaning of" the statute because "the term 'extraordinary' refers to unique *local* conditions in California that result from local emissions and local pollution concentrations"; they urged that "California does not 'need' its own emission standards to 'meet' global climate-change conditions that those emission standards will not meaningfully address."[9] True, the California emission standards directly regulated automobile manufacturers—not the fuel producers themselves. But, the fuel producers contended, the regulations had downstream (negative) effects on the market for liquid fuels, and invalidation of the EPA waiver would prevent those effects.[10]

---

[4] *Id.*

[5] *See id.*

[6] *See id.*

[7] *Id.* at 2130–31.

[8] *See* 42 U.S.C. § 7607(b)(1).

[9] Petitioners' Initial D.C. Circuit Brief, *supra* note 1, at 14–15 (emphasis added). Petitioners cited the APA's standard of review (*see id.* at 17–18) and contended that "the 2022 decision was arbitrary and capricious and exceeded the EPA's authority under Section 209(b)." Ohio v. EPA, 98 F.4th 288, 299 (D.C. Cir. 2024), *rev'd sub nom.* Diamond Alt. Energy, LLC v. EPA, 145 S. Ct. 2121 (2025).

[10] *See id.* at 16–17.

The EPA did not contest the fuel producers' Article III standing to sue, but California (which had intervened in the D.C. Circuit) argued that the fuel producers' injury was not redressable—and the D.C. Circuit agreed. Article III of the Constitution limits the reach of the federal judicial power to certain "cases" and "controversies,"[11] and the Supreme Court has interpreted this language to require that a plaintiff have "standing" to sue in federal court.[12] A plaintiff has Article III standing only if he seeks "a remedy that is likely to redress [the] injury" he claims to have suffered.[13] As California saw it, the fuel producers' injury flowed from the decisions of third parties (i.e., automobile manufacturers) to modify their vehicle fleets, and the fuel producers had provided no evidence that vacatur of the EPA waiver would inspire automobile manufacturers to change course.[14] Evaluating this argument, the D.C. Circuit noted that "[w]hether a petitioner has standing to challenge a particular government action depends, in part, upon whether the petitioner is 'an object of the action' at issue."[15] And in the D.C. Circuit's view, the fuel producers— not objects of the EPA waiver (and subsequent California emission standards) because their injury hinged on actions taken by third-party manufacturers—had not adduced evidence showing that the objects of the regulation (the manufacturers) were likely to do anything in response to vacatur.[16] The waiver concerned regulations for model years 2017 to 2025, and the D.C. Circuit issued its opinion in 2024; thus, the D.C. Circuit was skeptical both that automobile manufacturers would respond to vacatur of the waiver by changing their fleets in a way that would alleviate the fuel producers' injuries, and "that automobile manufacturers would do so relatively quickly—by Model Year 2025."[17]

The Supreme Court reversed. The Court determined that "[t]he fuel producers . . . might be considered an object of the California

---

[11] U.S. Const. art. III, § 2.

[12] *See* Lujan v. Def. of Wildlife, 504 U.S. 555, 560 (1992).

[13] Uzuegbunam v. Preczewski, 592 U.S. 279, 285 (2021).

[14] *See* Brief of State and Local Government Respondent-Intervenors at 13–15, Ohio v. EPA, No. 22-1081 (D.C. Cir. Feb. 13, 2023).

[15] *Ohio*, 98 F.4th 288, 300 (quoting *Lujan*, 504 U.S. at 561), *rev'd sub nom.* Diamond Alt. Energy, LLC v. EPA, 145 S. Ct. 2121 (2025).

[16] *See Ohio*, 98 F.4th at 300.

[17] *Id.* at 302.

regulations because the regulations explicitly seek to restrict the use of gasoline and other liquid fuels in automobiles."[18] Thus, looking to "commonsense economic realities," the Court inferred that the California regulations would have a tangible impact on automobile manufacturers' market-affecting conduct by forcing "automakers to produce a fleet of vehicles that, as a whole, uses significantly less gasoline and other liquid fuels."[19] That inference was bolstered by "statements of the fuel producers, California, EPA, and the vehicle manufacturers."[20] The Court allowed "that there may conceivably be some atypical instances where a market has permanently and dramatically changed such that invalidating a challenged regulation would have no effect on the market in question."[21] Yet it observed "that governments do not usually continue to enforce and defend regulations that have no continuing effect in the relevant market" and noted that California's cramped "view of redressability fails to account for dynamic markets and the effects of interrelated economic forces and regulatory programs that change over time."[22] At bottom, the Court held that vacatur was likely to redress the fuel producers' injury.

B. The Objects of Regulation

The upshot of *Diamond Alternative Energy* is a relaxed standing inquiry for third-party plaintiffs in regulatory cases. And Justice Kavanaugh's majority opinion in the case has some nuggets that will be useful to the regulatory litigation bar. The Court cleared the way for the use of inferences—both economic and otherwise—when assessing redressability for purposes of Article III standing. Here, the Court's use of "commonsense economic principles" established an important default rule for Article III standing cases involving government regulation. Moreover, the Court's evaluation of record evidence will require government regulators (and their allies) to tread carefully against the backdrop of potential litigation. Finally, the Court was not bothered that the fuel producers could

---

[18] Diamond Alt. Energy, LLC v. EPA, 145 S. Ct. 2121, 2135 (2025).

[19] *Id.* at 2136–37.

[20] *Id.* at 2138.

[21] *Id.* at 2139.

[22] *Id.* at 2139–40.

not get regulated parties to file affidavits in support of the lawsuit—lowering the evidentiary burden for unregulated plaintiffs when standing is in doubt.

The Court determined that the fuel producers, despite their unregulated status, were likely to be injured by the California regulations. To get there, the Court relied most heavily on "commonsense [economic] inferences."[23] True, the Court allowed that invalidating the EPA waiver would "not *certainly* . . . make a difference for [the] fuel producers."[24] But the Court explained that the "predictable" behavior of the third-party automobile manufacturers in response to the California regulations (manufacturing "more electric vehicles and fewer gasoline-powered vehicles") was at least likely to occur.[25] Therefore, if the Court invalidated the EPA waiver, then the resulting invalidation of "California's regulations would likely mean more gasoline-powered automobiles, which would in turn likely mean more sales of gasoline and other liquid fuels by the fuel producers."[26]

The premise of the Court's straightforward theory of redressability was that government regulation has an effect on parties. So, because the fuel producers could not show exactly what would happen in the absence of California's regulation, the Court followed a default rule: "[T]he fact that a regulation was designed to produce a particular effect on the market ordinarily means that the likely result of vacating that regulation would be to reduce that effect on the market."[27] The Court thus chastised the EPA and California for arguing "that even if the California regulations are invalidated, automakers would not likely manufacture or sell more gasoline-powered cars than they do now" (based on how the vehicle market had developed over the years).[28] As the Court asked rhetorically, "[I]f invalidating the regulations would change nothing in the market, why are EPA and California enforcing and defending the regulations?"[29]

---

[23] *Id.* at 2136.

[24] *Id.* at 2137 (emphasis added).

[25] *Id.* at 2136.

[26] *Id.* at 2137.

[27] *Id.*

[28] *Id.*

[29] *Id.*; *see also id.* at 2139 ("[W]e can assume that governments do not usually continue to enforce and defend regulations that have no continuing effect in the relevant market.").

The opinion then looked to "record evidence" to confirm its analysis. On this point, the Court zeroed in on four pieces of evidence—of which two were essentially what the Court perceived to be admissions against interest by the government. The Court highlighted statements by California and the EPA to support the conclusion that the fuel producers had standing. The Court pointed out that California had described its regulations as "'critical' . . . for 'greater emission reductions *in the future*'" and noted that the EPA had also "stated that the California regulations are likely to reduce consumption of fuel."[30] The decision is yet another reminder that the government can undermine its own litigating position through its communications efforts.[31]

The Court also held that the fuel producers did not need to "introduce evidence . . . from directly regulated third parties to show how third parties would likely respond to a government regulation or invalidation thereof."[32] Here, Justice Kavanaugh's majority opinion displayed an appreciation for the realities of regulatory litigation. The Court took the position that requiring "affidavits from regulated parties" would make unregulated plaintiffs' lawsuits "dependent on the happenstance of whether the plaintiff and the relevant regulated parties are aligned and share litigation interests—and whether the regulated party is willing to publicly oppose (and possibly antagonize) the government regulator by supporting the plaintiff's suit."[33] For a regulated party that would prefer to stay in the government's good graces, filing an affidavit in a case brought by an unregulated party against the regulator could be a risky endeavor. Justice

[30] *Id.* at 2137–38.

[31] In *West Virginia v. EPA*, for example, the Supreme Court held that the EPA's Clean Power Plan contravened the major questions doctrine—a canon of statutory interpretation that counsels against novel agency assertions of significant regulatory authority. 597 U.S. 697, 732, 735 (2022). In explaining why the doctrine applies, the Court cited a White House fact sheet about the regulation at issue in the case (the Clean Power Plan); the fact sheet "stated that the Clean Power Plan would 'drive a[n] . . . aggressive transformation in the domestic energy industry.'" *Id.* at 714 (quoting White House Fact Sheet, App. in Am. Lung Ass'n. v. EPA, No. 19-1140 etc. (D.C. Cir.), at 2076). Talk of an "aggressive transformation," as Justice Neil Gorsuch pointed out in a concurrence, raised the specter of the major questions doctrine's applicability. *Id.* at 745–46 (Gorsuch, J., concurring).

[32] *Diamond Alt. Energy*, 145 S. Ct. at 2139.

[33] *Id.*

Kavanaugh translated this practical reality into Article III standing doctrine.

Notably, *Diamond Alternative Energy* was not a one-off; in a concurrence in another case this Term, Justice Amy Coney Barrett acknowledged the Court's "relaxed redressability inquiry in administrative-law procedural injury cases."[34] For the purposes of Article III standing, administrative law might just be different.

C. Redressable — Under the Assumption of Vacatur

The Court's opinion elided a more fundamental question: Could a court invalidate the EPA waiver under the APA? In *Diamond Alternative Energy*, the fuel producers' asserted injury was redressable because invalidation of the EPA waiver would nullify the California regulations. Thus, redressability depended on the availability of invalidation—that is, vacatur—as an APA remedy. The Court explicitly assumed that such a remedy was available. That assumption rested on the Court's understanding of the phrase "set aside" in the APA. And the Court's assumption was a necessary one; if the APA does not authorize vacatur, then a favorable judgment on behalf of the fuel producers could not redress the asserted injury.

In their initial brief before the D.C. Circuit, the fuel producers asked that the court "set aside EPA's action rescinding the withdrawal of California's preemption waiver."[35] The term "set aside" comes from Section 706 of the APA, which the fuel producers cited in the "Standard of Review" section of their brief.[36] Section 706 provides that a "reviewing court shall hold unlawful and *set aside* agency action . . . found to be," among other things, "not in accordance with law."[37] Under D.C. Circuit precedent, the APA's instruction to "set aside" agency action means "that '[w]hen a reviewing court determines that agency regulations are unlawful, the ordinary result is that the rules are vacated—not that their application to the

---

[34] Gutierrez v. Saenz, 145 S. Ct. 2258, 2269 (2025) (Barrett, J., concurring in part and concurring in the judgment).

[35] Petitioners' Initial D.C. Circuit Brief, *supra* note 1, at 64; *see also id.* at 57 ("[I]f this Court agrees that the waiver exceeds EPA's statutory authority, EPA's reinstatement of that waiver must be set aside.").

[36] *See id.* at 17.

[37] 5 U.S.C. § 706(2) (emphasis added).

individual petitioners is proscribed.'"[38] The fuel producers hoped that the court would vacate the EPA's action reinstating its waiver for California, thereby preempting California's regulations.

At the Supreme Court, the majority in *Diamond Alternative Energy* assumed that "set aside" meant vacate. The Court opined that the fuel producers' injury was redressable—for Article III standing purposes—because "invalidating the California regulations would likely redress at least some of the fuel producers' monetary injuries."[39] On this point, the Court clarified that in its opinion, it would "use the term 'invalidated' as shorthand to describe the result from setting aside EPA's approval of the California regulations."[40] In part, the footnote explains that the agency action at issue is the EPA's reinstatement of its waiver—not the California regulations; thus, formally, the direct object of the verb "invalidating" is the EPA's action, not California's regulation. But the footnote also communicates something more fundamental: For the purposes of the opinion, the Court assumed that the D.C. Circuit was correct that "set aside" means invalidate.

The Court's redressability holding depended on this assumption. If a court invalidated the EPA's waiver, and thereby nullified the California regulations, then the automakers would not be forced "to produce a fleet of vehicles that, as a whole, uses significantly less gasoline and other liquid fuels"—likely leading to "more gasoline-powered automobiles, which would in turn likely mean more sales of gasoline and other liquid fuels by the fuel producers."[41] The alternative, however, would not provide complete relief to the fuel producers. If "set aside" means only that the agency action's "application to the individual petitioners is proscribed" (an interpretation that the D.C. Circuit rejected in *National Mining Association*), then the fuel producers would likely lack standing. If the EPA waiver did not apply to the fuel producers, then the California regulations would be preempted and could not apply to the fuel producers. But the California regulations *already* do not apply to the unregulated fuel

---

[38] Nat'l Mining Ass'n v. U.S. Army Corps of Eng'rs, 145 F.3d 1399, 1409 (D.C. Cir. 1998) (quoting Harmon v. Thornburgh, 878 F.2d 484, 495 n.21 (D.C. Cir. 1989)).

[39] *Diamond Alt. Energy*, 145 S. Ct. at 2135.

[40] *Id.* at 2135 n.3.

[41] *Id.* at 2137.

producers. Thus, proscribing the application of those regulations to the petitioner fuel producers—and only the fuel producers—would be an ineffectual remedy that would fail to redress the asserted injury. As unregulated challengers, the fuel producers needed vacatur.

II. The Vacatur Debate and Unregulated Third-Party Plaintiffs

The Supreme Court has not definitively held that the APA authorizes vacatur of agency action.[42] The Justices disagree about whether it does. On one side, Justice Kavanaugh—incidentally, the author of *Diamond Alternative Energy*—defends the D.C. Circuit's approach: Vacatur is the appropriate remedy under the APA. Justice Gorsuch, however, has led the way in arguing for an alternative approach: The term "set aside" merely requires courts to disregard the agency action when deciding disputes. In the long run of regulatory cases, the meaning of "set aside" defines the scope of the remedy. Had the automobile manufacturers sued the EPA and asked that the court set aside the waiver, the "set aside" debate would determine who enjoys the remedy. If "set aside" means vacate, then all automakers would be free from the California regulations. But if "set aside" means disregard, then only the automobile manufacturers before the court would evade the regulatory burden.

The upshot of the "set aside" debate is, however, far more consequential for the fuel producers and other regulatory litigants who are themselves unregulated. If courts adopt Justice Gorsuch's view, then the fuel producers and similarly situated litigants might be unable to bring APA lawsuits even though agency actions have caused them injury. To a textualist, this consequence may be irrelevant to the question of statutory interpretation around which the debate revolves. Nevertheless, this potential consequence could be of interest to Congress, to the extent that the legislature considers amending the APA. Against the backdrop of a high-stakes judicial disagreement about the meaning of "set aside" in the APA, Congress can provide much-needed clarity by revising the law.

A. Surveying the Landscape on Vacatur

This essay takes stock of the debate over the term "set aside" in the APA without attempting to resolve it. On one side is what might be

---

[42] *See* Trump v. CASA, Inc., 2025 WL 1773631, at *8 n.10 (U.S. June 27, 2025).

described as the traditional view—"set aside" means vacate. Justice Kavanaugh is the leading proponent of this understanding, and scholars like Mila Sohoni are fellow adherents. On the other side, however, is an emerging view—"set aside" means disregard as to the litigant. Justice Gorsuch has expressed sympathy for this understanding, and he is joined by John Harrison and the Department of Justice, among others. The Supreme Court has come close to resolving the debate, but it has declined to do so.

One possible reading of "set aside" in Section 706 of the APA is as an instruction to courts to invalidate unlawful agency action altogether. As Jonathan Mitchell sees it, Section 706 establishes "a veto-like power that enables the judiciary to formally revoke an agency's rules, orders, findings, or conclusions—in the same way that an appellate court formally revokes an erroneous trial-court judgment."[43] The D.C. Circuit has long understood Section 706 to authorize this remedy,[44] and at least one judge has opined that the statute requires it.[45] Justice Kavanaugh (formerly of the D.C. Circuit) penned a concurrence in a recent case—*Corner Post, Inc. v. Board of Governors of the Federal Reserve System*—to advocate for this interpretation of the law.[46] And Justice Kavanaugh's interpretation has scholarly support. Mila Sohoni has laid out the historical argument for the proposition that "[t]he APA authorizes the universal vacatur of rules."[47] Ron Levin has bolstered Sohoni's claims by arguing that "the phrase 'set aside' has the same simple, straightforward meaning that most people—with the exception of a few heretics—have always thought it has,"

---

[43] Jonathan F. Mitchell, *The Writ-of-Erasure Fallacy*, 104 VA. L. REV. 933, 1012 (2018).

[44] *See Nat'l Mining Ass'n*, 145 F.3d at 1409 (quoting *Harmon*, 878 F.2d at 495 n.21).

[45] *See* Checkosky v. SEC, 23 F.3d 452, 492 (D.C. Cir. 1994) (Randolph, J., separate opinion) (determining that Section 706, under D.C. Circuit precedent, "requires" courts to vacate impermissible agency action).

[46] *See* 603 U.S. 799, 826 (2024) (Kavanaugh, J., concurring) ("[T]he APA authorizes vacatur of agency rules.").

[47] Mila Sohoni, *The Past and Future of Universal Vacatur*, 133 YALE L.J. 2305, 2311 (2024); *see generally* Mila Sohoni, *The Power to Vacate a Rule*, 88 GEO. WASH. L. REV. 1121 (2020). One commentator has uncovered evidence of state-law origins for the phrase "set aside," further supporting the conclusion that "the APA's 'set aside' provision contemplates universal vacatur." Fred Halbhuber, *The State-Law Origins of the APA's 'Set-Aside' Power*, YALE J. ON REGUL.: NOTICE & COMMENT (June 11, 2025), https://www.yalejreg.com/nc/the-state-law-origins-of-the-apas-set-aside-power-by-fred-halbhuber/.

while allowing that "the sentence should be read as *authorizing* set-aside relief, not as commanding it in every instance."[48]

But another view of "set aside" has gained some high-profile backers in recent years. John Harrison has contended that vacatur is inconsistent with the original meaning of the APA.[49] Rather, as Harrison sees it, unlawful agency actions are invalid from the moment that they are undertaken.[50] Thus, "[w]hen the regulated party is the defendant, the court should disregard unlawful regulations" because they are "non-binding."[51] The Department of Justice has taken this position in litigation; indeed, the department issued Litigation Guidelines in 2018 instructing the department's civil litigators to advance this alternative reading of the statute.[52] The Court eventually confronted this position at oral argument in *United States v. Texas*,[53] prompting an incredulous reaction from Chief Justice John Roberts and "palpable surprise" from several others.[54] Yet Justice Gorsuch was joined by Justices Barrett and Clarence Thomas when he concurred in the case to note that "[t]here are many reasons to think [Section] 706(2) uses 'set aside' to mean 'disregard' rather than 'vacate.'"[55] So, according to one view—ascendant on the Court, attaining scholarly acceptance, and central to the Justice Department's view of the APA—the "set aside" language in Section 706 means that a court must merely disregard an agency action in an individual case.

[48] Ronald M. Levin, *Vacatur, Nationwide Injunctions, and the Evolving APA*, 98 Notre Dame L. Rev. 1997, 2021 (2023).

[49] *See* John Harrison, *Vacatur of Rules Under the Administrative Procedure Act*, 40 Yale J. on Regul.: Bull. 119, 120 (2023).

[50] *See* John Harrison, *Remand Without Vacatur and the Ab Initio Invalidity of Unlawful Regulations in Administrative Law*, 48 BYU L. Rev. 2077, 2079 (2023).

[51] *Id.* at 2140.

[52] *See* Sohoni, *The Power to Vacate a Rule, supra* note 47, at 1123 (discussing Memorandum from the Off. of the Att'y Gen. to the Heads of Civ. Litigating Components U.S. Att'ys, Litig. Guidelines for Cases Presenting the Possibility of Nationwide Injunctions 7–8 (Sept. 13, 2018), https://www.justice.gov/opa/press-release/file/1093881/download).

[53] 599 U.S. 670 (2023).

[54] *See* Sohoni, *The Past and Future of Universal Vacatur, supra* note 47, at 2309 ("At oral argument tor *United States v. Texas*, . . . the Solicitor General contended that the Administrative Procedure Act . . . does not authorize a federal court to vacate a rule universally. Several of the Justices reacted to this argument with palpable surprise. Chief Justice Roberts exclaimed, 'Wow.'" (footnotes omitted)).

[55] *Texas*, 599 U.S. at 696 (Gorsuch, J., concurring).

B. What about the Fuel Producers in Diamond Alternative Energy?

Reading "set aside" to mean disregard as opposed to vacate would have practical consequences. In particular, lawsuits like that of the fuel producers in *Diamond Alternative Energy* might have a redressability problem. Determining that courts should disregard an agency action like the EPA waiver is not likely to provide complete relief to unregulated plaintiffs. That lack of complete relief differs from lawsuits like the one in *Corner Post,* which sparked a disagreement between Justice Kavanaugh and John Harrison about the need for vacatur in lawsuits brought by regulatory-beneficiary plaintiffs. Yet the theory of the case in *Diamond Alternative Energy* is well-known in administrative law. Getting rid of such lawsuits would remove an arrow in the quiver of the regulatory litigation bar by narrowing the universe of litigants that can challenge agency action.

In practice, the fuel producers need vacatur. If a court vacates the EPA waiver, then the automakers would not be required to abide by California's regulatory scheme. Those regulations, however, could not lead to a situation in which a court would need to disregard the EPA waiver as to the fuel producers. If Harrison is right, and the agency action is void *ab initio,* then a judgment that "hold[s] unlawful" that agency action might be redundant—to say nothing of the practical likelihood that automakers might be reluctant to alter their course of action on the basis of one district court's decision.[56] Thus, the fuel producers (and similarly situated litigants) would struggle to challenge agency actions like the EPA waiver. To be sure, this is just a policy consequence of interpreting "set aside" one particular way. And the Court has eschewed consideration of policy consequences when interpreting statutes.[57] This essay does not contend that the interpretation of "set aside" should turn on the availability of suits by unregulated entities. But when the regulatory bar considers the implications of a different approach to the statutory text, the fate of lawsuits like that in *Diamond Alternative Energy* is relevant.

---

[56] *Cf.* Trump v. CASA, Inc., 2025 WL 1773631, at *13 n.17 (U.S. June 27, 2025) (observing "the reality that district court opinions lack precedential force even vis-à-vis other judges in the same judicial district").

[57] *See, e.g.,* Corner Post, Inc. v. Bd. of Govs. of the Fed. Rsrv. Sys., 603 U.S. 799, 823 (2024).

The fuel producers' situation is different from that of regulatory beneficiaries. In connection with *Corner Post*, Justice Kavanaugh and John Harrison appeared to disagree about the implications of vacatur's availability to the regulatory challengers in the case. *Corner Post* involved a challenge by a truck-stop merchant to a Federal Reserve regulation that established the maximum "interchange fee" that banks can charge merchants when customers use those banks' debit cards to buy the merchants' goods.[58] Corner Post argued that the interchange fees were too high and that the Federal Reserve should set a stricter cap.[59] At the Supreme Court, the case involved a question about the statute of limitations under the APA. Yet in his concurrence, Justice Kavanaugh observed that "Corner Post can obtain relief in this case only because the APA authorizes vacatur of agency rules."[60] As he explained, "an injunction barring the agency from enforcing the rule against [Corner Post] would not help [it], because [Corner Post] is not regulated by the rule in the first place."[61] Rather, as an unregulated plaintiff, Corner Post could "obtain meaningful relief only if the APA authorizes vacatur of the agency rule, thereby remedying the adverse downstream effects of the rule on" the merchant.[62] John Harrison took a different view; in a blog post, he contended that "[i]f a regulatory beneficiary who claims that an agency has regulated too little prevails, a court can give that party full relief without itself vacating any rule the agency has adopted."[63] Harrison argued that because the case involved an agency's failure to act, the appropriate remedy would be to enter "a mandatory injunction directing an agency to regulate more than the agency already has, or to consider doing so pursuant to the court's directions."[64] Vacatur is not necessary.

---

[58] *See id* at 805.

[59] *See id.*

[60] *Id.* at 826 (Kavanaugh, J., concurring).

[61] *Id.*

[62] *Id.*

[63] John Harrison, *Agency Action, Agency Failure to Act, and Universal Relief in* Corner Post v. Board of Governors of the Federal Reserve System, Yale J. on Regul.: Notice & Comment (Mar. 25, 2024), https://www.yalejreg.com/nc/agency-action-agency-failure-to-act-and-universal-relief-in-corner-post-v-board-of-governors-of-the-federal-reserve-system-by-john-harrison/.

[64] *Id.*

But *Diamond Alternative Energy* did not involve a suit by regulatory beneficiaries seeking more stringent regulation. In his *Corner Post* concurrence, Justice Kavanaugh warned that "[e]liminating vacatur as a remedy would terminate entire classes of administrative litigation that have traditionally been brought by unregulated parties."[65] Yet Justice Kavanaugh's examples of such "classes of administrative litigation" largely involved lawsuits that challenged "the allegedly unlawful under-regulation of other[s]."[66] The theory of the case in *Diamond Alternative Energy* exemplifies a separate class of administrative litigation in which vacatur is required—without the problem of Harrison's objection to regulatory beneficiaries' need for vacatur. And the fuel producers' lawsuit is not the only such case in which the unregulated object of a regulation challenges that regulation. In one regulatory suit that predated the APA, for example, "[a] manufacturer of corn syrup" challenged a regulation that "established a definition and standard of identity for sweetened condensed milk" that "did not authorize the use of corn syrup" in the milk—the manufacturer contended that he would suffer an injury because "canners of milk sold in interstate commerce would no longer buy" his corn syrup.[67] At bottom, interpreting "set aside" to mean disregard as opposed to vacate would call an entire class of suits into question.

Some Justices discuss vacatur as going unnecessarily beyond the parties in the case, but suits like *Diamond Alternative Energy* provide a counterexample. In *Trump v. CASA, Inc.*, the Supreme Court emphasized that "'[c]omplete relief' is not synonymous with 'universal relief.'"[68] And in his *United States v. Texas* concurrence, Justice Gorsuch contrasted vacatur with "party-specific relief" that "affects nonparties . . . only incidentally."[69] But in *Diamond Alternative Energy*, vacatur seems to be the only way that the fuel producer plaintiffs

---

[65] *Corner Post*, 603 U.S. at 833 (Kavanaugh, J., concurring).

[66] *Id.* Justice Kavanaugh did give a brief nod to the essentiality of vacatur "when a State challenges an agency action that does not regulate the State directly but has adverse downstream effects on the State." *Id.* at 836–37 (citing, as an example, Dep't of Com. v. New York, 588 U.S. 752 (2019)).

[67] Note, *Competitors' Standing to Challenge Administrative Action Under the APA*, 104 U. PA. L. REV. 843, 850 (1956) (discussing A.E. Staley Mfg. Co. v. Sec'y of Agri., 120 F.2d 258 (7th Cir. 1941)).

[68] 145 S. Ct. at 2557.

[69] 599 U.S. at 693 (Gorsuch, J., concurring in the judgment).

can obtain complete relief. As other courts have recognized in separate contexts, vacatur may be "necessary to grant complete relief" to
a party.[70] And so it appears to be here.

C. Considerations for Congress

If Congress is concerned about the alternative approach to "set
aside" taking hold, it can change the law. In particular, Congress can
clarify when vacatur is available. To be sure, Congress would need
to grapple with constitutional constraints on its power to authorize
wide-ranging remedies. But with a potential opening for APA reform in Congress, the legislature could take a crack at resolving the
"set aside" debate. Indeed, the Supreme Court's tendency toward
statutory interpretation in administrative law cases has "preserve[d]
space for Congress to change the law if it wants to [address] courts'
remedial powers in regulatory litigation."[71]

In recent years, Congress has signaled that it might be willing to
amend the APA,[72] and the legislature might want to take a closer look
at the potential problem of unregulated plaintiffs. One possible fix is
the establishment of a special statutory review provision for unregulated plaintiffs—who are nevertheless the objects of regulation—to
challenge regulations that adversely affect them and obtain vacatur. Additionally, Congress could take a side in the ongoing debates
about the meaning of "set aside." Or, it could pass a law stating that
whatever the meaning of "set aside," unregulated plaintiffs may obtain vacatur when it would provide them complete relief in a regulatory challenge. Such a move could alleviate the tension between
narrow conceptions of APA remedies and a robust understanding of
the right for unregulated entities like the fuel producers to challenge
regulations that target them.

---

[70] Florida v. United States, 660 F. Supp. 3d 1239, 1284 (N.D. Fla. 2023) (quoting
Health Freedom Def. Fund, Inc. v. Biden, 599 F. Supp. 3d 1144, 1177 (M.D. Fla. 2022),
vacated as moot sub nom. Health Freedom Def. Fund v. President of the U.S., 71 F.4th
888 (11th Cir. 2023)).

[71] Jennifer L. Mascott & Eli Nachmany, *Answered by Text*, 48 HARV. J.L. & PUB. POL'Y
33, 48 (2025).

[72] *Cf. id.* at 42 n.30 (discussing congressional consideration of bills to amend the
APA in light of the Supreme Court's elimination of deference to agencies in statutory
interpretation).

Article III of the Constitution looms in the background, but authorizing vacatur for certain unregulated plaintiffs would likely satisfy this constitutional requirement. The Supreme Court in *CASA* did not invoke Article III when opining that the Judiciary Act of 1789 likely does not authorize universal injunctions; rather, the Court relied only on the statute itself.[73] And jurists who have expressed skepticism about APA vacatur's consistency with Article III have focused on the notion that judges only have the power "to decide cases and controversies," and thus they should "avoid trenching on the power of the elected branches to shape legal rights and duties more broadly."[74] The key objection is that courts, when issuing the remedy of vacatur, assert an "authority to issue decrees that purport to define the rights and duties of sometimes millions of people who are not parties before them."[75] But even if that result is the incidental effect of vacatur in a case involving an unregulated plaintiff like the fuel producers, "there is no doubt that an Article III court 'may administer complete relief between the parties, even [if] this involves the determination of legal rights which otherwise would not be within the range of its authority.'"[76]

---

[73] *See CASA*, 145 S. Ct. at 2550 (describing the issue as "whether, under the Judiciary Act of 1789, federal courts have equitable authority to issue universal injunctions"). Indeed, the resolution of the universal injunctions issue fit with a broader theme at the Supreme Court of "focus[ing] on statutory interpretation as opposed to reaching for . . . constitutional holdings." Mascott & Nachmany, *supra* note 71, at 36.

[74] *Texas*, 599 U.S. at 694 (Gorsuch, J., concurring in the judgment).

[75] *Id.*

[76] *Health Freedom Def. Fund, Inc.*, 599 F. Supp. 3d at 1177 (quoting Kinney-Coastal Oil Co. v. Kieffer, 277 U.S. 488, 507 (1928), and then citing Trump v. Hawaii, 138 S. Ct. 2392, 2427 (2018) (Thomas, J., concurring), as "explaining that historic equity permitted relief to benefit third parties if it was 'merely a consequence of providing relief to the plaintiff'"), *vacated as moot sub nom.* Health Freedom Def. Fund v. President of the U.S., 71 F.4th 888 (11th Cir. 2023). *But cf.* Jameson M. Payne & GianCarlo Canaparo, *Is Vacatur Unconstitutional?* (July 2, 2025) (contending that vacatur may violate Article III by operating on the agency action instead of enjoining the relevant government official). Available at SSRN: https://papers.ssrn.com/sol3/papers.cfm?abstract_id=5333468.

Conclusion

In some APA cases, the remedy of vacatur is necessary to provide complete relief to a party. *Diamond Alternative Energy, LLC v. EPA* is an example—an unregulated challenger that is concerned about the downstream economic consequences of a regulation. But some jurists and scholars have called into question whether the APA authorizes vacatur—that is, they argue, the phrase "set aside" in the APA means disregard, not invalidate. If that argument wins the day, then cases like *Diamond Alternative Energy* may struggle to get off the ground. Although that policy consequence may not bear on the meaning of the term "set aside" (from the standpoint of statutory interpretation), it is nevertheless relevant to regulatory litigators and, perhaps, Congress.

Kennedy v. Braidwood Management: The "Inferior Officer" Clause Loses Some Bite

*Thomas Berry and Charles Brandt**

The Appointments Clause lies at the heart of the separation of powers, ensuring the Washington bureaucracy remains accountable to the President and the People he serves. It dictates that the President "shall appoint" officers of the United States, but provides that "the Congress may *by Law vest* the Appointment of such inferior Officers, as they think proper, in the President alone, in the Courts of Law, or in the Heads of Departments."[1]

The Supreme Court's 2024-2025 Term sparked an unexpected debate over what is required in order for Congress to "vest" an inferior officer appointment "by law." In *Becerra v. Braidwood Management*, the Court granted certiorari to address whether members of the U.S. Preventive Services Task Force (Task Force) were inferior or non-inferior (i.e. principal) officers under the Appointments Clause.[2]

After oral argument, the Court requested supplemental briefing on the question of whether Congress had "by law" vested the Secretary of Health and Human Services (HHS) with the authority to appoint Task Force members.[3] The order asked the parties to address two precedents—*United States v. Hartwell* and *United States v. Smith*.[4]

In an opinion authored by Justice Brett Kavanaugh, the Court held that Task Force members are inferior officers because they are sufficiently supervised by the HHS Secretary, who may review and

---

* Director and legal associate, Robert A. Levy Center for Constitutional Studies, Cato Institute.

[1] U.S. CONST. art. II, § 2, cl. 2 (emphasis added).

[2] 145 S. Ct. 1038 (2025).

[3] *Kennedy v. Braidwood Mgmt.*, 145 S. Ct., 1957 (2025).

[4] *Id.* (citing *United States v. Hartwell*, 73 U.S. 385 (1867); *United States v. Smith*, 124 U.S. 525 (1888)).

block their decisions and remove them without cause.[5] As to the question put to the parties in the supplemental briefing order, the Court found that Congress had "expressly vested" Task Force appointments in the Secretary—first, by authorizing the Director of the Agency for Healthcare Research and Quality (AHRQ) to "convene" the Task Force;[6] and second, by transferring the AHRQ Director's functions to the Secretary.[7]

Justice Clarence Thomas, joined by Justices Samuel Alito and Neil Gorsuch, dissented. Charging the majority with treating the Appointments Clause "as an inconvenient obstacle to be overcome, not a constitutional principle to be honored," the dissent would have required greater "clarity" from Congress "to depart from the default rule established by the Appointments Clause."[8] "[T]o vest appointment power for an office in a department head," the dissent explained, "Congress must pass a statute giving him the authority to assign a person to that office."[9] Furthermore, "[t]he vesting of appointment authority must be explicit."[10] Because the statutes relied upon by the majority did not give assignment authority to the Secretary "explicitly," Justice Thomas concluded that the appointment prerogative must remain with the President.

In our view, the Court's decision in *Braidwood* misreads the significance of *United States v. Hartwell* while completely ignoring *United States v. Smith*—a more relevant precedent that undermines the Court's holding. In *Smith*, the government advanced—and the Court rejected—an argument eerily similar to the vesting theory accepted in *Braidwood*. But the *Braidwood* Court does not purport to overrule *Smith*. Indeed, *Smith* garnered not a single citation, which is strange considering the Court *expressly* requested briefing on *Smith*. By contrast, the dissent mentions *Smith* and advances a clear statement rule faithful to it.

The article will proceed in six parts. Section One will explore the facts and holdings of *Hartwell* and *Smith*. Section Two will present a model approach to the vesting question taken by the Court

---

[5] *Kennedy v. Braidwood Mgmt.*, 145 S. Ct. 2427, 2439 (2025).

[6] *Id.* at 2453–54 (referencing 42 U.S.C. § 299b-4(a)(1)).

[7] *Id.* (referencing 80 Stat. 1610 & 98 Stat. 2705).

[8] *Id.* at 2462 (Thomas, J., dissenting).

[9] *Id.* at 2467.

[10] *Id.*

of Appeals for the Armed Forces (CAAF). Section Three will draw upon these insights to argue against the Court's *Braidwood* holding. Section Four will offer an account of which constitutional values might be advanced by the dissent's clear statement rule. Section Five will provide some potential implications. Lastly, Section Six will briefly conclude.

I. Hartwell and Smith

A. United States v. Hartwell

In *United States v. Hartwell*,[11] the Court considered the legal status of a bank clerk who was appointed by an assistant treasurer with the "approbation" (i.e. approval) of the Treasury Secretary.[12] The question was whether this bank clerk was an officer of the United States *within the meaning of a criminal statute*.[13] The defendant bank clerk was indicted under a statute which made it a crime for "officers" charged with the safekeeping of public money to embezzle or convert such funds.[14] The defendant sought to quash the indictment on the theory that was he not an "officer or person" subject to the act's prohibition.[15] The Court disagreed.

---

[11] 73 U.S. (6 Wall.) 385 (1867).

[12] A statute expressly required the Secretary's approbation for the clerk's appointment. 14 Stat. 191, 202 ("[I]n lieu of the clerks heretofore authorized, the assistant treasurer of the United States at Boston is hereby authorized to appoint, with the approbation of the Secretary of the Treasury, [the following clerks at the following salaries.]")

[13] *Hartwell*, 73 U.S. at 390 (framing the inquiry as whether "the defendant [was] an officer or person 'charged with the safe-keeping of the public money' *within the intent of the act of 1846*?") (emphasis altered).

[14] *Id.* at 393. The statute provided that "all officers and other persons, charged . . . with the safe-keeping, transfer, and disbursement, of the public moneys are hereby required to keep an accurate entry of each sum received, and of each payment or transfer; and . . . if any one of the said officers, . . . shall convert to his own use, in any way whatever, or shall use, by way of investment in any kind of property or merchandise, or shall loan, with or without interest, or shall deposit in any bank, or shall exchange for other funds, except as allowed by this act, any portion of the public moneys intrusted to him for safe-keeping, disbursement, transfer, or for any other purpose, every such act shall be deemed and adjudged to be an embezzlement . . .; and if any officer charged with the disbursements of public moneys shall accept, or receive, or transmit to the treasury department to be allowed in his favor, any receipt or voucher from a creditor of the United States, without having paid to such creditor, . . . every such act shall be deemed to be a conversion by such officer." 9 Stat. 59, 63.

[15] *Hartwell*, 73 U.S. at 393.

"An office," the Court explained, "is a public station, or employment, conferred by the appointment of government" that "embraces the ideas of tenure, duration, emolument, and duties."[16] Because the statute in question[17] "authorized the assistant treasurer . . . to appoint a specified number of clerks" (with the Secretary's assent), defined their duties, and set their salaries, the Court deemed the defendant an "officer" *for statutory purposes.*[18]

To be sure, the *Hartwell* Court briefly nodded to the Appointments Clause, stating: "The defendant was appointed by the head of a department within the meaning of the constitutional provision upon the subject of the appointing power."[19] But this statement is both dictum[20] and *ipse dixit*. It was accompanied by no analysis, and indeed, it was irrelevant to the question presented, which concerned *statutory* distinctions between officers (both principal and inferior), who were subject to indictment, and employees, who were not.[21] The apparent lack of judicial engagement with the constitutional question thus makes sense.

One other factor might explain the Court's scanty treatment of the Appointments Clause: Hartwell's counsel failed to attack the validity of his client's appointment.[22] Instead of challenging the indictment on *constitutional* grounds, counsel focused merely on the statute and whether its "terms" applied to Hartwell's clerkship.[23] In the absence of relevant "adversarial testing"—on which courts rely for "sound judicial decisionmaking"—*Hartwell* is seriously undermined as an Appointments Clause precedent.[24] Fortunately, *United States v. Smith,* discussed below, is significantly more illuminating.

---

[16] *Id.*

[17] General Appropriation Act of 1866, 14 Stat. 191, 202.

[18] *Hartwell,* 73 U.S. at 393.

[19] *Id.* at 393–94.

[20] *See Morrison v. Olson,* 487 U.S. 654, 719, 721 (1988) (Scalia, J., dissenting); *Seminole Tribe of Florida v. Florida,* 517 U.S. 44, 67 (1996) (explaining that under the doctrine of *stare decicis,* courts are only "bound" by "those portions of the opinion necessary to that result").

[21] *See Morrison,* 487 U.S. at 719 (Scalia, J., dissenting).

[22] *Hartwell,* 73 U.S. at 389–91 (providing a recapitulation of counsel's arguments with no reference to the Appointments Clause).

[23] *E.g., id.* at 391 (arguing that "[t]he terms of the sixteenth section . . . apply to principal officers alone; not to subordinates appointed by them.").

[24] *Sessions v. Dimaya,* 584 U.S. 148, 190 (2018) (Gorsuch, J., concurring in part and concurring in judgment); *see also Greenlaw v. United States,* 554 U.S. 237, 243–44 (2008) (discussing the importance of adversarial representation).

B. *United States v. Smith*

In *United States v. Smith*,[25] the Court meaningfully analyzed the vesting question that *Hartwell* only nodded to. Smith was a clerk for the collector of customs, and he was indicted for converting public monies to personal use.[26] Unlike Hartwell, Smith was not appointed under any statute that required the Secretary's approbation.[27] His appointment was made instead by the collector of customs, an inferior officer, and the indictment merely "averred" that "the appointment of the defendant as clerk was made with [the Secretary's assent]."[28] Also, unlike Hartwell, Smith actually moved to quash his indictment on the constitutional ground that he had not been "appointed by the head of a department."[29]

Given the similarities to the government's argument in *Braidwood*, we will break down the line of reasoning advanced by it in *Smith*. As recapitulated in the case caption, the government's argument that Smith was properly appointed proceeded in four parts:

First, "by authorizing the Secretary of the Treasury to fix the number [of clerks] to be employed and the compensation to be paid them," "[s]ection 2634 of the Revised Statutes establishe[d] the office of clerk."[30]

Second, "by a permanent appropriation," "[s]ection 3687 . . . provides for the payment of the expenses of collecting the revenue from customs, and [section] 2639 includes in those expenses clerk hire."[31]

Third, each department head was authorized under section 169 to "employ in his Department such number of clerks . . . at such rates of compensation respectively as may be appropriated for by Congress from year to year."[32]

Fourth, section 249 vested the duty of "superintend[ing] . . . the collection of the duties on imports and tonnage" in the Secretary.[33]

---

25 124 U.S. 525 (1888).

26 *Id.* at 525.

27 *Id.* at 532–33.

28 *Id.* at 533.

29 *Id.* at 527.

30 *Id.* at 530.

31 *Id.*

32 *Id.*

33 *Id.*

By establishing the office, appropriating funds for the salaries of the officer, authorizing assignment to the post, and granting general supervisory authority to a department head, the government argued that Congress had provided "a sufficient grant of power . . . to appoint."[34] As the indictment alleged that Smith was appointed with secretarial assent, the government concluded that the indictment was valid and the defendant's demurrer should be overruled.[35]

The Court rejected the government's implicit authority theory and held Smith's appointment invalid. Because the clerk's appointment was neither made nor approved by a principal officer pursuant to explicit statutory authority, the defendant could not be considered "appointed by the head of any department within the meaning of the [Appointments Clause]".[36] Treating *Hartwell*'s cursory treatment of the Appointments Clause as precedential, the Court distinguished it on the ground that that case involved a statute that expressly required secretarial assent to the appointment.[37]

In *Smith*, by contrast, there was *no law* vesting the Secretary with the power to appoint nor conditioning appointments on his approbation. That the indictment alleged the Secretary to have rubber-stamped Smith's hiring was irrelevant. Even if true, the allegation "could not add to the character, or powers, or dignity of the clerk."[38] *Smith* thus embraces a clear statement rule: In the absence of a statute that at least conditions an inferior's appointment on a principal's approval, Congress has not "vested" that appointment "by law" in a "head of department."

II. A Model Approach—United States v. Janssen

The Court of Appeals for the Armed Forces (CAAF) took what we consider to be the correct approach to the vesting question in *United States v. Janssen*, an approach faithful to *Smith* (despite not citing it).[39]

[34] *Id.*

[35] *Id.* at 533.

[36] *Id.*

[37] *Id.* at 532.

[38] That is, the character, powers, and dignity of an office find their source in statutory law, not executive action taken irrespective or in violation of statute. *Id.* at 533. *Accord United States v. Trump*, 740 F. Supp. 3d 1245, 1284 (S.D. Fla. 2024) (stating that the Executive may not "wrest[] from Congress its constitutionally prescribed role in the officer-appointing process").

[39] 73 M.J. 221 (C.A.A.F. 2014).

The CAAF, as will be shown, treats the inquiry as one of statutory interpretation—a measured approach that accounts for unique context and eschews one-size-fits-all jurisprudence.

Janssen considered whether a member of the Court of Criminal Appeals (CCA) was properly appointed under the Appointments Clause. The defendant was convicted by court martial and his conviction affirmed by CCA.[40] The panel that reviewed the sentence included a judge appointed by the Secretary of Defense. The defendant attacked the validity of that appointment, "asserting that the Secretary . . . lacked the statutory authority."[41]

The CCA disagreed, finding implicit authority for the appointment and affirming the sentence.[42] On appeal to the CAAF, the question presented was whether "Congress 'by law' vest[ed] the Secretary of Defense, the head of a department, with the authority to appoint a civilian as an appellate military judge."[43]

The CAAF found the appointment invalid, reversing the decision below. True, Congress had enacted statutes authorizing the Secretary to "employ such number of employees . . . as Congress may appropriate for from year to year"—"employee" being defined to include "officer[s]."[44] But in light of the statutory context, those general "'housekeeping' statutes" did not contain "the necessary authority" for making an appointment.[45]

"Congress," the court explained, "legislated with great specificity on the powers of the Secretary of Defense and the structure of the department," "rais[ing] the obvious question of why Congress would go to the trouble" if the Secretary already possessed an open-ended appointment power.[46] Indeed, "three positions within the Office of the Secretary" expressly required secretarial appointment under various statutes.[47] The court also pointed to another statute which "specifically provided for the appointment of administrative

---

[40] *Id.* at 222.

[41] *Id.* at 223.

[42] *Id.* at 222–23.

[43] *Id.* at 224.

[44] *Id.* (quoting 5 U.S.C. §§ 301, 2105(a), 3101).

[45] *Id.*

[46] *Id.* at 224, 225.

[47] *Id.* at 225 & n.9 (citing statutes).

law judges."[48] Particularly in light of the statutory scheme, "language *specifically granting* the head of a department the power to appoint inferior officers" would be required to override the default method of appointment (namely presidential nomination and Senate consent).[49]

The analysis in *Janssen* tracks with the Supreme Court's in *Smith*. Both cases recognized potentially implicit sources of appointment authority and both cases rejected such measures as insufficient to depart from the default rule of presidential nomination with Senate consent. What *Janssen* adds to the analysis is a greater sensitivity to statutory context and structure—tools that, had they been employed in *Braidwood*, would likely have carried the case the other way.

III. Where Braidwood Went Wrong

The Court erred in *Braidwood* in five noteworthy ways: (1) it failed to cite, let alone distinguish, *Smith*—notwithstanding the precedent's embrace of a clear statement rule; (2) it misconceived the significance of *Hartwell*, whose treatment of the Appointments Clause is nonprecedential; (3) it disregarded inconvenient statutory context that suggests Congress never intended to vest Task Force appointments in the HHS Secretary; (4) it rushed to judgment in denying lower courts the opportunity to weigh the issue first; and (5) it misused the doctrine of constitutional avoidance in shoring up its interpretation. We take up each error in turn.

A. Failure to Grapple with Smith

Despite the request for supplemental briefing on *Smith*,[50] Justice Kavanaugh's opinion for the Court never cited it. Evidently, six of the Justices agreed with the government's contention that *Smith* was "inapposite."[51] It is hard to see how.

Under *Smith*, the matter of vesting appointments is not up for legislative implication. Yet in *Braidwood*, the government advanced a hodgepodge of statutes—enacted decades apart with strange

---

[48] *Id.* at 225 (citing 5 U.S.C. § 3105).

[49] *Id.* at 224, 225 (emphasis added).

[50] *Kennedy v. Braidwood Management*, 145 S. Ct. 1957 (2025).

[51] Letter Brief for the United States at 8, *Braidwood Mgmt. v. Kennedy*, 145 S. Ct. 2427 (2025) (No. 24-316).

procedural wrinkles—and interpreted them, holistically, to provide "a sufficient vesting" and "a sufficient grant of power . . . to appoint."[52] The government's theory proceeded in three parts:

1. Section 299b-4(a)(1) of Title 42 authorized the AHRQ Director to "convene" the Task Force, which implied the power to appoint members.[53]

2. Section 299(a) made the Director an officer of the Public Health Service (PHS) and an agent of the HHS Secretary acting on the Secretary's behalf.[54]

3. Reorganization Plan No. 6 of 1966 transferred all of the functions of PHS officers to the Secretary,[55] and after doubt was cast on the plan's validity, Congress enacted a new statute ratifying and affirming the transfer.[56]

Together, the government argued, these three enactments provided "a reasonable basis for concluding that Congress vested the power to appoint Task Force members . . . in the Secretary himself."[57]

This line of reasoning harkens back to the implicit authority argument that the Court rejected in *Smith*. There, the government contended that while "[s]ometimes" Congress creates an office "in express terms," "more frequently," it will establish inferior offices "by implication."[58] The government then pieced together various statutes, including delegations for the Treasury Secretary to (1) fix the number of clerks, (2) set their compensation, and (3) "direct the superintendence of the collection of duties on imports and tonnage[.]"[59] The government argued that, read together, these measures provided "a sufficient vesting" and "grant of power . . . to appoint."[60]

---

[52] *Smith*, 124 U.S. at 530.

[53] Letter Brief for the United States, *supra*, at 1.

[54] *Id.*

[55] *Id.* (citing § 1(a), 80 Stat. 1610).

[56] *Id.* (quoting Reorganization Plan, Act of Oct. 19, 1984, Pub. L. No. 98-532, § 1, 98 Stat. 2705)

[57] *Id.* at 2.

[58] *Smith*, 124 U.S. at 529–30.

[59] *Id.* at 530 (quoting Rev. Stat. § 249, codified at 19 U.S.C. § 3).

[60] *Id.* at 530.

The *Smith* Court could easily have interpreted the statutes to "impose" by implication "the duty to carry out the selection" of clerks on the Secretary.[61] If the customs office fell under secretarial superintendence, and if the Secretary could fix the number of clerks as he saw fit (subject to appropriations), then presumably the Secretary could select clerks *acting through the customs office.* In the face of the default rule for officer appointments, however, this fact did not matter. The collage of statutes pieced together by the government furnished an authority too implicit, *even if plausible,* to override the Constitution's default method of appointment. In other words, only a statute explicitly "authorizing the head of a department to appoint" could satisfy the Excepting Clause.[62] So too the Court should have held in *Braidwood.*

Section 299b-4(a)(1), like Section 2634 from *Smith,* creates an office and authorizes the hiring of persons to fill the post. Section 299(a), like Section 249 from *Smith,* creates an agency relationship between a cabinet secretary and the officer responsible for appointing the putative inferior. Under *Smith,* neither measure is sufficient, independently or in conjunction, to vest Task Force appointments in the Secretary by law. Furthermore, the government's suggestion that "no law [in *Smith*], akin to the Reorganization Plan, . . . invested the Treasury Secretary himself with the selection of the clerks of the collector" is dubious.[63] Arguably, there *was* such a law;[64] the Court simply rejected the government's implicative construction of it.

True, the statute in *Braidwood* included a transfer-of-functions provision more specific than the superintendence measure from *Smith*— which could arguably distinguish it.[65] Whereas "superintendence" connotes the ability of a supervisor to reach down and direct the conduct of an inferior, "transfer" suggests the dislodging of power from an inferior in favor of principal. So, while in *Smith* the Secretary could direct the clerk's officer in choosing whom to hire, in *Braidwood* the Secretary could, following this theory, actually *wield* that power

---

[61] *Cf.* Letter Brief for the United States, *supra,* at 8.

[62] *Smith,* 124 U.S. at 530.

[63] Letter Brief for the United States, *supra,* at 8 (internal quotation marks omitted).

[64] 14 Stat. 191, 202 ("The Secretary of the Treasury shall direct the superintendence of the collection of the duties on imports and tonnage as he shall judge best.").

[65] 80 Stat. 1610 (transferring functions); 98 Stat. 2705 (ratifying transfer of functions post-*Chadha*).

for himself. But this difference is insufficient to distinguish *Smith* or to override the default rule for executive appointments.

Recall that the statute in *Braidwood* never used the word "appoint," instead employing the term "convene."[66] So, the "function" transferred from the Director to the Secretary was not the appointment of the Task Force, but the convening of its members. As Justice Thomas explains in dissent, the ordinary meaning of "convene"—"to cause to assemble"—does not encapsulate appointment or assignment, particularly in view of statutory context.[67] After all, Task Force members are unpaid, part-time volunteers who meet three times per year. It was to facilitate those meetings that Congress empowered the Director to "convene" the Task Force.[68] As such, the transfer-of-functions argument fails.

In contrast, the statutes in *Smith* used the language "employ," which more closely approximates "appoint" than "convene." The statute also provided greater control to the Secretary over the relevant interior officer, by delegating the power to fix the number of available posts.[69] And yet, in the absence of "a law authorizing the head of a department to appoint clerks of the collector,"[70] neither of these facts proved sufficient to vest the clerk's appointment in the Secretary. In short, if the statutes in *Smith* did not vest an appointment, it is hard to see how the statutes in *Braidwood* do so; they neither use the term "employ" (or "appoint"), nor allow the Secretary to tweak the number of members on the Task Force.

B. Misconception of Hartwell

The Court treats *Hartwell's* Appointments Clause analysis as if precedential,[71] based on a favorable citation in *Free Enterprise Fund v.*

---

[66] *Braidwood Mgmt.*, 145 S. Ct. at 2439 (internal quotation marks omitted).

[67] *Id.* at 2469 (Thomas, J., dissenting) (cleaned up).

[68] *Id.* at 2469–70.

[69] On the facts of this case, one can imagine an analogous power of the HHS Secretary to fix the number Task Force members.

[70] *Smith*, 124 U.S. at 533.

[71] Recall the full extent of *Hartwell's* vesting analysis: "The defendant was appointed by the head of a department within the meaning of the constitutional provision upon the subject of the appointing power." 73 U.S. at 393–94. As discussed in Section I.A., *supra*, *Hartwell* was a statutory criminal law case that hinged on the difference between officers (both principal *and* inferior), who were indictable, and employees, who were not.

PCAOB.[72] There, the Court invoked *Hartwell* for the proposition that secretarial assent to an inferior officer's appointment of another inferior "satisfies the Appointments Clause."[73] But an approving citation in a subsequent case cannot transform what was *dictum* into holding, particularly when doing so would contravene *actually binding* precedent.[74] Nor can the Court be charged with ignorance—it cited to the *very pincite* of Justice Antonin Scalia's *Morrison* dissent in which he ridiculed the relevant analysis from *Hartwell* as nonbinding and "sketchy."[75]

C. Disregard of Statutory Context

For all its emphasis on "context,"[76] the Court's analysis in *Braidwood* is, in one important respect, divorced from statutory context. HHS, one of the largest cabinet departments, is governed by Title 42—a vast collection of complex and detailed statutes. Notably, throughout the title, Congress employs unambiguous—indeed, explicit—language in order to vest appointment powers in the HHS Secretary.[77] Elsewhere, Congress delegates a general appointment authority in order to carry out designated functions.[78]

Title 42 thus "sets out in great detail the officials who make up the Office of the Secretary . . . and the procedures to be employed for their appointment."[79] Naturally, then, one would expect a similarly explicit grant of authority for secretarial appointment of the

---

[72] 561 U.S. 477 (2010)

[73] *Id.* at 512 n.13.

[74] *See generally Smith, supra.*

[75] *Braidwood Mgmt.*, 145 S. Ct. at 2443; *Morrison*, 487 U.S. at 719, 721 (Scalia, J., dissenting).

[76] *Id.* at 2454.

[77] *See, e.g.*, § 300jj-11 ("The Office shall be headed by a National Coordinator who shall be appointed by the Secretary . . ."); § 300u(a) ("The Secretary shall appoint a Director for the Office of Disease Prevention and Health Promotion established pursuant to paragraph (11) of this subsection."); § 209(i) ("The appointment of any officer or employee of the Service made in accordance with the civil-service laws shall be made by the Secretary . . . .")

[78] *See, e.g.*, 42 U.S.C. § 913 ("[T]he Secretary is authorized to appoint and fix the compensation of such officers and employees and to make such expenditures as may be necessary for carrying out the functions of the Secretary under this chapter.").

[79] *Janssen*, 73 M.J. at 225.

Task Force. But Chapter 6A contains no such provision, nor does it contain "any provision conferring a general appointment power."[80]

Congress knows what language to use when it wants to vest appointments in the HHS Secretary. But none of the statutes advanced by the government in *Braidwood* contained "the clarity typical of past statutes used for that purpose."[81] By accepting the government's tortuous vesting theory regardless, the Court did an interpretative disservice to the carefully crafted handiwork of Congress.

D. Rush to Judgment

In a recent statement respecting the denial of certiorari in *Snope v. Brown*, Justice Kavanaugh stressed the importance of percolation of questions in the lower courts, stating: "Opinions from [the] Courts of Appeals . . . assist this Court's ultimate decisionmaking."[82] In *Braidwood*, the Justice showed no such restraint.

It is often said that the Supreme Court is "a court of review, not of first view."[83] But, as Justice Thomas observed in dissent, neither the district court nor the Fifth Circuit addressed whether Congress properly vested Task Force appointments by law.[84] Indeed, the lower courts had no occasion to address the question: Having classified Task Force members as principal officers (incorrectly, it turns out), they mooted the vesting question, which is relevant only to inferior officers.

Rather than rushing to judgment, the Court should have remanded the case for consideration of the vesting question. By relying solely on the parties' supplemental briefs, the Court denied itself the helpful insights of its lower court colleagues—some of whom have addressed this very question in prior cases.

While the counterfactual is impossible to know, had the Court remanded to the Fifth Circuit, presumably that court would have applied or distinguished its own precedent on the vesting issue,[85] thus better refining the relevant legal questions for Supreme Court

---

[80] *Id.*

[81] *Trump v. United States*, 603 U.S. 593, 648 (2024) (Thomas, J., concurring).

[82] 145 S. Ct. 1534, 1535 (2025) (statement of Kavanaugh, J., respecting denial of certiorari).

[83] *Cutter v. Wilkinson*, 544 U. S. 709, 718 n.7 (2005).

[84] *Braidwood Mgmt.*, 145 S. Ct. at 2465 (Thomas, J., dissenting).

[85] *Willy v. Admin. Rev. Bd.*, 423 F.3d 483, 492 (5th Cir. 2005).

review. Alas, the Court could not resist reaching the merits, the absence of these insights notwithstanding.[86]

E. Misuse of Constitutional Avoidance

As a final backstop against the dissent, the Court invoked constitutional avoidance. "[I]f there were any doubt" as to the constitutionality of the vesting, the Court explained, "the canon of constitutional avoidance . . . [would] dispel it."[87] While "reading the statutes at issue to vest appointment authority in the AHRQ Director alone would . . . render them 'clearly unconstitutional'," interpreting them holistically to "vest the Secretary with authority to appoint" was "at a minimum reasonable," and thus preferable as a matter of statutory construction.[88]

The problem with this argument is its failure to account for *Smith*, where constitutional avoidance did not save the appointment, notwithstanding the plausible basis for the government's saving construction. Furthermore, where the constitutional question is about the *language* Congress must use in order to depart from a default constitutional principle, statutory and constitutional dimensions fold into one and "avoidance" becomes little more than a thumb on the scale for government. Applying the canon here, as the Court does, is in effect to reject the necessity of a clear statement on the merits.[89]

IV. What a Clear Statement Rule Accomplishes

"Canons . . . are often expressed as clear statement rules that require a court to interpret a statute to avoid a particular result unless Congress speaks explicitly to accomplish it."[90] A clear statement rule under the Excepting Clause would advance important constitutional values: unitary executive control and senatorial oversight of appointments.

---

[86] *But cf. Snope*, 145 S. Ct. at 1535 (statement of Kavanaugh, J.).

[87] *Braidwood Mgmt.*, 145 S. Ct. at 2460.

[88] *Id.* at 2461 (internal quotation marks omitted).

[89] On the other hand, because *Smith* was a criminal prosecution, it is possible that the rule of lenity came into play—encouraging the Court to adopt a narrow construction. However, the Court gave no indication that this was the case. *But cf. Hartwell*, 73 U.S. at 395 ("We are not unmindful that penal laws are to be construed strictly.").

[90] Amy Coney Barrett, *Substantive Canons and Faithful Agency*, 90 B.U. L. Rev. 109, 118 (2010).

First, a clear statement rule would advance unitary executive control of federal officers to the benefit of democratic accountability. The unitary executive provides a focal point "for the jealousy and watchfulness of the people."[91] By putting the onus on Congress to depart from *presidential* nomination by clear textual command, the rule would empower the President to superintend the conduct of *all* officers—principal and inferior—through direct removal in the absence of any statute, presumably signed by the President,[92] divesting him of that power in favor of a principal officer. When Congress vests executive appointments—and by implication, removals[93]—in cabinet secretaries, it renders them the direct object of an inferior officer's loyalty, *not* the President.[94] With each additional appointment vested in someone other than the President, there results an attenuation of presidential control and a diffusion of accountability.[95] If Congress desires that result, it should have to speak clearly. Otherwise, the power of appointment should presumably remain with the President—"the sword of the community"[96] and the only federal officer "elected by the entire Nation."[97]

Second, a clear statement rule would safeguard the Senate's advice and consent prerogative. The Excepting Clause's default method of appointment contains two elements: presidential nomination and senatorial confirmation. The Senate's power to review executive

---

[91] The Federalist No. 70, at 412 (Alexander Hamilton) (Royal Classics ed. 2020).

[92] Of course, Congress can override a presidential veto by a two-thirds supermajority in each house. *See* U.S. Const., art. I., § 2, cl. 2. But in today's age, Congress rarely does so. During President Trump's first term and President Obama's two terms, Congress overrode one presidential veto each. During President's Biden's term in office, Congress overrode none. That makes two veto overrides since 2009, for an average of one every eight years. *Vetoes, 1789 to Present*, U.S. Senate (last visited Aug. 8, 2025), https://tinyurl.com/5fu7wt7v.

[93] *See Ex Parte Hennen*, 38 U.S. (13 Pet.) 230, 259 (1839).

[94] *See* Neomi Rao, *Removal: Necessary and Sufficient for Presidential Control*, 65 Ala. L. Rev. 1205, 1228 (2014) ("[A] simple truth of administration [is] that an officer will seek to please the person that decides whether the officer stays or goes.").

[95] *Cf.* Aditya Bamzai & Saikrishna Bangalore Prakash, *The Executive Power of Removal*, 136 Harv. L. Rev. 1756, 1835 (2023) (raising the possibility of Congress "consolidating all existing departments into a single behemoth, staffed with thousands of tenure-protected inferior officers").

[96] The Federalist No. 78, at 499 (Alexander Hamilton) (Royal Classics ed. 2020).

[97] *Trump v. United States*, 603 U.S. 593, 622 (2024). The Vice President, of course, is also elected nationwide on the same ticket as the President. U.S. Const., amend. XII.

nominations was intended to prevent "unfit characters" from assuming positions of power merely for reasons of loyalty.[98]

A presumption should exist that advice and consent remains intact to guard against unfit presidential picks, unless Congress overrides it by unambiguous language. Vesting appointments by implication may leave the Senate in the dark about whether a statute divests it of its confirmation power. If a collection of statutes, enacted over several decades, may vest an inferior appointment in a principal office, that means the Senate may—also by implication—forfeit its right of reviewing that inferior's nomination. In contrast, a clear statement rule would force the enacting Congress to grapple with the potentially untoward consequences of waiving advice and consent, and to waive it *knowingly.*

Furthermore, the clear statement need not be specific to the inferior's office. Congress could, for instance, enact a broad yet unambiguous delegation to appoint officers in order to carry out designated functions.[99] That, too, would suffice under our proposed clear statement rule.

V. Implications

Braidwood carries several important implications—both specific to the Appointments Clause and more broadly relevant to the Court's jurisprudence.

First, *Smith* has in effect been overruled *sub silentio,* at least to the extent that precedent is read, as we think, to embrace a clear statement rule for inferior appointments. Second, *Hartwell's* putative rule to the contrary—which was unreasoned *dictum*—has assumed the stature of binding precedent for Appointments Clause purposes. Under *Hartwell* and *Braidwood,* Congress may vest inferior appointments by implication, and the courts will not insist on clear legislative intent. So long as the statute might reasonably be read to require principal officer approval for the inferior appointment, the courts will deem the appointment "vested" "by law" in the sense of the Appointments Clause.[100] Courts may also employ constitutional avoidance to rescue questionable "vestings" of appointment.

---

[98] THE FEDERALIST NO. 76, at 441 (Alexander Hamilton) (Royal Classics ed. 2020).

[99] *See, e.g.,* 42 U.S.C. §§ 300jj-11; 300u(a); 209(i); *see also* 42 U.S.C. § 913.

[100] U.S. CONST. art. II, § 2, cl. 2 (capitalization normalized).

More broadly, *Braidwood* sends some interesting signals about the current Court. First, it arguably shows—once more—that the Justices will afford the Affordable Care Act charitable treatment—construing its provisions to comply with constitutional commands notwithstanding a more plausible construction to the contrary.[101] When construing the ACA, the Court thus sits more as a partner to Congress, not an independent check. Second, *Braidwood* suggests that the Court will not always remand for the lower courts to address constitutional issues they left untouched, even when the Court might benefit.

Third and lastly, while some issues—like gun control and the Second Amendment—warrant percolation in the lower courts before getting teed up for certiorari, other issues—like the vesting of inferior appointments—apparently do not. It is unclear how to grapple with this apparent inconsistency. Perhaps the Court was disinclined to remand the matter to a court of appeals that has been frequently reversed the last few Terms. Or perhaps the Court did not want to leave an important component of a healthcare subsidy program in legal limbo. Either way, it is unclear under what circumstances an issue might benefit from lower court percolation, at least according to Justice Kavanaugh.

VI. Conclusion

Justice Thomas summed up the fatal flaw in *Braidwood* best: "because the Appointments Clause's default rule, as a constitutional provision, is of greater dignity than a statute, we should not presume that Congress meant to set it aside if the question is doubtful."[102] By holding that appointments may be vested by implication, the Court has done just that, in disservice to the Appointments Clause.

---

[101] *See NFIB v. Sebelius*, 597 U.S. 519 (2012); *cf. also King v. Burwell*, 576 U.S. 473, 515 (2015) (Scalia, J., dissenting).

[102] *Braidwood Mgmt.*, 145 S. Ct. at 2467 (Thomas, J. dissenting) (cleaned up).

Danger, Safety, and the Fourth Amendment: *Barnes v. Felix*

Matthew P. Cavedon[1]

Introduction

Danger to human life is constantly offered in law and the popular imagination as a rationale for limiting the reach of the Fourth Amendment. In defense of the Constitution, one could simply cite Benjamin Franklin: "They who can give up essential liberty to obtain a little temporary safety, deserve neither liberty nor safety."[2] Another, gentler response is that constitutional safeguards for the rights of the accused in fact *further* safety rather than endangering it. While the protection of human life and limb was not addressed by the majority in *Barnes v. Felix*,[3] it was raised by the concurrence as a limiting principle on Fourth Amendment protections. Renewed emphasis on safety as a Fourth Amendment value is a faithful understanding of that provision and a way of promoting cross-ideological support for its guarantees. Constitutionally compliant policing is more than just the law. It protects the safety of suspects, civilians, and officers.

[1] Director, Project on Criminal Justice, Cato Institute. The author was the main drafter of Cato's *amicus* briefs at the certiorari and merits stages of *Barnes v. Felix*, as well as in support of the petitions for certiorari in *Jimerson v. Lewis* and *Pennigton v. West Virginia*. He thanks his wife Julie and his daughter Ellie for enriching his life. This article was aided by research assistance from Rebekah Canty as well as feedback from Kay Levine, Mike Fox, Brent Skorup, Quinton Crawford, and the editors. Generous support for it was provided by the McDonald Agape Foundation. This article is dedicated to Hunter Rodgers.

[2] ONLINE LIBR. OF LIBERTY, *Quote: Benjamin Franklin on the Trade Off between Essential Liberty and Temporary Safety (1775)*, https://oll.libertyfund.org/quotes/benjamin-franklin-on-the-trade-off-between-essential-liberty-and-temporary-safety-1775 (quoting 7 THE WORKS OF BENJAMIN FRANKLIN: LETTERS AND MISC. WRITINGS 1775–1779).

[3] 145 S. Ct. 1353 (2025).

I. Safety Is Treated as Reason to Limit the Fourth Amendment

The specter of danger is a constant threat to constitutional liberty. Many people believe that the rule of law is no match for existential danger. Amidst the Great Depression, the Supreme Court made short shrift of the Contracts Clause by holding, "While emergency does not create power, emergency may furnish the occasion for the exercise of power" in ways ordinarily prohibited by the Constitution.[4] Authorities including Justice Robert Jackson and a later majority of the Court insisted that neither the First Amendment nor due process can be understood as "a suicide pact"—both must give way before danger.[5] Outside the American context, too, "emergencies" have been given as a reason to suspend constitutional provisions.[6]

In the years of the Weimar Republic, before he became the foremost Nazi jurist, Carl Schmitt developed a theory that law cannot decide "exceptional" situations.[7] To justify 20th-century authoritarianism, he revived ancient Roman justifications for "commissarial dictatorship," or empowering one man to rule the state to save it from mortal danger.[8] Schmitt's claims about law being unfit for dangerous situations have come back into scholarly vogue in part due

---

[4] Home Bldg. & Loan Ass'n v. Blaisdell, 290 U.S. 398, 426 (1934).

[5] Terminiello v. Chicago, 337 U.S. 1, 37 (1949) (Jackson, J., dissenting) (criticizing the "doctrinaire logic" of the majority that led it to uphold freedom of speech for an anti-Semitic, anti-communist political diatribe that triggered an uproar); Kennedy v. Mendoza-Martinez, 372 U.S. 144, 159–60 (1963) (invoking the "suicide pact" notion in defending military conscription before holding that draft-dodging cannot be punished with loss of citizenship).

[6] Christian Bjørnskov & Stefan Voigt, *Why Do Governments Call a State of Emergency? On the Determinants of Using Emergency Constitutions*, 54 EURO. J. POL. ECON. 110, 110 (2018) ("[B]etween 1985 and 2014, 137 countries declared a state of emergency at least once. This implies that roughly 2/3 of all sovereign nations declared a state of emergency during that period.").

[7] *See generally* CARL SCHMITT, POLITICAL THEOLOGY: FOUR CHAPTERS ON THE CONCEPT OF SOVEREIGNTY (George Schwab trans., 2d ed. 1934); CARL SCHMITT, DICTATORSHIP: FROM THE ORIGIN OF THE MODERN CONCEPT OF SOVEREIGNTY TO THE PROLETARIAN CLASS STRUGGLE (Michael Hoelzl & Graham Ward trans., 7th ed. 1978).

[8] *See* Carlos Pérez-Crespo, *An Apocalyptic Speech Outlining a Theory of Dictatorship: Carl Schmitt Inspired by Juan Donoso Cortés*, 26 REDESCRIPTIONS 21, 22 (2023); Ellen Kennedy, *Emergency Government Within the Bounds of the Constitution: An Introduction to Carl Schmitt, "The Dictatorship of the Reich President According to Article 48 R.V.,"* 18 CONSTELLATIONS 284, 287 (2011).

to the work of Harvard Law professor Adrian Vermeule.[9] Danger as a reason to suspend the rule of law has found its way into presidential discourse, too. During his first administration, President Donald Trump dismissed due process concerns about seizing firearms: "Take the guns first, go through due process second."[10] More recently, he has echoed Schmitt (and Emperor Napoleon Bonaparte): "He who saves his Country does not violate any Law."[11] Danger—to the community and to the political order more broadly—is seen as the line beyond which the Constitution must yield.

Arguments from danger are particularly common in the Fourth Amendment context. For decades, constitutional protections for Americans suspected of criminal activity have been portrayed in popular culture as an obstacle to safety. Consider the "Dirty Harry"-esque police officers of action films who can protect the public only by setting aside niceties like probable cause.[12] Television dramas and lawmakers alike have imagined scenarios in which a "ticking time bomb" can be defused only by officers who "take matters into their own hands" and commit illegal searches and seizures.[13] Legal "technicalities" are cast as obstacles to rescuing abducted children and thwarting terrorist plots.[14] Popular culture portrays constitutional constraints on criminal investigations as dangerous.

---

[9] ADRIAN VERMEULE, COMMON GOOD CONSTITUTIONALISM 158 (2022); Adrian Vermeule, *Our Schmittian Administrative Law*, 122 HARV. L. REV. 1095, 1100–01 (2009).

[10] Brett Samuels, *Trump: "Take the Guns First, Go Through Due Process Second,"* THE HILL (Feb. 28, 2018), https://thehill.com/homenews/administration/376097-trump-take-the-guns-first-go-through-due-process-second/.

[11] Maggie Haberman et al., *Trump Suggests No Laws Are Being Broken if His Motive Is to "Save His Country,"* N.Y. TIMES (Feb. 16, 2025), https://www.nytimes.com/2025/02/15/us/politics/trump-saves-country-quote.html.

[12] Michael Stokes Paulsen, *Dirty Harry and the Real Constitution*, 64 U. CHI. L. REV. 1457, 1457–60 (1997) (book review) (summarizing sympathetically Dirty Harry's take on Fourth Amendment law).

[13] Ron E. Hassner, *The Myth of the Ticking Bomb*, 41 WASH. Q. 83, 83–84 (2018).

[14] Andrew E. Taslitz, *Respect and the Fourth Amendment*, 94 J. CRIM. L. & CRIMINOLOGY 15, 17 (2003); *cf.* Wendy Kaminer, *When Justice Becomes Mere Technicality*, THE ATLANTIC (May 4, 2011), https://www.theatlantic.com/national/archive/2011/05/when-justice-becomes-mere-technicality/238344/ ("Traditional law-and-order, lock-'em-up-and-throw-away-the-key advocates have always harbored contempt for legal technicalities—by which they mean the Fourth, Fifth, and Sixth Amendment rights of the accused.").

These depictions may well appeal more to lay Americans than to lawyers, but their theories about the limited applicability of the Constitution resemble more legally sophisticated accounts. Consider *Caniglia v. Strom*.[15] In that case, the Court unanimously rejected a standalone "caretaking" exception to the warrant requirement for home entries.[16] While warrantless entry could be justified by an exigent circumstance like the presence of an injured person or imminent risk of injury, the Constitution lacks "an open-ended license" for officers to enter homes for non-law-enforcement purposes.[17] This straightforward holding was accompanied by concurring opinions emphasizing that the Fourth Amendment must often yield before danger. Chief Justice John Roberts, joined by Justice Stephen Breyer, wrote that officers can still enter homes without a warrant to prevent violence and disorder.[18] Justice Samuel Alito noted that the Court's holding did not extend to mental-health assessments, short-term seizures of guns pursuant to "red flag" laws, or home entries meant to determine whether someone was medically incapacitated.[19] Justice Brett Kavanaugh wrote "to underscore and elaborate on" the Chief Justice's concerns, saying that warrantless entries are constitutional "when police officers have an objectively reasonable basis to believe that there is a current, ongoing crisis for which it is reasonable to act now."[20]

Cabining Fourth Amendment protections with concerns about danger is nothing new, nor is it only judicial conservatives who are worried. In *Georgia v. Randolph*, a majority of the Court held that "a physically present co-occupant's stated refusal to permit entry prevails" over the consent given by another home resident.[21] Its opinion confirmed the "undoubted right of the police to enter in order to protect a victim" of domestic violence.[22] Justice Breyer concurred,

---

[15] Caniglia v. Strom, 593 U.S. 194 (2021).

[16] *Id.* at 196.

[17] *Id.* at 198–99.

[18] *Id.* at 199 (Roberts, C.J., concurring).

[19] *Id.* at 201–03 (Alito, J., concurring).

[20] *Id.* at 204, 206 (Kavanaugh, J., concurring).

[21] Georgia v. Randolph, 547 U.S. 103, 106 (2006).

[22] *Id.* at 118–19.

highlighting the need for flexibility in stopping domestic violence.[23] Unlike *Caniglia*, *Randolph* also featured a dissent concerning danger. Chief Justice Roberts, joined by Justice Antonin Scalia, warned that the majority's holding enabled domestic violence by letting "the abuser whose behavior prompted the request for police assistance" refuse officers entry.[24]

The concerns about danger raised in *Barnes*, *Caniglia*, and *Randolph* are by no means baseless. By its terms, the Fourth Amendment protects people against "unreasonable searches and seizures."[25] Scholars have long debated whether reasonableness is measured in terms of specific historical rules or using broader judicial discretion.[26] Either way, the presence of danger in contexts ranging from traffic stops to suicidality to domestic violence *is* relevant to constitutional standards. To expect officers to remain indifferent to danger facing themselves, suspects, or civilians is unreasonable and ahistorical.[27]

What is remarkable is the one-dimensionality of the Court's narratives. Danger is always the constitutional caveat—the reason to limit the Fourth Amendment—rather than a concern justifying constitutional protections. While no right is unqualified, Fourth Amendment protections are routinely qualified in the same breath as they are voiced (or not even voiced at all, as in the case of the *Randolph* dissent). Constitutional limits on searches and seizures are deemed ill-suited to a dangerous world. The concurrence to the Court's recent decision in *Barnes v. Felix* follows this rights-skeptical approach.

[23] *Id.* at 126–27 (Breyer, J., concurring).

[24] *Id.* at 139 (Roberts, C.J., dissenting).

[25] U.S. CONST. amend. IV.

[26] *See generally* Nikolaus Williams, Note, *The Supreme Court's Ahistorical Reasonableness Approach to the Fourth Amendment*, 89 N.Y.U. L. REV. 1522 (2014) (surveying perspectives).

[27] *See, e.g.*, Mackenzie R. Lyons, Note, *Revising the Scope of the Fourth Amendment Community Caretaking Exception on Behalf of Older Adults*, 47 S. ILL. U. L.J. 149 (2022); James A. Albert, *The Liability of the Press for Trespass and Invasion of Privacy in Gathering the News—A Call for the Recognition of a Newsgathering Tort Privilege*, 45 N.Y. L. SCH. L. REV. 331, 363 (2002) ("[I]nspections of hospitals, nursing homes, and surgical centers are not at all unreasonable or in violation of the Fourth Amendment. They are in fact necessary to protect life."); John F. Decker, *Emergency Circumstances, Police Responses, and Fourth Amendment Restrictions*, 89 J. CRIM. L. & CRIMINOLOGY 433 (1999).

II. Safety Is Seen as a Fourth Amendment Countervalue by the *Barnes v. Felix* Concurrence

Barnes features the conventional take on danger, safety, and the Fourth Amendment—and highlights why that now-conventional wisdom comes up short. The case concerned a death arising out of a 2016 traffic stop on a Houston freeway.[28] Respondent Roberto Felix Jr., a constable, received an alert about a car with unpaid toll violations.[29] He pulled over the driver, Ashtian Barnes.[30] Mr. Barnes told Constable Felix the car had been rented by his girlfriend.[31] After Constable Felix asked Mr. Barnes to produce identification, Mr. Barnes opened the car trunk and turned off the ignition.[32] Constable Felix rested his hand on his gun holster and told Mr. Barnes to exit, at which point Mr. Barnes turned the ignition back on.[33] Constable Felix unholstered his gun—then jumped onto the car's doorsill above the running board.[34] The car began to move forward.[35] Within two seconds of jumping onto the car, while still unable to see inside, Constable Felix yelled at Mr. Barnes not to move, then fired two shots.[36] Mr. Barnes died on the spot.[37]

Mr. Barnes's mother filed a federal lawsuit under 42 U.S.C. § 1983, alleging that Constable Felix violated her late son's Fourth Amendment right to be free of excessive force.[38] The district court granted summary judgment in favor of Constable Felix and his codefendants, finding that Fifth Circuit precedent forbade it from considering "the officer's conduct precipitating the shooting—which included jumping onto a moving vehicle and blindly firing his weapon inside."[39] Circuit authority also prevented the district court from considering

[28] *Barnes*, 145 S. Ct. at 1356.

[29] *Id.*

[30] *Id.*

[31] *Id.*

[32] *Id.*

[33] *Id.*

[34] *Id.*

[35] The district court made no finding as to whether the car had started moving when Constable Felix jumped onto it. Barnes v. Felix, 532 F. Supp. 3d 463, 466 (S.D. Tex. 2021).

[36] *Barnes*, 145 S. Ct. at 1356.

[37] *Id.*

[38] *Id.*

[39] *Barnes*, 532 F. Supp. 3d at 466.

the severity of Mr. Barnes's alleged offense and whether he was trying to escape, limiting its inquiry to whether Constable Felix "was in danger *at the moment of the threat*" triggering his use of deadly force.[40] The only fact that mattered was that at the time Constable Felix opened fire, he "was still hanging onto the moving vehicle and believed it would run him over."[41] The district court complained that the Fifth Circuit had "effectively stifled a more robust examination of the Fourth Amendment's protections," but the court deemed itself bound to apply binding authority.[42]

The Fifth Circuit affirmed based on the binding "moment of threat" doctrine, but added more misgivings.[43] Judge Patrick Higginbotham—who wrote the panel's opinion—issued a separate concurring opinion, beginning with indignation: "A routine traffic stop has again ended in the death of an unarmed black man, and again we cloak a police officer with qualified immunity, shielding his liability."[44] Judge Higginbotham believed the moment-of-threat doctrine contradicted the Supreme Court's direction that courts had to assess the reasonableness of deadly force using the totality of the circumstances.[45] Ignoring an officer's decisions leading up to his use of deadly force cheapened human life and weakened the Fourth Amendment.[46] After all, the traffic violations Mr. Barnes allegedly committed did not even authorize his arrest under Texas law.[47] Judge Higginbotham thought it was significant that the Supreme Court limited the use of deadly force against fleeing *felons*, while the Fifth Circuit analyzed deadly force against even petty offenders only with respect to "the precise millisecond" at which an officer used it.[48] This made his court's references to the totality of the circumstances "merely performative."[49]

---

[40] *Id.* at 468–69 (emphasis in original) (citation omitted).

[41] *Id.* at 471.

[42] *Id.* at 472.

[43] Barnes v. Felix, 91 F.4th 393, 398 (5th Cir. 2024).

[44] *Id.* (Higginbotham, J., concurring).

[45] *Id.*

[46] *Id.*

[47] *Id.* at 399.

[48] *Id.* (citing Tennessee v. Garner, 471 U.S. 1, 9, 21 (1985)).

[49] *Id.* at 400.

The Supreme Court granted certiorari.[50] In a unanimous decision by Justice Elena Kagan, the Court held the moment-of-threat rule incompatible with the totality-of-the-circumstances analysis required by the Fourth Amendment.[51] Such a comprehensive inquiry does not have a "time limit," and while "the situation at the precise time of the shooting will often be what matters most," "earlier facts and circumstances" can be relevant.[52] The Court reserved for a future case a further question, "whether or how an officer's own 'creation of a dangerous situation' factors into the reasonableness analysis."[53]

Justice Kavanaugh concurred, joined by Justices Alito, Amy Coney Barrett, and Clarence Thomas.[54] He emphasized that the Fourth Amendment's reach is limited by "the dangers of traffic stops for police officers."[55] Officers' lives are at risk when they approach someone sitting in a car, as the suspect has a tactical advantage.[56] The concurrence recounted several instances of officers being killed during traffic stops—reserving for a footnote the reality that "officers sometimes use excessive force during traffic stops" too and "of course should be held to account for their actions."[57]

The concurrence continued that officers cannot "let their guard down and assume that any particular traffic stop will be safe—even if a driver is pulled over for nothing more than a speeding violation, a broken taillight, or the like."[58] Drivers could be intoxicated or even preparing to commit acts of extreme violence.[59] For example, Oklahoma City bomber Timothy McVeigh was ultimately arrested following a traffic stop for a missing license plate, while serial killer Ted Bundy resisted an officer who pulled him over on suspicion of driving a stolen vehicle.[60] A motorist like Mr. Barnes who tries to

---

[50] *Barnes*, 145 S. Ct. at 1357.

[51] *Id.*

[52] *Id.* at 1358.

[53] *Id.* at 1360 (citation omitted).

[54] *Id. et seq.* (Kavanaugh, J., concurring).

[55] *Id.*

[56] *Id.* at 1360–61.

[57] *Id.* at 1361 n.2.

[58] *Id.* at 1361.

[59] *Id.*

[60] *Id.*

drive away from a stop could endanger others, and doing so to avoid consequences for a minor offense like a toll violation could even be evidence of particular danger.[61] "He could have an abducted child in the car" or be about to commit a terrorist attack by plowing into a crowd.[62] An officer has "no particularly good or safe options" when faced with a driver who tries to leave.[63] Fourth Amendment jurisprudence has to give officers executing traffic stops broad deference due to "extraordinary dangers."[64]

Justice Kavanaugh's opinion took a standard line: Fourth Amendment protections and danger are opposing values that have to be weighed against each other. Who can say whether someone pulled over for a taillight violation might be Jack the Ripper, with a victim tied up in the trunk? How was Constable Felix to know whether Mr. Barnes started his ignition because he wanted to avoid paying for tickets he did not incur or because he was about to mow down pedestrians? Best not to let legal scrupulosity put too many limits on an officer's ability to kill.

The *Barnes* decision was a straightforward rejection of an artificial doctrinal test, one of several recent decisions instructing lower courts to stop inventing them.[65] In context, though, the case raised anew enduring questions about the reach of constitutional rights in the face of danger. While the concurrence hardly blazed a new route in setting liberty against safety, Fourth Amendment rules should often protect both—and disregarding rights can be dangerous as well. When officers disregard constitutional limits, they can

---

[61] *Id*

[62] *Id.* at 1362.

[63] *Id.* at 1363.

[64] *Id.*

[65] *See, e.g.*, Ames v. Ohio Dept. of Youth Servs.,605 U.S. 303, 305–06 (2025) ("[T]his additional 'background circumstances' requirement is not consistent with Title VII's text or our case law construing the statute."); Seven Cnty. Infrastructure Coal. v. Eagle Cnty., 145 S. Ct. 1497, 1507 (2025) (holding the National Environmental Policy Act to be "purely procedural" and so forbidding courts from imposing additional substantive requirements). Justice Thomas's concurrence in *Ames*, joined by Justice Neil Gorsuch, "highlight[ed] the problems that arise when judges create atextual legal rules and frameworks," accusing these of "distort[ing] the underlying statutory text, impos[ing] unnecessary burdens on litigants, and caus[ing] confusion for courts." *Ames*, 605 U.S. at 313 (Thomas, J., concurring). He criticized "improper judicial lawmaking." *Id.* at 314.

endanger themselves, suspects, and civilians. More than being merely compatible with safety, the Fourth Amendment exists in part to further it.

III. Safety Is Actually a Fourth Amendment Value

Not long ago, the Court was accustomed to thinking of the Fourth Amendment as a shield for safety rather than a danger in its own right. In the watershed excessive force case *Tennessee v. Garner,* the Court held that the Fourth Amendment forbids the use of deadly force to stop an unarmed suspected felon from fleeing "unless it is necessary to prevent the escape and the officer has probable cause to believe that the suspect poses a significant threat of death or serious physical injury to the officer or others."[66] The *Garner* Court emphasized the importance of constitutional limits in safeguarding suspects' lives.[67] "The intrusiveness of a seizure by means of deadly force is unmatched. The suspect's fundamental interest in his own life need not be elaborated upon."[68] In addition to a person's own life interest, society has an interest in protecting the life of the accused so that a court can determine guilt and punishment.[69] The respect for human life reflected by the Fourth Amendment could even overcome some concerns about law enforcement effectiveness: "It is not better that all felony suspects die than that they escape."[70]

Garner did set the Fourth Amendment's outer limit as the protection of life, holding that deadly force would be justifiable when the suspect is a threat to others.[71] But it also explored how constitutional constraints advance safety. *Garner* noted the early common law rule categorically authorizing the killing of fleeing suspected felons.[72] It found this rule not to be controlling due to the radical expansion in offenses qualifying as felonies—especially noncapital crimes for which death would not be the routine punishment (or even a legally

---

[66] *Garner,* 471 U.S. at 3.
[67] *Id.* at 7–8.
[68] *Id.* at 9.
[69] *Id.*
[70] *Id.* at 11.
[71] *Id.* at 11–12.
[72] *Id.* at 12.

available one)—and the introduction of handguns allowing officers to kill suspects who were not immediate threats.[73] The Court also noted that the common law limited seizures for the sake of safety, banning the slaying of a fleeing suspected misdemeanant.[74] While *Garner* has been criticized for treating safety as "but one factor in a general policy discussion of proper police conduct"—thus relying on "grisly instrumentalism"—at least it recognized that Fourth Amendment rights can safeguard life.[75]

This theme frequently appeared in earlier cases concerning the seizure of fleeing suspects and homes entries.[76] To begin with seizures like the one at issue in *Garner*, while that Court correctly noted the common law's broad allowance of deadly force to stop fleeing suspected felons, late-19th and early-20th century American authorities also held that deadly force could not be used "simply to prevent an escape."[77] Like *Garner*, they noted the need to save suspects' lives to honor due process.[78] Killing a fleeing suspected misdemeanant was murder.[79] An officer had "no more right to kill him than he would have if the offender were to lie down and refuse to go."[80] "The law value[d] human life too highly to give an officer the right to proceed to the extremity of shooting one whom he is attempting to arrest for a violation" of a petty law.[81]

---

[73] *Id.* at 13–15.

[74] *Id.* at 15.

[75] T. Alexander Aleinikoff, *Constitutional Law in the Age of Balancing*, 96 YALE L.J. 943, 990–91 (1987); *see also* Kufere Laing, Note, Killer Cops, *Killer Laws: Fourth Amendment Jurisprudence and Separate, but Equal Policing*, 65 How. L.J. 267, 307 (2021) ("We must also replace *Garner*'s 'balancing' framework . . . . Under no circumstances is it reasonable for the government to kill with no imminent threat to life—flight alone can never justify taking a human life.").

[76] The discussion that follows draws on three Cato Institute amicus briefs written by this article's author: Br. for Cato Inst. et al. as Amicus Curiae, Barnes v. Felix, 145 S. Ct. 1353 (2025); Br. for Cato Inst. as Amicus Curiae, Jimerson v. Lewis, No. 24-473 (U.S. Nov. 29, 2024); Br. for Cato Inst. as Amicus Curiae, Pennington v. West Virginia, No. 22-747 (U.S. Mar. 13, 2023).

[77] Caldwell v. State, 41 Tex. 86, 98 (1874).

[78] *Garner*, 471 U.S. at 12 (citing State v. Smith, 103 N.W. 944, 945 (Iowa 1905)); *see also* State v. Campbell, 12 S.E. 441, 443 (N.C. 1890).

[79] Holloway v. Moser, 136 S.E. 375, 376 (N.C. 1927) (quoting 2 BISHOP ON CRIMINAL LAW §§ 662–63).

[80] Head v. Martin, 3 S.W. 622, 624 (Ky. 1887).

[81] Holmes v. State, 62 S.E. 716, 718 (Ga. Ct. App. 1908).

Some common law cases even extended protection to suspects re-sisting arrest, forbidding an arrestor's use of "any greater force than [was] reasonably and apparently necessary for his protection."[82] Suspects could be protected even if they triggered an arrestor's use of excessive force.[83] Whenever possible, officers had to secure people "without resorting to the use of fire-arms or dangerous weapons."[84] They could not take life without "diligence and caution."[85] Not even a suspect's use of deadly force categorically authorized deadly force in response—necessity remained the touchstone.[86] An officer who used excessive force would be guilty of assault and battery.[87] "Human life is too sacred," read one decision, to approve of the needless use of deadly force.[88] *Garner's* explicit treatment of life as a Fourth Amendment value reflected much older authorities.[89]

American courts were also quick to emphasize the importance of protecting safety in the context of searches. Pre-Independence English common law courts recognized that home entries could involve "destruction or breaking."[90] A homeowner facing a chaotic entry and not realizing it was part of a lawful search had "a right to consider it as an aggression on his private property, which he will be justified in resisting to the utmost."[91] The common law required

---

[82] *Head*, 3 S.W. at 623 (cited approvingly by *Holloway*, 136 S.E. at 377).

[83] *Id.* at 624.

[84] Reneau v. State, 70 Tenn. 720, 722 (1879) (cited approvingly by *Garner*, 471 U.S. at 12).

[85] *Id.; see also Smith*, 103 N.W. at 946 (holding that killing someone engaged in felony escape was justifiable only if it was "the only reasonably apparent method" available "for the honest and non-negligent purpose of preventing the felony, and not for some other reason").

[86] *Head*, 3 S.W. at 623 ("If the offender puts the life of the officer in jeopardy, the latter may *se defendendo* slay him; but he must not use any greater force than is reasonably and apparently necessary for his protection.").

[87] *Holmes*, 62 S.E. at 718.

[88] *Head*, 3 S.W. at 623.

[89] That said, an early commentary did describe *Garner* as the first Supreme Court decision that "explicitly recognized that the fourth amendment protects an individual's interest in life as well as her interests in property and privacy." *The Supreme Court, 1984 Term: I. Constitutional Law. [Part 2 of 2]*, 99 HARV. L. REV. 120, 248 (1985) (mentioning also Winston v. Lee, 470 U.S. 753, 761 (1985) ("[A] search for evidence of a crime may be unjustifiable if it endangers the life . . . of the suspect.")).

[90] Wilson v. Arkansas, 514 U.S. 927, 935–36 (1995) (quoting Semayne's Case, 77 Eng. Rep. 194, 196 (K.B. 1603)).

[91] Ker v. California, 374 U.S. 23, 58 (1963) (op. of Brennan, J.) (quoting Launock v. Brown, 106 Eng. Rep. 482, 483 (1819)).

a knock on the door and an announcement to "protect the arresting officers from being shot as trespassers."[92]

Protecting the lives of suspects and officers alike was articulated as a rationale for Fourth Amendment limits on searches, too. In a 1948 opinion, Justice Robert Jackson foresaw "grave troubles" from unjustified home entries.[93] Innocent homeowners in such cases could well think officers are criminal intruders, and their "natural impulse would be to shoot."[94] Alternatively, an officer "seeing a gun being drawn on him might shoot first"—though Justice Jackson thought this could well be deemed murder.[95] He hoped warrant requirements would end operations that were "reckless" and "fraught with danger and discredit."[96] Later justices also expressed concern, warning that "practical hazards of law enforcement militate strongly against any relaxation" of constitutional rules limiting home entries.[97] The Court's 1980 decision in *Payton v. New York* described the search warrant requirement as preventing "the danger of needless intrusions."[98]

This framing of the Fourth Amendment has not entirely disappeared. The Court's 2006 decision in *Hudson v. Michigan* cited Justice Jackson's *McDonald* concurrence and briefly noted that one historical reason for the knock-and-announce rule is protecting "human life and limb, because an unannounced entry may provoke violence in supposed self-defense by the surprised resident."[99] Even in that case, though, discussion of safety as a Fourth Amendment interest was minimal. Justice Anthony Kennedy's concurring opinion focused instead on "privacy and security in the home" more generically.[100] Justice Breyer's dissent mentioned only "the privacy of the home"— and the possibility of a constitutionally exceptional no-knock warrant "diminishing any danger to the officers" who execute it.[101]

---

[92] *Id.*

[93] McDonald v. United States, 335 U.S. 451, 460 (1948) (Jackson, J., concurring).

[94] *Id.* at 460–61.

[95] *Id.* at 461.

[96] *Id.*

[97] *Ker*, 374 U.S. at 57 (Brennan, J., concurring in part and dissenting in part).

[98] Payton v. New York, 445 U.S. 573, 585–56 (1980).

[99] Hudson v. Michigan, 547 U.S. 586, 594 (2006) (citing, *inter alia*, *McDonald*, 335 U.S. at 460–61 (Jackson, J., concurring)).

[100] *Id.* at 603 (Kennedy, J., concurring in part and concurring in the judgment).

[101] *Id.* at 621, 624 (Breyer, J., dissenting).

What the Fourth Amendment does *not* require, rather than what it does, protects safety.

From English common law courts to state decisions from the 1800s and early 1900s, to the Supreme Court's own 20th-century opinions, safety appeared as a reason to both authorize *and* to limit searches and seizures. Safety was a way of striking balances, not a hydraulic mechanism pressing only against constitutional constraints.

The Court's recent neglect of that nuanced understanding is troubling.

Empirical reality suggests the wisdom of the older approach. Returning to the context at issue in *Barnes*, research suggests that fears about the dangerousness of traffic stops may be overstated. To be sure, the "dominant narrative in policing is that each one of these stops is not just highly dangerous but also potentially fatal."[102] For this reason, the Court has endorsed giving officers "unquestioned command" over drivers and passengers.[103] Officers are also trained to assume that any stop can become deadly "if they become complacent on the scene or hesitate to use force."[104] In spite of these assumptions, however, a landmark study

> found that the rate for a felonious killing of an officer during a routine traffic stop for a traffic violation was only 1 in every 6.5 million stops. The rate for an assault that results in serious injury to an officer was only 1 in every 361,111 stops. Finally, the rate for an assault (whether it results in officer injury or not) was only 1 in every 6,959 stops. Less conservative estimates suggest that these rates may be much lower.
>
> In addition, the vast majority (over 98%) of the evaluated cases in the study resulted in no or minor injuries to the officers. Further, only a very small percentage of cases (about 3%) involved violence against officers in which a gun or knife was used or found at the scene, and the overwhelming majority of those cases resulted in no or minor injuries to an officer. Less than 1% of the evaluated cases involved guns or knives and resulted in serious injury to or the felonious killing of an officer.[105]

[102] Jordan Blair Woods, *Policing, Danger Narratives, and Routine Traffic Stops*, 117 Mich. L. Rev. 635, 637 (2019).

[103] Arizona v. Johnson, 555 U.S. 323, 330 (2009) (quoting Maryland v. Wilson, 519 U.S. 408, 414 (1997)).

[104] Woods, *supra* note 103, at 638.

[105] *Id.* at 640.

Assuming danger weighs only *against* the Fourth Amendment— and that officers face grave danger every time they pull over a car— unreasonably undermines the safety of the driving public.

Danger is often the excuse that erodes constitutional government, and one-sided fear weighs against Fourth Amendment protections. Recovering its safety-enhancing side would provide fresh reasons for Americans of different ideological persuasions to respect it.

IV. Safety Should Be a Cross-Ideological Fourth Amendment Principle

Commentators representing different philosophical approaches have identified safety as an important aspect of the Fourth Amendment. Emphasizing this shared belief is especially important in a time of deep fracturing concerning the meaning and legitimacy of constitutional rights. A few years ago, the Black Lives Matter movement and the deaths motivating it inspired scholarship on how Fourth Amendment limits protect life. Breonna Taylor's death at the hands of police officers who entered her apartment based on stale information led one commentator to ask whether enforcing drug prohibition could ever be "an equitable exchange" for a human life.[106] Civil rights scholar Mitchell Crusto has criticized Fourth Amendment doctrines for contributing to a "Blue Shield" that makes it "practically impossible to successfully prosecute a police officer for using lethal force"—a protest that could benefit from appreciating the contrary possibilities of Fourth Amendment jurisprudence.[107] Crusto seeks a remedy in due process doctrines rather than the Fourth Amendment.[108] However, he recognizes that constitutionally compliant policing would protect "lives of innocent civilians while also saving the lives of police officers."[109] This "interest convergence," whereby both sides of a policing encounter are made safer,

---

[106] Micah Mooring, Comment, *No-Knock Warrants: Protective or Predatory for North Carolinians?*, 45 CAMPBELL L. REV. 26, 282 (2023)

[107] Mitchell F. Crusto, *Black Lives Matter: Banning Police Lynchings*, 48 HASTINGS CONST. L.Q. 3, 53 (2020).

[108] *See generally* Mitchell F. Crusto, *Right to Life: Interest-Converging Policing*, 71 RUTGERS U. L. REV. 63 (2018).

[109] *Id.* at 68.

is another basis for seeing Fourth Amendment limits as potential common ground.[110]

Convincing law enforcement officers that stronger Fourth Amendment limits could protect their lives would go a long way toward strengthening support for the Constitution. Safety concerns could also motivate other groups to appreciate rights. Unconstrained policing poses extraordinary danger to another group of Americans who tend to lean conservative: gun owners. Right-of-center intellectual David French has written about cases in which "poor tactics and unwise choices" led to the needless deaths of civilians at the hands of officers who overestimated danger based on the suspects' possessing a gun.[111] In one such case, for a man awakened in his car by officers, "death was likely the moment the cops arrived and saw his gun."[112] Regarding another case, French quoted the officer's rationale for fatally shooting a man who was complying with instructions to retrieve his driver's license, but who also announced he had a lawfully owned gun nearby: "if [he] has the . . . guts and the audacity to smoke marijuana in front of a five-year-old girl and risk her lungs and risk her life by giving her secondhand smoke and the front-seat passenger doing the same thing then what, what care does he give about me?"[113] Considering a third killing, French summarized the danger of lawless policing to Americans exercising their Second Amendment rights:

> [M]y home is my castle. It's where my wife and kids are, and it's hard to imagine a situation where there's loud pounding, that late [at night], that doesn't involve a degree of urgency. I have a constitutional and a human right, guaranteed under

[110] *Id.* One of the signers of the Cato Institute's *Barnes* amicus brief was the Law Enforcement Action Partnership, "whose members include police, prosecutors, judges, corrections officials, and other law enforcement officials advocating for criminal justice . . . reforms that will make our communities safer and more just." Br. for Cato Inst. et al. as Amicus Curiae, Barnes v. Felix, *supra* note 77.

[111] David French, *The Underexamined Factor in Too Many Police Shootings*, NAT'L REV. (Apr. 4, 2019), https://www.nationalreview.com/2019/04/the-underexamined-factor-in-too-many-police-shootings/ (discussing the killing of Willie McCoy).

[112] *Id.*

[113] David French, *The Unwritten Law That Helps Bad Cops Go Free*, NAT'L REV. (June 21, 2017), https://www.nationalreview.com/2017/06/philando-castile-shooting-police-must-display-reasonable-fear/ (quoting Officer Jeronimo Yanez's rationale for killing Philando Castile).

> the Second Amendment, to defend my family, my life, and my home. Unless, of course, the people pounding on the door are cops who 1) had no search warrant, 2) didn't turn on their emergency lights, 3) didn't identify themselves as police, 4) misunderstood a neighbor's directions, and 5) showed up at the wrong house, the house of a completely innocent man. Then, my right to defend myself turns into a right to die in two seconds flat, without firing a shot or even clambering [sic] a round.[114]

The Fourth Amendment makes it safer to exercise Second Amendment rights.[115]

Showcasing how the Fourth Amendment should protect life could also activate those who adhere to the "consistent life ethic." U.S. Catholic bishops teach that all vulnerable lives "require our respect, protection, and action."[116] This stance has contributed to efforts by Catholics and Evangelical Protestants to oppose capital punishment, linking efforts to abolish it with concerns about abortion and euthanasia.[117] While much of the pro-life movement does not yet name policing reform a core agenda item, some activists do criticize excessive force.[118] Understanding how the Fourth Amendment protects

---

[114] David French, *Another Federal Court of Appeals Attacks the Second Amendment*, Nat'l Rev. (Mar. 20, 2017), https://www.nationalreview.com/2017/03/andrew-scott-case-second-amendment-attacked-eleventh-circuit-appeals-court/ (discussing the killing of Andrew Scott).

[115] Unfortunately, not all Second Amendment supporters are as ready to recognize this as French. *See* Jacob Sullum, *NRA Breaks Its Silence on Philando Castile Shooting*, Reason (July 10, 2017), https://reason.com/2017/07/10/nra-breaks-silence-on-philando-castile-s/ ("... Should Yanez have been calmer and more careful, or was the onus on Castile to put the officer at ease after announcing that he was carrying a gun? [NRA spokeswoman Dana Loesch] splits the difference by saying 'there were a lot of things that I wish would have been done differently.'").

[116] John L. Carr, *The Consistent Life Ethic: A Look Back, A Look Around, A Look Ahead*, 2 U. St. Thomas L.J. 256, 261 (2005).

[117] Ben Jones, *The Republican Party, Conservatives, and the Future of Capital Punishment*, 108 J. Crim. L. & Criminology 223, 237–39 (2018); see also Kevin M. Barry, *The Death Penalty and the Fundamental Right to Life*, 60 B.C. L. Rev. 1545, 1547–48 (2019).

[118] *See Police Brutality*, Rehumanize Int'l, https://www.rehumanizeintl.org/police-brutality (accessed July 5, 2025); *Responding to Police Brutality as Pro-Life Advocates*, The Minimise Project, (June 4, 2020), https://theminimiseproject.ie/2020/06/04/responding-to-police-brutality-as-pro-life-advocates/; Rachel MacNair, *Voices on Police Brutality in the Aftermath of the Murder of George Floyd*, Consistent Life Network (June 2, 2020), https://consistent-life.org/blog/index.php/2020/06/02/police-brutality/.

safety could mobilize new advocacy against dangerous policing and deepen appreciation for constitutional principles.

Constitutional rights have been questioned by intellectuals holding different ideological positions. Vermeule has urged critics of American democracy to "abandon[] the defensive crouch of originalism and . . . refuse[] any longer to play within the terms set by legal liberalism," rejecting a constitutional jurisprudence that seeks to "minimize the abuse of power" in favor of one ensuring that "the ruler has the power needed to rule well."[119] Left-wing criticism of constitutional criminal procedure as under-protective abounds.[120] Appreciating the positive role safety should already hold in Fourth Amendment law could help address these criticisms.[121]

Conclusion

Long before the New Deal Court's embrace of emergency exceptions, *The Federalist's* Publius argued that America needed a Supreme Court "to act as a final barrier for protecting the long-range 'interests' of the people from their temporary 'inclinations,' . . . and overall, to preserve the integrity of what he called 'a limited Constitution,' without which the goal of the 'real welfare' of the people could not

---

[119] Adrian Vermeule, *Beyond Originalism*, The Atlantic (Mar. 31, 2020), https://www.theatlantic.com/ideas/archive/2020/03/common-good-constitutionalism/609037/.

[120] *See, e.g.,* Jessica Beckman, *Extending Fourth Amendment Protections and Bivens Claims for Damages to Non-Citizens in Cross-Border Killing Context*, 53 UIC J. Marshall L. Rev. 343 (2020); Devon W. Carbado, *From Stopping Black People to Killing Black People: The Fourth Amendment Pathways to Police Violence*, 105 Calif. L. Rev. 125, 164 (2017) (". . . Fourth Amendment law helped to stage [Eric] Garner's trajectory from life to death. Which is to say, the extraordinary violence [Officer Daniel] Pantaleo mobilized against Garner grew out of an ordinary police interaction whose life-and-death boundaries Fourth Amendment law helps to produce."); Mary Ellen O'Connell, *Ending the Excessive Use of Force at Home and Abroad*, 31 Temp. Int'l & Comp. L.J. 87, 105–06 (2017); Joëlle Anne Moreno, *Flagrant Abuse: Why Black Lives (Also) Matter to the Fourth Amendment*, 21 Berkeley J. Crim. L. 36 (2016); Josephine Ross, *Warning: Stop-and-Frisk May Be Hazardous to Your Health*, 25 Wm. & Mary Bill of Rts. J. 689 (2016); Laing, *supra* note 74, at 306–07 (criticizing *Terry* frisks and even *Garner's* rules concerning deadly force). *See also* this author's Br. for Cato Inst. as Amicus Curiae, Cooper v. United States, No. 24-5381 (U.S. Sept. 23, 2024) (criticizing *Terry* as antioriginalist).

[121] *Cf.* Brandon Garrett & Seth Stoughton, *A Tactical Fourth Amendment*, 103 Va. L. Rev. 211, 213–14 (2017) ("From politicians, to community groups, to policing organizations, leading voices have called into question the Fourth Amendment's 'objective reasonableness' standard, arguing that it is insufficiently protective of life and a poor guide for law enforcement. We agree, but argue that need not be the case.").

be met."[122] In other words, Publius saw the need for safety in the face of danger as a justification for the constitutional rule of law—not a reason to limit it.

Experience proves what the Founders and the judges who followed them knew: safety can be endangered not just by recognizing Fourth Amendment limits but also by abandoning them. Recently, the Supreme Court has cast the Fourth Amendment only as a threat and not as a shield. A more balanced approach may bring more Americans to appreciate the Constitution, rather than dismissing it as an obstacle to normative values and urgent needs.

---

[122] Benjamin Lozano, *A Limited Constitution: Publius, the State of Emergency, and "One Supreme Tribunal"*, 37 BOUNDARY 2 215, 229 (2010).

Through the Federal Accountability Looking Glass

*Patrick Jaicomo and Anya Bidwell**

The Supreme Court confronted a simple question in *Martin v. United States*: "If federal officers raid the wrong house, causing property damage and assaulting innocent occupants, may the homeowners sue the government for damages?"[1] The answer, the Court explained, "is not as obvious as it might be."[2] Or, perhaps, not as obvious as it *should* be. As a result, the innocent Martin family's search for a remedy in the aftermath of a mistaken FBI raid on their home has led them on a surreal adventure through the federal-accountability looking glass. And what the Supreme Court found there reveals a bizarre landscape of immunities through which the Martins continue their journey in search of a remedy.

Introduction

> *"Oh, what fun it'll be, when they see me through the glass in here, and can't get at me!"*

—Lewis Carroll[3]

For half a century, the path to legal remedies for rights violations has been overgrown by a thicket of immunities and exceptions. Courts have steadily increased protections for government officials,

* Friends and senior attorneys at the Institute for Justice, leading its Project on Immunity and Accountability. This term, we, along with our colleagues Dylan Moore and Jared McClain, represented Curtrina Martin, her minor son Gabe, and her former partner, Hilliard Toi Cliatt (collectively, "the Martins"), before the Supreme Court. As our coauthors and cocounsel on the Martins' briefing, we thank and credit Dylan and Jared here. We also extend our gratitude to our colleagues Jeffrey Cieslikowski, Mary Fetter, Sean Hroncich, Daniel Nelson, and Daniel Nivens for their thoughtful comments, suggestions, and help with this article.

1 Martin v. United States, 145 S. Ct. 1689, 1694 (2025).

2 *Id.*

3 LEWIS CARROLL, THROUGH THE LOOKING-GLASS AND WHAT ALICE FOUND THERE ch. I (1871).

while decreasing the availability of causes of actions through which to hold officials accountable.[4] Consider qualified immunity, a doctrine conceived by the Supreme Court in 1967.[5] Once a modest defense to constitutional claims, requiring government officials to show good faith and reasonableness,[6] the doctrine grew into one that demands victims prove their rights were "clearly established" by pointing to binding judicial precedent involving materially identical facts.[7] Similarly, *"Bivens* claims"[8]—implied causes of action against federal officers for constitutional violations—were once so robust as to prompt the Supreme Court's creation of the clearly established test[9] but have since been marked "disfavored"[10] and all but prohibited.[11] Federal officials now operate in a "Constitution-free zone,"[12] an immunity wonderland where the rules bend to federal discretion.

The Supreme Court often cites the constitutional separation of powers to justify its animosity toward these implied causes of action. "[C]reating a cause of action," it argues, "is a legislative endeavor."[13] Yet, even when Congress *has* endeavored to create a cause of action, as it did through the Federal Tort Claims Act (FTCA),[14] the road to a remedy is difficult to find in American courthouses.

Congress passed the FTCA in 1946 to ensure remedies for certain state tort claims against the United States for the wrongs committed by its employees. The FTCA was the years-long culmination of congressional efforts to address a growing problem: remediless

[4] *See infra* Part II.

[5] *See* Pierson v. Ray, 386 U.S. 547, 554–57 (1967).

[6] *See id.*

[7] Harlow v. Fitzgerald, 457 U.S. 800, 815–19 (1982).

[8] Bivens v. Six Unknown Named Agents, 403 U.S. 388 (1971); *see also* Butz v. Economou, 438 U.S. 478, 485–504 (1978).

[9] *See Harlow,* 457 U.S. at 813–19.

[10] Ashcroft v. Iqbal, 556 U.S. 662, 675 (2009).

[11] Egbert v. Boule, 596 U.S. 482, 486 (2022) ("[P]rescribing a cause of action is a job for Congress[.]").

[12] Byrd v. Lamb, 990 F.3d 879, 884 (5th Cir. 2021) (Willett, J., concurring).

[13] *Egbert,* 596 U.S. at 491. *But see* The Apollon, 22 U.S. (9 Wheat.) 362, 367 (1824) (holding that the judiciary can create a cause of action, if "justice demands," so an "injured party [may] receive a suitable redress").

[14] 28 U.S.C. §§ 1346(b)(1), 2671–80.

wrongs that resulted from the actions of government officials as they performed their work. As with qualified immunity and *Bivens*, however, the FTCA remedy—once widely available—began to shrink. Over the past several decades, the courts have denied the FTCA's promise in many ways, draining what was once a reservoir of remedies.[15] Sometimes they have done so at the request of the Department of Justice—as with the expansion of the FTCA's "discretionary function" exception,[16] which the government argues should operate like qualified immunity.[17] Other times, the courts have done it themselves—as with the Eleventh Circuit's creation of a Supremacy Clause bar that prohibits all FTCA claims that "have some nexus with furthering federal policy and can reasonably be characterized as complying with the full range of federal law."[18]

Alice's bizarre journey through the looking glass seems mundane compared to the misadventure of suing the federal government. Even an innocent family, mistakenly raided by the FBI, can be left without recourse as courts stack exceptions, bars, and immunities atop one another.[19]

But in this Term's *Martin v. United States*, the Supreme Court reached through the looking glass. It unanimously rejected the Eleventh Circuit's Supremacy Clause bar to FTCA claims.[20] It also directed the lower court to revisit critical questions surrounding the

---

[15] *See, e.g.*, Brownback v. King, 592 U.S. 209, 218 (2021) (holding that jurisdictional dismissal of an FTCA claims can trigger a judgment bar that defeats other, unrelated claims); *id.* at 222 (Sotomayor, J., concurring) (noting that this may "produce[] seemingly unfair results by precluding meritorious claims when a plaintiff's FTCA claims fail for unrelated reasons").

[16] 28 U.S.C. § 2680(a).

[17] *See* Brief for Respondents at 36, Martin v. United States, 145 S. Ct. 1689 (2025) (No. 24-362), 2025 WL 1011691 (quoting *Harlow*, 457 U.S. at 818) ("The scope of the exception thus mirrors the doctrine of qualified immunity, under which 'government officials performing discretionary functions [] generally are shielded from liability for civil damages insofar as their conduct does not violate clearly established statutory or constitutional rights.'").

[18] Denson v. United States, 574 F.3d 1318, 1348 (11th Cir. 2009); *see also* Kordash v. United States, 51 F.4th 1289, 1293–94 (11th Cir. 2022).

[19] Martin v. United States, No. 23-10062, 2024 WL 1716235 (11th Cir. Apr. 22, 2024) (*Martin Appeal*).

[20] *See Martin*, 145 S. Ct. at 1700.

discretionary-function exception in cases of "wrong-house raids and similar misconduct."[21] Noting several circuit splits along the way, the Court hinted at a broader interest in clearing the path to federal remedies via the FTCA.[22]

In Part I of this tale, we review the facts of the *Martin* raid. Next, in Part II, we situate the expansion of the discretionary-function exception within the ever-growing landscape of government defenses, focusing on the contradicting interpretations created by the circuit courts. In Part III, we explain the lower court decisions in *Martin*. Finally, in Part IV, we discuss the Supreme Court's unanimous decision in *Martin v. United States*, its implications, and the potential paths back to the remedies Congress provided through the FTCA.

With qualified immunity still a formidable queen, *Bivens* a disfavored pawn, and the accumulation of federal power adding more pieces to the government's side of the board each year, "the stakes of clarifying the scope of the discretionary-functions exception grow ever greater."[23] Victims of federal abuse "must increasingly rely on the FTCA" to find their way back through the looking glass and "vindicate their constitutional rights."[24]

I. The Raid of the Martin House

"How would you like to live in Looking-glass House?"[25]

In suburban Atlanta sits a house at 3756 Denville Trace. Built on a quarter-acre lot in 2000, the four-bedroom, three-bathroom home has an attached two-car garage, tasteful landscaping, and a manicured lawn. In 2017, it was home to a family: Hilliard Toi Cliatt; his partner, Curtrina Martin; and her seven-year-old son, Gabe.

A. The Raid

Before dawn on October 18, FBI Special Agent Lawrence Guerra led a six-agent SWAT team to 3756 Denville Trace. Guerra, failing to

---

[21] *Id.* at 1703.

[22] *See id.*

[23] Xi v. Haugen, 68 F.4th 824, 844 (3d Cir. 2023) (Bibas, J., concurring).

[24] *Id.*

[25] CARROLL, *supra* note 3, at ch. I.

confirm the address visible on the mailbox, mistakenly believed he had arrived at 3741 Landau Lane—the home of a gang member for which Guerra had a search warrant. Ignoring conspicuous features that should have averted their mistake, the heavily armed SWAT team battered down the Martins' door, detonated a flashbang grenade in their home, and stormed inside.

The explosion startled the Martins awake, filling them with the dread that dangerous criminals were invading their home. Trina's first instinct was to run to her son's room, but Toi, acting to protect his partner, grabbed Trina and pulled her into a closet. Meanwhile, seven-year-old Gabe cowered under his covers, where he heard his mother's desperate cries: "I need to go get my son, . . . I need to go get my son."

Masked government agents shoved open the door to the closet where Toi and Trina had barricaded themselves. Agents dragged Toi out and handcuffed him, and Trina, half naked, collapsed before a room full of hostile strangers. As she pleaded to see her son, agents pointed guns at her and Toi.

B. The Realization

Agents peppered Toi with questions. But when he told them his address—3756 Denville Trace—the chaos abruptly stopped. Realizing his colossal error, Agent Guerra unshackled Toi and said, "I'll be right back."

He and his team went down the block to 3741 Landau Lane and executed another raid at the *correct* address. Guerra then galumphed back to 3756 Denville Trace, apologized, documented the damage, and left a calling card with his supervisor's information. The Martins were left in stunned disbelief.

The cause of this terrible and life-threatening mistake? Agent Guerra later claimed his GPS, purportedly set for 3741 Landau Lane, had instead directed him to 3756 Denville Trace. But Guerra could not prove this; he threw the GPS away before the Martins could examine it in discovery.[26]

---

[26] This telling of the facts is modeled on Brief for Petitioners at 11–13, Martin v. United States, 145 S. Ct. 1689 (2025) (No. 24-362), 2025 WL 788935.

C. The Repercussions

"Left with personal injuries and property damage—but few explanations and no compensation,"[27] the Martins sued. They brought individual *Bivens* claims against Agent Guerra and the unnamed SWAT-team members for their violation of the Fourth Amendment and FTCA claims against the United States for the Georgia-law torts committed during the raid.

In another moment the Martins were through the looking glass—into a world where reason dissolved and blame vanished. In this checkerboard-landscape, the federal government plays the immunity game against its victims.

Here we pause the Martins' story to survey this topsy-turvy fiefdom.

II. The Immunity Game

"It's a great huge game of chess that's being played."[28]

Over the years, the federal government has systematically fortified its immunities and defenses, while simultaneously eroding avenues for people to hold it accountable. A formidable wall now stands between rights and remedies, built primarily with three tools: the expansion of qualified immunity, the constriction of *Bivens*, and the inversion of the FTCA through its discretionary-function exception.[29]

A. Qualified Immunity

"Curiouser and curiouser! . . . I'm opening out like the largest telescope that ever was!"[30]

Qualified immunity emerged from the Supreme Court in 1967's *Pierson v. Ray*.[31] Initially envisioned as a "defense of good faith and

---

[27] *Martin*, 145 S. Ct. at 1695.

[28] CARROLL, *supra* note 3, at ch. II.

[29] 28 U.S.C. § 2680(a).

[30] LEWIS CARROLL, ALICE'S ADVENTURES IN WONDERLAND ch. II (1865).

[31] 386 U.S. 547, 554–58 (1967).

probable cause,"[32] this "qualified immunity" from liability required an officer to prove both reasonableness and good faith.[33] Though first applied to state police under 42 U.S.C. § 1983,[34] the Court soon extended good-faith immunity to all government workers—local, state, and federal.[35] Foreshadowing a dark future for accountability, the Court wrote that "any lesser standard would deny much of the promise of § 1983."[36]

Then, in 1982, the Supreme Court adopted a lesser standard, dramatically reshaping qualified immunity in *Harlow v. Fitzgerald*. Driven by its own policy concerns in the *Bivens* case against Nixon administration officials,[37] the Court abandoned the subjective "good faith" inquiry for the objective "clearly established test." The Supreme Court announced, "[G]overnment officials performing discretionary functions generally are shielded from liability for civil damages insofar as their conduct does not violate clearly established statutory or constitutional rights of which a reasonable person would have known."[38] This clearly established test "completely reformulated qualified immunity along principles not at all embodied in the common law[.]"[39]

The clearly established test quickly grew into a disorienting hedge maze, requiring a victim of government abuse to prove that the legal principles in her case have such a "clear foundation in then-existing precedent" that they are "beyond debate," and "every reasonable official would interpret [them] to establish the particular rule the plaintiff seeks to apply" to the "particular circumstances" of the

---

[32] *Id.* at 557.

[33] *See* Wood v. Strickland, 420 U.S. 308, 321–22 (1975).

[34] *See Pierson*, 386 U.S. at 550, 555–58; *see also* Civil Rights Act of 1871, ch. 22, § 1, 17 Stat. 13. *But see generally* Patrick Jaicomo & Daniel Nelson, *Section 1983 (Still) Displaces Qualified Immunity*, 49 Harv. J.L. & Pub. Pol'y (forthcoming 2026), https://papers.ssrn.com/sol3/papers.cfm?abstract_id=5124275.

[35] *See* Procunier v. Navarette, 434 U.S. 555, 568–69, 556 nn.1–2 (1978); Butz v. Economou, 438 U.S. 478, 507 (1978).

[36] *Wood*, 420 U.S. at 322.

[37] *Harlow*, 457 U.S. at 816.

[38] *See id.* at 818.

[39] Anderson v. Creighton, 483 U.S. 635, 645 (1987).

victim's situation with "a high degree of specificity."[40] Were that not enough, the Supreme Court continued to adorn qualified immunity with additional, government-friendly features like the right to an immediate interlocutory appeal and the ability to win without having to defend the constitutionality of the government actions.[41]

We could say much more,[42] but we must not be late!

B. The Bivens *Cause of Action*

"What a curious feeling! . . . I must be shutting up like a telescope."[43]

As qualified immunity grew, the Supreme Court cut *Bivens* back to the roots, making it nigh impossible to sue individual federal

---

[40] District of Columbia v. Wesby, 583 U.S. 48, 63 (2018) (citations omitted) (cleaned up). In practice, qualified immunity imposes a two-part hurdle: A plaintiff must show (1) the violation of a constitutional right (the merits) and (2) that the right was clearly established at the time of its violation (the clearly established test). Pearson v. Callahan, 555 U.S. 223, 232 (2009). Despite its opening promise that qualified immunity would not "license [] lawless conduct," *Harlow*, 457 U.S. at 819, or shield "the plainly incompetent," Malley v. Briggs, 475 U.S. 335, 341 (1986), the doctrine routinely does both and allows courts and government officials to sidestep accountability through nonsensical distinctions of earlier precedent. *See, e.g.*, Benning v. Comm'r, 71 F.4th 1324, 1332–34 (11th Cir. 2023) (shielding prison officials who confiscated and censored emails because earlier precedent involved physical, not electronic, mail); Frasier v. Evans, 992 F.3d 1003, 1015 (10th Cir. 2021) (shielding police who forced a man to delete a video he recorded of them using force on a suspect, even though they had been trained that doing so violated the First Amendment because "judicial decisions are the only valid interpretive source of the content of clearly established law"); Baxter v. Bracey, 751 F. App'x 869, 872 (6th Cir. 2018) (shielding officers who allowed their dog to bite a surrendered suspect because the suspect in an earlier case had positioned his body differently).

[41] For example, the Court has formally extended qualified immunity from the federal officers to their state and local colleagues, Davis v. Scherer, 468 U.S. 183, 194 n.12 (1984); granted government defendants a right to immediate interlocutory appeals whenever immunity is denied, Mitchell v. Forsyth, 472 U.S. 511, 524–30 (1985); and allowed courts to avoid deciding the constitutional merits by determining that a right is not clearly established, *Pearson*, 555 U.S. at 236.

[42] And we have. *See generally* Patrick Jaicomo & Anya Bidwell, *Recalibrating Qualified Immunity*, 112 J. CRIM. L. & CRIMINOLOGY 105 (2022) (providing a fuller discussion of qualified immunity's dark history and discussing our optimism for a brighter future in light of indications from the Supreme Court). As have others. *See generally, e.g.*, William Baude, *Is Qualified Immunity Unlawful?*, 106 CALIF. L. REV. 45 (2018) (providing comprehensive overview of qualified immunity).

[43] CARROLL, *supra* note 30, at ch. I.

officials for violating the Constitution.[44] The Court formally authorized the *Bivens* cause of action in 1971, after Webster Bivens sued federal narcotics agents who invaded his home without a warrant, handcuffed him in front of his family, and arrested him on baseless charges.[45] (Sound familiar?) To ensure state-federal constitutional parity, the Court ruled that the Constitution itself implied a right to sue for its violation, affirming that courts must "be alert to adjust their remedies so as to grant the necessary relief."[46]

Over the following decade, the Court directly approved *Bivens* claims in two more cases—*Davis v. Passman*[47] and *Carlson v. Green*[48]—and implicitly blessed many more.[49] By 1982, *Bivens* claims were so widespread and robust that *Harlow* constructed the clearly established test to temper the Court's policy concerns with holding federal officials to their constitutional obligations.[50] *Bivens*, however, remained generally available.[51]

But in 1983, the tide began to turn. The Supreme Court first ruled that an "elaborate, comprehensive scheme" by Congress addressing some harm—however remotely—displaced *Bivens* claims in the same arena.[52] By 1988, even congressional *inaction* could displace *Bivens*, since "special factors counselling hesitation in the absence of affirmative action by Congress has proved to include an appropriate judicial deference to indications that congressional inaction

---

[44] *See generally* Patrick Jaicomo & Anya Bidwell, *Unqualified Immunity and the Betrayal of* Butz v. Economou, 126 Dick. L. Rev. 719 (2022) (detailing the history of claims against federal officers and the Court's inconsistent approach to qualified immunity and *Bivens*). *See also generally, e.g.,* Steven I. Vladeck, *The Inconsistent Originalism of Judge Made Remedies Against Federal Officers,* 96 Notre Dame L. Rev. 1869, 1887–89 (2021).

[45] *See Bivens,* 403 U.S. at 389–90.

[46] *Id.* at 392 (citations omitted).

[47] Davis v. Passman, 442 U.S. 228 (1979).

[48] Carlson v. Green, 446 U.S. 14 (1980).

[49] *See* Jaicomo & Bidwell, *Unqualified Immunity, supra* note 44, at 763–64 app. A (collecting 31 Supreme Court cases recognizing, implying, or allowing to go forward constitutional claims against federal officers).

[50] *See Harlow,* 457 U.S. at 820 n.36.

[51] *See* Jaicomo & Bidwell, *Unqualified Immunity, supra* note 44, at 735–43.

[52] Bush v. Lucas, 462 U.S. 367, 380–90 (1983); *see also* Chappel v. Wallace, 462 U.S. 296, 298–304 (1983) (citing Congress's authority in the field of military discipline structure as a "special factor" counseling hesitation against extending *Bivens*).

has not been inadvertent."[53] And the Court's stated concern shifted from institutional competency to the separation of powers.[54] Even when Congress passed the Westfall Act in 1988,[55] explicitly allowing claims against "employee[s] of the Government . . . brought for a violation of the Constitution of the United States,"[56] the judicial erosion of claims against federal officers continued apace.[57]

Then, in the 2000s, the Supreme Court began walking *Bivens* to the gallows. In *Correctional Services Corp. v. Malesko*,[58] the Court reimagined *Bivens* as generally *unavailable* and announced that, unless the Court had previously extended the cause of action into a specific context, none existed.[59]

In *Ziglar v. Abbasi*, the Court went further, unveiling a restrictive two-step test to assess *Bivens* availability: A plaintiff must (1) demonstrate that his case does not present a "new context" (often based on picayune distinctions),[60] and, if it does, (2) show there are no "special

[53] Schweiker v. Chilicky, 487 U.S. 412, 423 (1988) (internal quotation marks omitted).

[54] *Contra, e.g.*, The Apollon, 22 U.S. (9 Wheat.) 362, 367 (1824) ("[T]his Court can only look to the questions, whether the laws have been violated; and if they were, justice demands, that the injured party should receive a suitable redress.").

[55] Federal Employees Liability Reform and Tort Compensation Act of 1988, Pub. L. No. 100-694, 102 Stat. 4563 (1988) (citing as its impetus Westfall v. Erwin, 484 U.S. 292 (1988)).

[56] 28 U.S.C. § 2679(b)(2)(A).

[57] The Supreme Court recently acknowledged that the Westfall Act "left *Bivens* where it found it" in 1988. Hernandez v. Mesa, 589 U.S. 93, 111 n.9 (2020). But the effect of this acknowledgement (*i.e.*, where Congress found *Bivens*) is still a mystery that has not been answered by the courts. *But see* Buchanan v. Barr, 71 F.4th 1003, 1015–18 (D.C. Cir. 2023) (Walker, J., concurring) ("I'm not certain whether the Westfall Act is best read to allow state tort suits for constitutional injuries. But that reading finds support in the text of the statute, accords with Founding-era principles of officer accountability, and closes a remedial gap—ensuring relief for those injured by federal officers' unconstitutional conduct.").

[58] Corr. Servs. Corp. v. Malesko, 534 U.S. 61 (2001).

[59] *Id.* at 70, 74.

[60] Ziglar v. Abbasi, 582 U.S. 120, 136 (2017). The new-context analysis is eerily like the clearly established test. *See supra* note 40. It asks whether a case is "different in a meaningful way from previous *Bivens* cases decided by this Court" considering a nonexhaustive list of factors. *Ziglar*, 582 U.S. at 1859. Courts have taken this to mean that a case must "exactly mirror the facts and legal issues" of an earlier decision. Ahmed v. Weyker, 984 F.3d 564, 568 (8th Cir. 2020) (citing Farah v. Weyker, 926 F.3d 492, 498 (8th Cir. 2019)). Thus, when Veterans Administration police beat and choked an elderly veteran for failing to put his belongings in an x-ray machine quickly enough,

factors counseling hesitation" against the judiciary extending a cause of action into this new context.

Finally, in *Egbert v. Boule*, the Court stopped just short of overruling *Bivens* outright,[61] leaving the bench and bar to answer a riddle: "When might a court ever be 'better equipped' than the people's elected representatives to weigh the 'costs and benefits' of creating a cause of action?"[62] If this question is not merely rhetorical, no one seems to know the answer. But it's growing increasingly difficult to imagine a *Bivens* remedy available to anyone other than Webster Bivens himself.

C. The Federal Tort Claims Act and Its Exceptions

> *"[The Queen's] so extremely . . . likely to win, that it's hardly worthwhile finishing the game."*[63]

This brings us to the Federal Tort Claims Act[64]—the heart of *Martin v. United States* and a crucial piece in the complex immunity game played by the federal government against everyday people. Before qualified immunity, *Bivens*, and even Section 1983, there was the bar of sovereign immunity, founded on the ancient notion that "the King can do no wrong."[65] The FTCA, passed in 1946, partly in response to a U.S. Army airplane's deadly collision with

---

the Fifth Circuit concluded that the case presented a new context from *Bivens* because it took place in a hospital, not a private home; the officers were not investigating a narcotics crime; and the officers did not handcuff or strip-search the veteran. Oliva v. Nivar, 973 F.3d 438, 442–43 (5th Cir. 2020). The Fifth Circuit even treated the officers' *greater* violence (chokehold) as reason to deny relief because the narcotics officers in *Bivens* "did not place Webster Bivens in a chokehold." *Id.* at 443.

61 *Egbert*, 596 U.S. at 482. "While our cases describe two steps, those steps often resolve to a single question: whether there is any reason to think that Congress might be better equipped to create a damages remedy." *Id.* at 492. More pointedly, *Egbert* explained, "A court faces only one question: whether there is any rational reason (even one) to think that Congress is better suited to 'weigh the costs and benefits of allowing a damages action to proceed.'" *Id.* at 496 (citation omitted).

62 *Id.* at 503 (Gorsuch, J., concurring).

63 CARROLL, *supra* note 30, at ch. VIII.

64 This discussion of the FTCA draws heavily from Brief for Petitioners at 6–11, 19–21, Martin v. United States, 145 S. Ct. 1689 (2025) (No. 24-362), 2025 WL 788935.

65 We do not pause to consider why a nation that threw off its sovereign would turn around and adopt this legal principle, though others have. *See, e.g.*, David E. Engdahl, *Immunity and Accountability for Positive Governmental Wrongs*, 44 U. COLO. L. REV. 1, 2–21 (1972).

the Empire State Building,[66] was Congress's effort "to mitigate [the] unjust consequences of sovereign immunity" and address the "multiplying number of remediless wrongs . . . which would have been actionable if inflicted by an individual or a corporation but [were] remediless solely because their perpetrator was an officer or employee of the government."[67]

Congress designed the FTCA to waive sovereign immunity and permit remedies for a large swath of government harms. To accomplish these purposes, the FTCA permitted a federal cause of action for damages, "allow[ing] a plaintiff to bring certain state-law tort suits against the Federal Government."[68] The act provides a broad grant of jurisdiction and waiver of sovereign immunity for claims that satisfy six criteria:

> Subject to [28 U.S.C. § 2671–80], the district courts . . . shall have exclusive jurisdiction of civil actions on claims [1] against the United States, [2] for money damages, . . . [3] for injury or loss of property, or personal injury or death [4] caused by the negligent or wrongful act or omission of any employee of the Government [5] while acting within the scope of his office or employment, [6] under circumstances where the United States, if a private person, would be liable to the claimant in accordance with the law of the place where the act or omission occurred.[69]

Even so, a claim could still be defeated by sovereign immunity if it falls within the "Exceptions" in Section 2680, for which "[t]he provisions of [chapter 171] and section 1346(b) of this title shall not apply[.]"[70] These exceptions exclude 13 categories of claims from the FTCA's waiver of sovereign immunity.[71] Among these are the so-called "discretionary-function" and "intentional-tort" exceptions.[72]

---

[66] *See* Gregory C. Sisk, *The Continuing Drift of Federal Sovereign Immunity Jurisprudence,* 50 WM. & MARY L. REV. 517, 536 (2008); *see also* 28 U.S.C. 1346(b)(1) (making the FTCA retroactively effective for claims "accruing on and after January 1, 1945").

[67] Feres v. United States, 340 U.S. 135, 139–40 (1950).

[68] *Brownback,* 592 U.S. at 210–11.

[69] 28 U.S.C. § 1346(b)(1).

[70] *Id.* § 2680.

[71] *Id.*

[72] *Id.* § 2680(a), (h). Neither shorthand description is apt. *See* United States v. Gaubert, 499 U.S. 315, 324–25 & 325 n.7 (1991) (2680(a) includes some nondiscretionary acts and excludes some discretionary ones); Levin v. United States, 568 U.S. 503, 507 n.1 (2013) (2680(h) includes some negligent acts and excludes some intentional ones).

1. Section 2680(a): The discretionary-function exception

The discretionary-function exception reinstates sovereign immunity for any claim "based upon the exercise or performance or the failure to exercise or perform a discretionary function or duty on the part of a federal agency or an employee of the Government, whether or not the discretion involved be abused."[73] This exception was Congress's safeguard against courts second-guessing legislative or administrative policy decisions. Even so, the exception was merely a "clarifying amendment" to that end.[74]

Crucially, the discretionary-function exception precludes claims for acts based on federal regulations[75] or legally conferred discretion "based on considerations of public policy."[76] For acts in the latter category, just any discretion will not do. Because the exception concerns policy judgments, there are "obviously discretionary acts" that do not trigger the discretionary-function exception because they are not "based on the purposes that [a] regulatory regime seeks to accomplish."[77] The exception, in other words, is a term of art with boundaries that do not extend to every act involving discretion.[78]

---

[73] 28 U.S.C. § 2680(a).

[74] Dalehite v. United States, 346 U.S. 15, 26 (1953). As the Department of Justice liaison on the FTCA, Assistant Attorney General Francis Shea, explained to Congress, "[i]t is not probable that the courts would extend a Tort Claims Act into the realm of the validity of legislation or discretionary administrative action," but just in case they might, the exception "makes this specific." *Hearings on H.R.5573 and 6463 Before H. Comm. on the Judiciary*, 77th Cong., 2d Sess. 29 (1942).

[75] *Gaubert*, 499 U.S. at 324.

[76] *Id.* at 322–23 (cleaned up).

[77] *Id.* at 325 n.7.

[78] "Discretionary function" means the use of power conferred by law in certain circumstances to fulfill a definite, policy-based end. *See* BLACK'S LAW DICTIONARY 587, 827 (3d ed. 1933) ("When applied to public functionaries, discretion means a power or right conferred upon them by law of acting officially in certain circumstances," and "function" means, "[o]ffice; duty; fulfillment of a definite end or set of ends by correct adjustment of means."). This understanding is reinforced by the historical context of the FTCA's enactment and related statutes—such as the Reorganization Act of 1945 and Administrative Procedure Act of 1946, which used "function" to describe policy-driven agency actions. *See* Reorganization Act of 1945, Pub. L. No. 79-263, 59 Stat. 613 (1945); Administrative Procedure Act, Pub. L. No. 79-404, 60 Stat. 237 (1946); *see also* Off. of Att'y Gen., *Final Report of the Attorney General's Committee on Administrative Procedure* 119 (1941) (attorney general explaining that the purpose is to limit judicial interference with the types of policy determinations vested in the agencies' discretion).

Because the exception concerns policy judgments, many discretionary acts do not trigger the exception because they are not based on policy. Take, for instance, driving: Although driving requires constant discretion, a negligent car crash does not trigger the exception because decisions about when to break, change lanes, or turn on a car's headlights are not "grounded in regulatory policy."[79] By contrast, the exception would shield a government official's use of delegated authority to order the removal of a stop sign or increase of a speed limit, even if those decisions resulted in a car crash.

The discretionary-function exception's core purpose is to shield decisions rooted in social, economic, or political policy,[80] not bar ordinary common-law torts committed by government employees.[81] So, in the event of a catastrophic explosion caused by large fertilizer shipments to Europe after the Second World War, the exception shielded the cabinet-level decision to ship enormous amounts of potentially explosive fertilizer under dangerous conditions,[82] but it would not have shielded a government dockworker dropping a lit cigarette into a cargo hold.[83]

---

[79] *Gaubert*, 499 U.S. at 325 n.7. *Gaubert* sorts the discretionary-function exception into four buckets: (1) "[I]f a regulation mandates particular conduct, and the employee obeys the direction," 2680(a) reinstates sovereign immunity, and the claim is barred. (2) If "established governmental policy, as expressed or implied by statute, regulation, or agency guidelines, allows a Government agent to exercise discretion," 2680(a) presumptively reinstates sovereign immunity, and the claim is barred if the agent exercises discretion to further the established policy. (3) "If [an] employee violates [a] mandatory regulation," 2680(a) does not reinstate sovereign immunity, and the claim can proceed. (4) If no statute, regulation, or agency guideline confers discretion on an employee to take an action, 2680(a) does not reinstate sovereign immunity, and the claim can proceed. *Id.* at 324.

[80] United States v. Varig Airlines, 467 U.S. 797, 814 (1984) ("Congress wished to prevent judicial 'second-guessing' of legislative and administrative decisions grounded in social, economic, and political policy through the medium of an action in tort."); *Dalehite*, 346 U.S. at 27 (citation omitted) (explaining that the exception shields against tort suits that can be resolved only by forcing the judiciary to assess "the validity of legislation or discretionary administration action," such as "decisions of a regulatory nature," "the expenditure of Federal funds," or "the execution of a Federal project").

[81] *Dalehite*, 346 U.S. at 28 & n.19 ("Ordinary common-law torts" were "[u]ppermost in the collective mind of Congress" when it passed the FTCA.); *Varig Airlines*, 467 U.S. at 810 (The common law torts of employees of regulatory agencies, as well as of other Federal agencies," are "within the scope of" the FTCA.).

[82] *See id.* at 38–42.

[83] *See id.* at 23 ("Since no individual acts of negligence could be shown, the suits for damages that resulted necessarily predicated government liability on the participation of the United States in the manufacture and the transportation of FGAN.").

2. Section 2680(h): The intentional-tort exception and law-enforcement proviso

Congress did bar some ordinary common-law torts from the FTCA when it enacted the statute in 1946. To prevent claims "where some agent of the Government gets in a fight with some fellow . . . [a]nd socks him,"[84] Congress also enacted an intentional-tort exception, reinstating sovereign immunity for "[a]ny claim arising out of assault, battery, false imprisonment, false arrest, malicious prosecution, abuse of process, libel, slander, misrepresentation, deceit, or interference with contract rights."[85]

But as experience between 1946 and 1973 showed, the intentional-tort exception created a glaring injustice: "[A] Federal mail truck driver creates direct federal liability if he negligently runs down a citizen on the street but the Federal Government is held harmless if a federal narcotics agent intentionally assaults the same citizen in the course of an illegal 'no-knock' raid."[86]

Thus, in 1974, spurred by a pair of federal drug raids on innocent families in Collinsville, Illinois[87] (again, sound familiar?), Congress added a vital "law-enforcement proviso," or carve-out, to the intentional-tort exception.[88] This exception-to-the-exception-to-a-waiver-of-immunity ensures that the FTCA provides claims for "assault, battery, false imprisonment, false arrest, abuse of process, or malicious prosecution" when committed by a federal law enforcement officer.

The law-enforcement proviso's purpose, the Supreme Court explained in *Carlson v. Green*, was to ensure that "innocent individuals who are subjected to raids [of the type conducted in Collinsville and *Bivens*] will have a cause of action against . . . the Federal Government."[89] And although public outrage toward the

---

[84] United States v. Shearer, 473 U.S. 52, 55 (1985) (citation omitted).

[85] 28 U.S.C. § 2680(h).

[86] S. Rep. No. 93-588, at 3 (1973).

[87] The raids made national news. *See, e.g.*, Andrew H. Malcolm, *Drug Raids Terrorize 2 Families—by Mistake*, N.Y. TIMES (Apr. 29, 1973); *Hearings on Reorganization Plan No. 2 of 1973 Before the Subcomm. on Reorganization, Rsch., and Int'l Orgs. of the S. Comm. on Gov't Operations*, 93d Cong., 1st Sess., pt. 3, at 461–83 (1973) (testimony from victims of Collinsville raids); *see also generally* John C. Boger et al., *The Federal Tort Claims Act Intentional Torts Amendment*, 54 N.C. L. REV. 497, 499–517 (1976).

[88] 28 U.S.C. § 2680(h).

[89] *Carlson*, 446 U.S. at 20 (quoting S. Rep. No. 93-588, at 3).

Collinsville raids moved Congress to act, Congress did not cabin the proviso to the specific facts—or torts—at issue in those raids.[90] Instead, the language Congress enacted provides a remedy for a swath of tortious conduct by federal law enforcement officers that the FTCA could not otherwise address due to its intentional-tort exception.[91] Congress (in consultation with the Department of Justice) crafted the proviso as a statutory "counterpart to . . . *Bivens*" that extends beyond "constitutional tort situations[.]"[92]

3. The circuit splits

After its enactment of the law-enforcement proviso, Congress expected the FTCA to provide remedies for victims of federal police abuses like the families in Collinsville.[93] But the lower courts have since invented such a wide range of conflicting interpretations— weaving together what the law-enforcement proviso allows with what the discretionary-function exception prohibits—that what was once a springboard to remedies is now a trap door to their denial.

Soon after Congress enacted the proviso, courts read it in relative harmony with the discretionary-function exception. Consider the analysis in *Caban v. United States*.[94] There, the Second Circuit allowed a wrongful detention claim to proceed, reasoning that the agents' actions did not involve "weighing important policy choices."[95] Other circuits agreed. As the Fifth Circuit explained in a similar ruling, "if actions under the proviso must also clear the hurdle of the discretionary function exception . . . even *Bivens* and Collinsville would not pass muster and the law enforcement proviso would fail to create the effective legal remedy intended by Congress."[96] And the Ninth Circuit emphasized that, while law enforcement necessarily involves making discretionary decisions, they are not "the sort of generalized

[90] *See* S. Rep. No. 93-588, at 3–4.

[91] *Id.* at 1 (explaining that the purpose of the bill containing the proviso was "to provide a remedy against the United States for the intentional torts of its investigative and law enforcement officers").

[92] S. Rep. 93-588, at 3–4; *see also Carlson*, 446 U.S. at 20 ("Congress views FTCA and *Bivens* as parallel, complementary causes of action[.]").

[93] *See* S. Rep. 93-588, at 3–4.

[94] Caban v. United States, 671 F.2d 1230 (2d Cir. 1982).

[95] *Id.* at 1233.

[96] Sutton v. United States, 819 F.2d 1289, 1296 (5th Cir. 1987).

social, economic and political policy choices that Congress intended to exempt from tort liability."[97]

This harmony began to change after the Supreme Court's 1991 decision in *Gaubert v. United States*,[98] which tried to clarify—but apparently muddled—the test for applying the exception.[99] The lower courts seized on several phrases in the decision, largely (or entirely[100]) stripped them of context, and began treating almost any discretionary act as presumptively policy-driven, regardless of how mundane, misguided, or—even—unconstitutional the underlying decision was.[101] To limit this broad reading of the discretionary-function exception in light of the law-enforcement proviso, lower courts then invented various carve-outs to the discretionary-function exception, leading to several "longstanding, recurring circuit splits involving the discretionary-function exception."[102] The result has been a doctrinal Wonderland, wherein similar facts produce different outcomes depending on the circuit in which they are adjudicated.

"It's my own invention."[103]

First, "there is a split over whether claims that fall within the . . . law-enforcement proviso must also fall outside the discretionary-function

---

[97] Garcia v. United States, 826 F.2d 806, 809 (9th Cir. 1987) (citing *Caban*, 671 F.2d at 1230).

[98] *Gaubert*, 499 U.S. at 315.

[99] *Id.* at 335 (Scalia, J., concurring in part).

[100] C.M. v. United States, 672 F. Supp. 3d 288, 334 (W.D. Tex. 2023) (criticizing Shivers v. United States, 1 F.4th 924, 932–33 (11th Cir. 2021)).

[101] *See, e.g.*, Campos v. United States, 888 F.3d 724, 735 (5th Cir. 2018) (asserting that the exception applies "unless the official had clear guidance on what to do when presented with what is argued to be the relevant evidence."); Esquivel v. United States, 21 F.4th 565, 574 (9th Cir. 2021) (writing that when a federal officer exercises discretion, "it must be presumed that the agent's acts are grounded in policy when exercising that discretion."); *Shivers*, 1 F.4th at 931 (citations omitted) (declaring that the exception applies "*unless* a source of federal law 'specifically prescribes' a course of conduct."); *id.* at 932 ("[T]here is no 'constitutional-claims exclusion' to the statutory discretionary function exception. . . .").

[102] *Xi*, 68 F.4th at 842–43 (Bibas, J., concurring). This discussion of the splits is adapted from Petition for a Writ of Certiorari at 23–34, Martin v. United States, 145 S. Ct. 1689 (2025) (No. 24-362), 2024 WL 43774198.

[103] CARROLL, *supra* note 3, at ch. VIII.

exception."[104] Six circuits hold that an FTCA claim must clear the discretionary-function exception, even if it also falls within the law-enforcement proviso.[105] But the Eleventh Circuit determined that the proviso operates as an exception, not only to the intentional-tort exception, but to the discretionary-function exception too.[106] In the Eleventh Circuit's view, the discretionary-function exception is categorically inapplicable to claims brought under the law-enforcement proviso. Simply put, if a plaintiff brings a proviso claim, the discretionary-function analysis is moot.

Second, "there is a split over whether the exception applies when the challenged conduct was careless rather than a considered exercise of discretion."[107] Three circuits hold that—because careless action does not require the weighing of policy considerations—the exception does not apply to incompetent or lazy acts.[108] But another three circuits allow careless acts to trigger the exception.[109] In these circuits, a federal employee's carelessness is irrelevant because "the government is not required to prove either that an affirmative decision was made, or that any decision actually involved the weighing of policy considerations, in order to claim immunity."[110] In the circuits that exclude carelessness, the failure of prison guards to discover a nine-inch-long knife during a pat down would not trigger the exception,[111] but in the other circuits . . . it may.

Third, the courts are split over "whether unconstitutional conduct necessarily falls outside the exception."[112] Seven circuits hold that the discretionary-function exception does not apply when a

---

[104] *Xi*, 68 F.4th at 843 (Bibas, J., concurring).

[105] Caban v. United States, 671 F.2d 1230, 1234 (2d Cir. 1982); Medina v. United States, 259 F.3d 220, 226 (4th Cir. 2001); Joiner v. United States, 955 F.3d 399, 406 (5th Cir. 2020); Linder v. United States, 937 F.3d 1087, 1089 (7th Cir. 2019); Gasho v. United States, 39 F.3d 1420, 1433 (9th Cir. 1994); Gray v. Bell, 712 F.2d 490, 507–08 (D.C. Cir. 1983).

[106] Nguyen v. United States, 556 F.3d 1244, 1260 (11th Cir. 2009).

[107] *Xi*, 68 F.4th at 843 (Bibas, J., concurring).

[108] Coulthurst v. United States, 214 F.3d 106, 111 (2d Cir. 2000); Rich v. United States, 811 F.3d 140, 147 (4th Cir. 2015); Palay v. United States, 349 F.3d 418, 432 (7th Cir. 2003).

[109] Willis v. Boyd, 993 F.3d 545, 549 (8th Cir. 2021); Gonzalez v. United States, 814 F.3d 1022, 1033 (9th Cir. 2016); Kiehn v. United States, 984 F.2d 1100, 1105 (10th Cir. 1993).

[110] *Gonzalez*, 814 F.3d at 1033.

[111] *See Rich*, 811 F.3d at 147.

[112] *Xi*, 68 F.4th at 843 (Bibas, J., concurring).

federal officer's conduct is unconstitutional.[113] These courts reason that "[f]ederal officials do not possess discretion to violate constitutional rights[,]" so when they do, the discretionary-function exception does not affect a victim's ability to recover under the FTCA.[114] But in two circuits, including the Eleventh Circuit through its decision in *Shivers v. United States,* "the theme that 'no one has discretion to violate the Constitution' has nothing to do with the Federal Tort Claims Act[.]"[115] This interpretation also explains why, as discussed in Part III, the Eleventh Circuit's decision in *Martin* did not need to reach the merits of the Martins' constitutional claims—deciding only that the rights were not clearly established.[116] The constitutionality of Agent Guerra's raid on the wrong house was irrelevant to the FTCA's discretionary-function analysis, and, of course, *Pearson v. Callahan* made it optional for the qualified-immunity analysis too.

With the pieces thus set for the huge game of chess, we return to the story of the Martin family to see how they braved the gyre of immunities.

III. The Lower Court Denial of the Martins' Remedies

"Would you kindly tell me the meaning of the poem called 'Jabberwocky'?"[117]

The Martins invoked *Bivens* against the individual agents and the FTCA against the United States. Given the similarities to the *Bivens* and Collinsville raids, the Martins' case should have quickly proceeded to trial. Yet, through the accountability looking glass, justice is rarely so straightforward.

---

[113] Limone v. United States, 579 F.3d 79, 102 (1st Cir. 2009); Myers & Myers Inc. v. USPS, 527 F.2d 1252, 1261 (2d Cir. 1975); United States Fid. & Guar. Co. v. United States, 837 F.2d 116, 120 (3d Cir. 1988) (*USF&G*); Medina, 259 F.3d at 225; Raz v. United States, 343 F.3d 945, 948 (8th Cir. 2003); Nurse v. United States, 226 F.3d 996, 1002 (9th Cir. 2000); Loumiet v. United States, 828 F.3d 935, 943 (D.C. Cir. 2016).

[114] *USF&G*, 837 F.2d at 120.

[115] *Linder*, 937 F.3d at 1090; *see also Shivers*, 1 F.4th at 930 ("Congress left no room for the extra-textual 'constitutional-claims exclusion'[.]" (citation omitted)).

[116] *Martin Appeal*, 2024 WL 1716235, at *5.

[117] CARROLL, *supra* note 3, at ch. VI.

The federal government moved for summary judgment. The Fourth Amendment *Bivens* claims, it argued, "should be dismissed on qualified immunity grounds because Guerra was acting within the scope of his discretionary authority, and [the Martins] have failed to show that the alleged constitutional right was clearly established at the time of the incident."[118] And the government argued that the discretionary-function exception barred the Martins' negligence claims and, shockingly, that the Constitution's Supremacy Clause barred their intentional-tort claims for good measure.[119]

A. The Martins' Adventures in Districtcourtland

The district court agreed with the federal government and poured the Martins out of court.[120] Despite Supreme Court and Eleventh Circuit precedent establishing that officers violate the Fourth Amendment when they raid the wrong house, unless "objective facts available to the officers at the time suggest[] no distinction between" a search warrant's target and the place mistakenly searched,[121] the district court held these prior cases lacked "indistinguishable facts" to "clearly establish" the Martins' rights.[122] Because Agent Guerra had done "considerably more than nothing"[123] to prepare for the raid and the two homes "shared several conspicuous features" (though also "were dissimilar in some respects and separated by three or four homes"), qualified immunity barred the Martins' *Bivens* claims.[124]

---

[118] Martin v. United States, 631 F. Supp. 3d 1281, 1291 (N.D. Ga. 2022) (*Martin MSJ*).

[119] These arguments were made in successive motions and addressed in successive orders, but we discuss them together for simplicity. *See Martin MSJ*, 631 F. Supp. 3d 1281; Martin v. United States, No. 1:19-cv-4106, 2022 WL 18263039 (N.D. Ga. Dec. 30, 2022) (*Martin Reconsideration*).

[120] *Martin Reconsideration*, 2022 WL 18263039, at *5.

[121] Maryland v. Garrison, 480 U.S. 79, 88 (1987); *see also* Hartsfield v. Lemacks, 50 F.3d 950, 955 (11th Cir. 1995) (finding that an officer's actions "were simply not consistent with a reasonable effort to ascertain and identify the place intended to be searched" (citing *Garrison*, 480 U.S. at 88–89)).

[122] *Martin MSJ*, 631 F. Supp. 3d at 1292 (citing Smith v. LePage, 834 F.3d 1285, 1297 (11th Cir. 2016)).

[123] *Id.* at 1294 (internal quotation marks omitted) (citing *Hartsfield*, 50 F.3d at 955).

[124] *Id.* at 1294–95.

Turning to the FTCA, the district court noted that "the Eleventh Circuit has concluded that the investigation of the whereabouts and identity of the subject of an arrest warrant . . . is conduct that falls within the discretionary function exception."[125] And because "there was no statute, regulation or even internal operating procedure prescribing Guerra's course of action," his "decisions regarding *how* to execute the warrant" were "the epitome of discretion."[126] Accordingly, the Martins' FTCA claims fell within the discretionary-function exception.[127]

The district court acknowledged that the Martins had established valid intentional-tort claims under Georgia law—false imprisonment, assault, and battery—and recognized they were permitted by the law-enforcement proviso[128] (which Eleventh Circuit precedent held to override the discretionary-function exception).[129] But it still dismissed the claims under the Eleventh Circuit's mimsy Supremacy Clause bar, precluding all FTCA claims for actions that have "some nexus" with federal policy and can "reasonably be characterized" as compliant with "the full range of federal law."[130]

B. The Martins' Adventures in Circuitcourtland

The Eleventh Circuit affirmed the district court's decision, denying the Martins any remedy. In a brisk opinion, the panel upheld Agent Guerra's qualified immunity, reasoning that "[t]he FBI affords its agents discretion in preparing for warrant executions" because the FBI "has no official policy or practice with respect to how agents are to locate or navigate to the target address of a search warrant."[131] Accordingly, "the law at the time did not clearly establish that Guerra's preparatory steps before

---

125 *Id.* at 1296 (citing Mesa v. United States, 123 F.3d 1425, 1438 (11th Cir. 1997) (cleaned up)).

126 *Id.* at 1296.

127 *Id.* at 1297.

128 *Id.*

129 *Nguyen*, 556 F.3d at 1260 ("[W]here . . . the § 2680(h) proviso applies to waive sovereign immunity, the exception to waiver contained in § 2680(a) is of no effect.").

130 *Kordash*, 51 F.4th at 1293–94; *Martin Reconsideration*, 2022 WL 18263039, at *2–3.

131 *Martin Appeal*, 2024 WL 1716235, at *6.

the warrant execution would violate the Fourth Amendment."[132] And because *Pearson v. Callahan* allows the courts to skip the constitutional merits[133]—that is, whether Agent Guerra executed an unreasonable search by smashing down the door of the wrong house without checking the address—"the sole issue for [] resolution [wa]s whether his actions violated clearly established law."[134] The panel concluded they did not.

The United States also retained its immunity against the Martins' FTCA claims, thanks to the discretionary-function exception and Supremacy Clause bar. While the Eleventh Circuit offered a plaintiff-friendly interpretation of the law-enforcement proviso through its decision in *Nguyen v. United States* (holding that the proviso trumps the discretionary-function exception),[135] the Eleventh Circuit more than offset that ruling with defendant-adoring interpretations elsewhere.

Consider, first, the *Shivers* rule: In *Shivers v. United States*, the Eleventh Circuit transformed the FTCA's discretionary-function provision from a limited exception into a slithy default by holding that it "applies *unless* a source of federal law 'specifically prescribes' a course of conduct," citing *Gaubert* and *Berkowitz v. United States*.[136] This, even though "neither cited Supreme Court case uses 'unless' in that context,"[137] and both decisions made a broader point—that, while specifically prescribed conduct is indeed not discretionary, it's not the only category of nondiscretionary conduct.[138]

Consider, next, the *Denson* Supremacy Clause bar: In *Denson v. United States*, the Eleventh Circuit concocted a constitutional barrier to the FTCA itself.[139] Even though the act is a "Law[] of the

---

132 *Id.*

133 *Pearson*, 555 U.S. at 236; *see also supra* note 40.

134 *Martin Appeal*, 2024 WL 1716235, at *5.

135 *Nguyen*, 556 F.3d at 1260.

136 1 F.4th 924, 931 (11th Cir. 2021) (citing *Gaubert*, 499 U.S. at 322; Berkowitz v. United States, 486 U.S. 531, 536 (1988)).

137 *C.M.*, 672 F. Supp. 3d at 334.

138 *Gaubert*, 499 U.S. at 322.

139 *Denson*, 574 F.3d at 1344–49.

United States" and so "the supreme Law of the Land,"[140] *Denson* concluded that the Supremacy Clause actually bars all FTCA claims that "have some nexus with furthering federal policy and can reasonably be characterized as complying with the full range of federal law."[141] Drawing a "broader application" from the Supreme Court's decision in *In re Neagle*,[142] the Eleventh Circuit began from the premise that "an officer of the United States cannot be held in violation of state law while simultaneously executing his duties as prescribed by federal law."[143] Because the FTCA provides relief "in accordance with the law of the place where the act . . . occurred,"[144]—typically, state tort law—*Denson* concluded that "liability simply cannot attach to the acts taken by federal officers in the course of their duties and committed in compliance with federal law[.]"[145] The court then clarified in *Kordash v. United States* that these standards are satisfied whenever a federal employee acts within the scope of his "discretionary authority."[146] In other words, the Supremacy Clause bar was just the discretionary-function exception in disguise, renamed to undo *Nguyen's* holding that the exception could not bar FTCA claims permitted by the law-enforcement proviso.

The *Martin* panel noted how these immunity doctrines conveniently burble into a single justification that immunizes the government and its employees.[147] Since Agent Guerra was acting within his "discretionary authority," all the Martins' claims—constitutional, intentional-tort, and negligence-tort—were doomed by immunity of one sort or another.[148]

---

[140] U.S. Const. art. VI.

[141] *Denson*, 574 F.3d at 1348.

[142] 135 U.S. 1 (1890).

[143] *Denson*, 574 F.3d at 1346–47.

[144] 28 U.S.C. § 1346(b)(1).

[145] *Denson*, 574 F.3d at 1349.

[146] *Kordash*, 51 F.4th at 1294.

[147] *Martin Appeal*, 2024 WL 1716235, at *6 (explaining that "[s]imilar to the discretionary-function exception, the Supremacy Clause ensures that states do not impede or burden the execution of federal law") (citing *Denson*, 574 F.3d at 1336–37)).

[148] *Id.* at *8.

Citing the circuit splits over the discretionary-function exception, the Martins petitioned for certiorari, and the Supreme Court agreed to hear their case.[149]

IV. The Supreme Court Revival of the Martins' Remedies

"Shaking" and "Waking"[150]

The Supreme Court unanimously revived all the Martins' FTCA claims.[151] It addressed two pivotal issues: "(1) whether the law enforcement proviso overrides not just the intentional-tort exception but also the discretionary-function exception, and (2) whether the Supremacy Clause affords the United States a defense in FTCA suits."[152] With a vorpal blade, the Court "[c]lear[ed] away the two faulty assumptions on which the [Eleventh Circuit] has relied in the past"[153] and answered a resounding "no" to both—abrogating *Nguyen*'s interpretation of the law-enforcement proviso[154] and *Denson* and *Kordash*'s creation and extension of the Supremacy Clause

---

[149] Underscoring the rights-eating challenges posed by immunity doctrines more generally, the same day we filed our petition in *Martin*, we also filed one in *Jimerson v. Lewis*. Petition for a Writ of Certiorari, Jimerson v. Lewis, 145 S. Ct. 1220 (2025) (mem.) (No. 24-473), 2024 WL 4625629; *see also* Jimerson v. Lewis, 94 F.4th 423 (5th Cir. 2024). Both cases involved wrong-house raids in which police failed to confirm an address, and both resulted in the victims being denied a remedy. The crucial difference was the officers' employment. In *Jimerson*, unlike *Martin*, the officers executing the raid were local, not federal police. So rather than file a lawsuit under the FTCA (and *Bivens*), the family had to sue police officers under Section 1983. As a result, when the Fifth Circuit held—as the Eleventh Circuit had in *Martin*—that the Fourth Amendment violation suffered by the Jimersons was not clearly established because the officer who ordered the raid had done more than "nothing," *Jimerson*, 94 F.4th at 430 (citing *Hartsfield*, 50 F.3d at 955), it was sufficient to establish "reasonable effort[s] to ascertain and identify the place intended to be searched." *Id.* at 429 (citing *Garrison*, 480 U.S. at 88). While the Supreme Court was apparently unprepared to take up a wrong-house raid case in the qualified immunity context, it was interested in the FTCA. So, while it granted certiorari in *Martin*, it denied it in *Jimerson*. *Jimerson*, 145 S. Ct. at 1220 ("Justice Sotomayor and Justice Jackson would grant the petition for writ of certiorari.").

[150] CARROLL, *supra* note 3, at chs. X, XI.

[151] *Martin*, 145 S. Ct. at 1703.

[152] *Id.* at 1697.

[153] *Id.* at 1703.

[154] *Id.* at 1697–1700.

bar.[155] The Court also called into question the continued vitality of *Shivers*—and the entirety of the Eleventh Circuit's discretionary-function jurisprudence—while acknowledging the foregoing circuit splits.[156] Altogether, *Martin* is a victory for victims of wrong-house raids by federal police that shakes awake the judiciary, returning the FTCA to the real world.

A. The Quiet End of the Supremacy Clause Bar and Law-Enforcement Proviso Supremacy

> *"The Cat's head began fading away the moment he was gone, and, by the time he had come back with the Duchess, it had entirely disappeared."*[157]

The Supreme Court swiftly dispatched the Supremacy Clause bar. While the FTCA allows the government to "assert any defense based upon judicial or legislative immunity . . . as well as any other defenses to which the United States is entitled,"[158] *Martin* declared the Eleventh Circuit's Supremacy Clause defense indefensible. The FTCA, as federal law, is itself supreme. And since the FTCA "incorporates state law, in most cases there is no conflict for the Supremacy Clause to resolve."[159] As a result, Georgia law—"the law of the place" where the raid occurred—is incorporated as federal law for purposes of the FTCA and, because it "would permit a homeowner to sue a private person for damages if that person intentionally or negligently raided his house and assaulted him," it permits such FTCA claims too.[160] The Supremacy Clause is no longer a hurdle to the Martins or anyone else living in the long shadow of *Bivens* and Collinsville.

The Supreme Court similarly junked the idea that the law-enforcement proviso overrides the discretionary-function exception. Rather than categorically permit the six listed torts of the law-enforcement proviso, regardless of any of Section 2680's exceptions, the Court determined that the proviso countermands only the

---

[155] *Id.* at 1700–02.

[156] *Id.* at 1702–03.

[157] CARROLL, *supra* note 30, at ch. VIII.

[158] *Martin*, 145 S. Ct. at 1702 (citing 28 U.S.C. § 2674).

[159] *Id.* at 1700.

[160] *Id.* (citations omitted)

intentional-tort exception.[161] Relying heavily on the proviso's placement "in the same subsection (and the same sentence) as the intentional-tort exception," Section 2680(h), the Court concluded that the proviso does not apply to the discretionary-function exception.[162] On the way, it diminished our "resort to legislative history" via discussion of the Collinsville raids because, of course: "Legislative history is not the law."[163]

B. The Quiet Beginning of a New Era for the FTCA

"A boat beneath a sunny sky, Lingering onward dreamily . . ."[164]

So "[w]here does all that leave the case" of the wrong-house raid on the Martin family?[165] With a glimpse of a way back through the looking glass.

Though it confined its holdings to the two questions above, the Supreme Court provided instructions for the Eleventh Circuit on remand, directing it to "careful[ly] reexamin[e] this case in the first instance," free from "faulty assumptions."[166] By reversing the Eleventh Circuit's broad application of the discretionary-function exception to both the Martins' negligent- and intentional-tort claims,[167] the Supreme Court also sent an unmistakable message: The exception does not automatically apply just because an officer has some room for judgment.

The Supreme Court also flagged its interest in resolving the broader confusion over the discretionary-function exception, acknowledging the existence of multiple circuit splits and noting that "important questions surround whether and under what circumstances that exception may ever foreclose a suit like this one."[168]

---

[161] *Id.* at 1697–1700.

[162] *Id.* at 1703.

[163] *Id.* at 1699–1700.

[164] CARROLL, *supra* note 3, at ch. XII.

[165] *Martin*, 145 S. Ct. at 1702.

[166] *Id.* at 1703.

[167] *Compare Martin*, 145 S. Ct. at 1703, *with Martin Appeal*, 2024 WL 1716235, at *7 (citing *Shivers*, 1 F.4th at 929, and *Mesa*, 123 F.3d at 1438).

[168] *Martin*, 145 S. Ct. at 1703 (citing, *e.g.*, *Shivers*, 1 F.4th at 931 (presumption that exception applies); *Rich*, 811 F.3d at 147 (application of exception to careless or lazy acts);

"Before addressing" these questions, however, the Court directed the Eleventh Circuit to conduct a "proper inquiry" on remand.[169]

Justice Sonia Sotomayor, joined by Justice Ketanji Brown Jackson, concurred. Going further than the majority, Justice Sotomayor explained "there is reason to think the discretionary-function exception may not apply to these claims."[170] And, she clarified, "[e]ven where a federal employee retains an element of choice, . . . the exception does not apply reflexively. After all, it is rare for statutes or regulations to prescribe an official's required course of conduct down to the very last detail, so some degree of choice will almost invariably remain."[171] Noting the uncertainty among the lower courts and the Supreme Court's three-decade silence on the matter,[172] Justice Sotomayor was plain: "[I]t is long past time for this Court to weigh in on the exception's scope."[173]

Justice Sotomayor also questioned "the Eleventh Circuit's suggestion in the decision below [and *Shivers v. United States*] that the discretionary-function exception might apply 'unless a source of federal law specifically prescribes' a federal employee's course of conduct.'"[174] And she implored the lower court on remand not to "ignore the existence of the law enforcement proviso, or the factual context that inspired its passage, when construing the discretionary function exception."[175] Of course, "any interpretation should allow for liability in the very cases Congress amended the FTCA to remedy."[176] Given the clear parallels between Collinsville and the Martin raid, the discretionary-function exception must either deny a remedy to both or neither. It is difficult to imagine Congress intended the former conclusion when it enacted the law-enforcement proviso in response to the Collinsville raids.

Xi, 68 F.4th at 839 (application of exception to unconstitutional acts); *id.* at 843 (Bibas, J., concurring) (application of exception to ministerial acts)).

[169] *Martin*, 145 S. Ct. at 1703.

[170] *Id.* at 1704 (Sotomayor, J., concurring).

[171] *Id.*

[172] *See Gaubert*, 499 U.S. at 315.

[173] *Martin*, 145 S. Ct. at 1704–05 (Sotomayor, J., concurring).

[174] *Id.* at 1705 (cleaned up, citing, *e.g.*, *Shivers*, 1 F.4th at 931).

[175] *Id.* at 1706.

[176] *Id.*

On remand, then, the Eleventh Circuit's options are limited. Having had its application of the discretionary-function exception to the Martins' negligence claims reversed,[177] it cannot simply rely on past precedent to dismiss the Martins' case again. This leaves the Eleventh Circuit with a choice: realign the discretionary-function exception with its original meaning or join other circuits in holding that careless or unconstitutional acts cannot trigger the exception. Either course should lead to a better world.

Epilogue: The Concepts of a Conclusion

> *"Which dreamed it?"* [178]

Returning to where we began: "If federal officers raid the wrong house, causing property damage and assaulting innocent occupants, may the homeowners sue the government for damages?"[179] The answer, unfortunately, remains less than obvious. But at least the answer is not, as it was before *Martin*, a definitive "no." We will see where the adventure leads the Martins next, as we return to the Eleventh Circuit. But they have already come a long way.

Beyond *Bivens*, around qualified immunity, and on the shoulders of reluctant adventurers like Trina, Gabe, and Toi, the FTCA may yet lead the people of America back to a world where federal officials looking into a mirror must face the consequences of their actions, rather than imagining a looking-glass world of immunities free from self-reflection.

> *"Your majesty shouldn't purr so loud," Alice said, rubbing her eyes, and addressing the kitten, respectfully, yet with some severity. "You woke me out of oh! such a nice dream! And you've been along with me, Kitty—all through the Looking-Glass world. Did you know it, dear?*[180]

---

[177] *Martin Appeal*, 2024 WL 1716235, at *7.

[178] CARROLL, *supra* note 4, at ch. XII.

[179] *Martin*, 145 S. Ct. at 1694.

[180] CARROLL, *supra* note 3, at ch. XII.

Free Speech Coalition v. Paxton: A Departure, But Not a Roadmap

By Vera Eidelman*

In *Free Speech Coalition v. Paxton*, the Supreme Court was tasked with determining what level of scrutiny applies to a regulation of speech that is "harmful to" (or obscene from the perspective of) minors—content that is constitutionally protected for adults but not minors—when it interferes with adults' access in the name of protecting kids. The plaintiffs argued that, as a content-based regulation of adults' protected speech, the answer had to be "strict scrutiny," both as a matter of first principles and because that is the answer the Supreme Court gave in a number of cases asking a similar, and in some cases identical, question. These cases included two early-Internet cases brought by the ACLU and many others: *Reno v. ACLU* and *Ashcroft v. ACLU*.

In *Free Speech Coalition*, however, the Supreme Court disagreed, holding that the Texas law at issue—which requires publishers of websites where at least one-third of the content is "harmful to minors" to verify the age of all visitors before granting access—is subject only to intermediate scrutiny. To reach that surprising result, the Court issued two hard-to-square holdings: first, that the First Amendment does not protect the right to access content that is "harmful to minors" *even for adults* without having to first verify their age and, second, that burdens and bans can be subject to different tiers of scrutiny.

The opinion adds to the Court's expanding list of cases reflecting motivated reasoning and outcome-driven results. But the somewhat comforting—and critical—news is that these holdings are limited to regulations of "harmful to minors" content, both by their (arguably questionable) logic and by their explicit terms. And there are a couple

* Senior staff attorney with the ACLU's Speech, Privacy, and Technology Project. The author was one of the attorneys who represented Free Speech Coalition at the Supreme Court. This article reflects the views of the author, and not necessarily the ACLU.

of other silver linings sprinkled throughout the opinion: the Court emphasizes that strict scrutiny is really, truly strict; it ultimately affirms that burdens are indeed subject to First Amendment scrutiny; and it implies that the category of content that counts as "harmful to minors" cannot be determined through the eyes of a young child.

This article proceeds in five parts. First, it offers the background necessary to understand the Court's opinion: a primer on "harmful to minors" and obscenity doctrine, a review of the Court's *Reno* and *Ashcroft* decisions, and the details of the Texas law at issue in *Free Speech Coalition*. Second, it summarizes the Court's majority opinion. Third, it highlights the holdings that undergird the opinion—and break new ground. Fourth, it emphasizes that those holdings, much as they depart from prior precedent, are unlikely to pave the way for courts to uphold additional content-based restrictions on speech, since they must be limited to regulations of "harmful to minors" materials. Finally, it identifies a few other speech-protective aspects of the opinion.

I. Background

In 2023, Texas passed HB 1181, a law that requires publishers of websites where "more than one-third of [the published material] is sexual material harmful to minors" to "verify that an individual attempting to access the material is 18 years of age or older."[1]

Before the law took effect, a group of impacted speakers—including creators and distributors of adult content, and a performer whose content is featured on several adult websites—filed suit on First Amendment grounds. Building off of early-Internet precedent that struck down federal laws that burdened adults' access to sexually-explicit speech in an effort to stop minors from accessing it, the plaintiffs argued that the age-verification requirement unconstitutionally burdens adults' access to speech that is wholly protected for them.

The district court agreed and enjoined the law, but the Fifth Circuit reversed, holding that the law should only have been subject to rational basis review. When it reached the Supreme Court, there were two questions: what is the proper level of scrutiny to apply, and does the law satisfy it?

Before turning to the Court's answers, it is useful to have background on three things: first, the doctrine governing sexual speech

[1] TEX. CIV. PRAC. & REM. CODE § 129B.002(a).

that is "harmful to minors"; second, the early-Internet cases that plaintiffs argued already answered the questions; and third, the specifics of the Texas law at issue.

A. *"Harmful to Minors" Speech*

When it comes to sexually-explicit content—and only when it comes to sexually-explicit content—the First Amendment recognizes a distinction between the rights of adults and the rights of minors.

For adults, anything that falls short of obscenity is protected speech. Though the Supreme Court struggled for years to define what qualifies as "obscenity,"[2] it landed on a definition in *Miller v. California*: Speech is obscene, and therefore not protected by the First Amendment, if it (1) "depicts or describes . . . sexual conduct specifically defined by the applicable state law" "in a patently offensive way"; (2) "the average person, applying contemporary community standards[,] would find that the work, taken as a whole, appeals to the prurient interest"; and (3) "the work, taken as a whole, lacks serious literary, artistic, political, or scientific value."[3]

The government's authority to regulate minors' access to sexual content is broader. As the Court explained in *Ginsberg v. New York*, "minors under 17 [have] a more restricted right than that assured to adults to judge and determine for themselves what sex material they may read or see."[4] Specifically, the government has the power, without violating the First Amendment, to "adjust[ ] the definition of obscenity to social realities by permitting the appeal of this type of material to be assessed in terms of the sexual interests of such minors."[5]

In *Free Speech Coalition*, the Supreme Court articulated the definition as follows, incorporating *Ginsberg*'s rule of viewing the material from the perspective of a minor into the *Miller* definition of obscenity, which post-dated *Ginsberg*: material is "harmful to minors" if "(a) taken as a

---

[2] In the Court's own words, its pre-*Miller* efforts reflected "a variety of views among the members of the Court unmatched in any other course of constitutional adjudication." Miller v. California, 413 U.S. 15, 22 (1973) (quoting Interstate Cir., Inc. v. Dallas, 390 U.S. 676, 704–05 (1968) (Harlan, J., concurring and dissenting)).

[3] *Id.* at 24.

[4] Ginsberg v. New York, 390 U.S. 629, 637 (1968). The case was a challenge to a statute that made it illegal to knowingly sell to a minor under the age of 17 any "picture . . . which depicts nudity . . . and which is harmful to minors."

[5] *Id.* at 638 (internal quotation marks omitted).

whole, and under contemporary community standards, [it] appeal[s] to the prurient interest *of minors*; (b) [it] depict[s] or describe[s] specifically defined sexual conduct in a way that is patently offensive *for minors*; and (c) taken as a whole, [it] lack[s] serious literary, artistic, political, or scientific value *for minors*."[6] Restrictions on minors' access to such speech need only satisfy rational basis review.[7]

Somewhat confusingly, the Supreme Court named this category of speech "harmful to minors"—but, critically, it refers to the very specific category of sexually-explicit content defined above, not any content the government might argue "harms" kids. Outside of this specific category of sexual content, minors are entitled to the full universe of First Amendment protections.[8] The government cannot "create a wholly new category of content-based regulation that is permissible only for speech directed at children."[9] Instead, bedrock First Amendment principles apply "[e]ven where the protection of children is the object."[10] Indeed, the Supreme Court has made clear that, generally, the fact that a speaker or listener is young is reason not for the diminution of their rights, but "for scrupulous protection of [their] Constitutional freedoms . . . if we are not to strangle the free mind at its source and teach youth to discount important principles of our government as mere platitudes."[11] Even when children are involved, "we apply the limitations of the Constitution with no fear that freedom to be intellectually and spiritually diverse or even contrary will disintegrate the social organization."[12]

---

[6] Free Speech Coal., Inc. v. Paxton, 145 S. Ct. 2291, 2304 (2025) (citing *Miller*, 413 U.S. at 24; *Ginsberg*, 390 U.S. at 635).

[7] *Ginsberg*, 390 U.S. at 639.

[8] *See, e.g.*, Brown v. Ent. Merchs. Ass'n, 564 U.S. 786, 793–94 (2011) (rejecting government's argument that it can regulate violent speech communicated to minors just as it can sexual speech, because "speech about violence is not obscene" and *Ginsberg* only "approved a prohibition on the sale to minors of *sexual* material that would be obscene from the perspective of a child").

[9] *Id.* at 794.

[10] *Id.* at 804–05 (invalidating regulation of violent video games for minors). *See also, e.g.*, Erznoznik v. City of Jacksonville, 422 U.S. 205, 212–13 (1975) (invalidating restriction on drive-in movies designed to protect children from nudity); Reno v. ACLU, 521 U.S. 844, 874 (1997) (invalidating statute prohibiting indecent communications available to minors online).

[11] W. Va. State Bd. of Educ. v. Barnette, 319 U.S. 624, 637 (1943).

[12] *Id.* at 641.

B. Reno and Ashcroft

What makes this distinction between minors' and adults' rights to access sexual content critical in *Free Speech Coalition v. Paxton* is that one law can, in (purportedly or actually) seeking to prevent *minors'* access to such speech, also hinder *adults'* access to it—and that is what the Texas law at issue in the case does. It forces adults to verify their ages by providing documentation that exposes their identities and can make them vulnerable to privacy and security harms, including by creating a record of the sexual content they consume.

The Supreme Court previously dealt with this complexity in *Reno v. ACLU*[13] and *Ashcroft v. ACLU*,[14] both of which applied strict scrutiny to federal laws that sought to protect children from sexually-explicit speech published online because of the impact the laws had on adults' speech.[15] Background on these opinions is critical to understanding some of the doctrinal moves the Court makes in *Free Speech Coalition* since the Court was not writing on a blank slate.

i. Reno v. ACLU and the CDA

In *Reno*, the Supreme Court considered two provisions of the Communications Decency Act of 1996 (CDA), which Congress enacted to protect kids from sexual content sent or displayed over the Internet—then a sufficiently new medium that the Supreme Court devoted more than four pages of its opinion to explaining what it is—without first verifying recipients' or viewers' ages.[16] The first provision, the "indecent transmission provision," made it a crime to knowingly transmit "obscene or indecent" content to anyone under the age of 18.[17] The second, the "patently offensive display provision," made

---

[13] 521 U.S. 844 (1997).

[14] 542 U.S. 656 (2004).

[15] Though the legislative action has currently shifted to the states, historically, the federal government was more focused on such regulation.

[16] *See Reno*, 521 U.S. at 849–53 (explaining that the "[i]nternet is an international network of interconnected computers" and describing how "electronic mail (e-mail), automatic mailing list services ('mail exploders,' sometimes referred to as 'listservs'), 'newsgroups,' 'chat rooms,' and the 'World Wide Web' . . . constitute a unique medium—known to its users as 'cyberspace'"). The case also proved to be seminal in recognizing "the vast democratic forums of the Internet" and establishing that there is "no basis for qualifying the level of First Amendment scrutiny that should be applied to [the Internet]." *Id.* at 868–70.

[17] *Id.* at 859 (quoting 47 U.S.C. § 223(a)).

it a crime to knowingly send or display depictions or descriptions of "sexual or excretory activities or organs" "in terms patently offensive as measured by contemporary community standards" such that the depictions or descriptions were available to anyone under the age of 18.[18] For both provisions, "restrict[ing] access to covered material by requiring certain designated forms of age proof, such as a verified credit card or an adult identification number or code" constituted an affirmative defense.[19] Thus, the law made it illegal to transmit or display obscene, indecent, or patently offensive content to people online without first verifying their ages.

Twenty organizations, including the ACLU, sued as soon as the provisions were signed into law, and a second lawsuit by nearly 30 additional plaintiffs followed. After the plaintiffs obtained preliminary relief in the lower court, the government appealed to the Supreme Court.

The plaintiffs primarily focused on the burdens the law—framed as a protection for children—imposed on adults, and argued that it was unconstitutional both as a complete prohibition on protected speech among adults and as a content-based regulation of adults' protected speech.[20] In defending the statute, the federal government relied heavily on *Ginsberg*, arguing that it "establish[ed] that there is no First Amendment right to disseminate indecent material to children."[21]

The Supreme Court agreed with the plaintiffs and subjected the law to strict scrutiny, and specifically rejected the government's invitation to apply *Ginsberg*, for four reasons: First, while the law at issue in *Ginsberg*, which prohibited sales to minors, allowed parents to buy the banned materials for their kids, the CDA offered no such option.[22] Second, the law in *Ginsberg* only applied to commercial transactions.[23] Third, the *Ginsberg* statute reached only speech that was "utterly without redeeming social importance for minors,"

[18] *Id.* at 859–60 (quoting 47 U.S.C. § 223(d)).

[19] *Id.* at 860–61 (quoting 47 U.S.C. § 223(e)(5)(B)).

[20] *See* Brief of Appellees, *Reno v. ACLU*, 521 U.S. 844 (1997) (No. 96-511), 1997 WL 74378, at *21–24 (arguing that the CDA is unconstitutional because it "operates as a criminal ban on constitutionally protected speech among adults").

[21] Reply Brief of Appellants, *Reno v. ACLU*, 521 U.S. 844 (1997) (No. 96-511), 1997 WL 106544, at *2.

[22] *Reno*, 521 U.S. at 865.

[23] *Id.*

while the CDA neither offered any limiting definition of "indecent" nor cabined the ban on "patently offensive" materials to those that "lack serious literary, artistic, political, or scientific value."[24] Finally, the *Ginsberg* statute "defined a minor as a person under the age of 17, whereas the CDA, in applying to all those under 18 years, include[d] an additional year of those nearest majority."[25]

Thus, *Ginsberg*, the Court concluded, "surely do[es] not require us to uphold the CDA and [is] fully consistent with the application of the most stringent review of its provisions."[26] Instead, the Supreme Court emphasized courts' obligation to review such laws with rigor: "the mere fact that a statutory regulation of speech was enacted for the important purpose of protecting children from exposure to sexually explicit material does not foreclose inquiry into its validity."[27]

The Court struck down the two CDA provisions because they "effectively suppress[ ] a large amount of speech that adults have a constitutional right to receive and to address to one another . . . [i]n order to deny minors access to potentially harmful speech."[28] Citing to *Ginsberg*, the Court agreed that it has "repeatedly recognized the governmental interest in protecting children from harmful materials," but, it explained, "that interest does not justify an unnecessarily broad suppression of speech addressed to adults."[29] "[R]egardless of the strength of the government's interest" in protecting children, "[t]he level of discourse reaching a mailbox"—or inbox, or computer screen—"simply cannot be limited to that which would be suitable for a sandbox."[30]

With respect to the affirmative age-verification defense specifically, the Court held that it failed the tailoring requirement of strict scrutiny because (1) "it is not economically feasible for most noncommercial speakers to employ such verification"; (2) the government "failed to prove that the proffered defense would significantly reduce the heavy burden on adult speech produced by the prohibition

---

[24] *Id.* (quoting *Ginsberg*, 390 U.S. at 646).

[25] *Id.* at 865–66.

[26] *Id.* at 868.

[27] *Id.* at 875.

[28] *Id.* at 874.

[29] *Id.* at 875 (citing *Ginsberg*, 390 U.S. at 639).

[30] *Id.* (quoting Bolger v. Youngs Drug Prods. Corp., 463 U.S. 60, 74–75 (1983)).

on offensive displays"; and (3) "the Government failed to adduce any evidence that these verification techniques actually preclude minors from posing as adults." In other words, it was both too onerous and too ineffective to pass muster.[31]

The upshot? Content-based regulations of sexually-explicit speech are subject to strict scrutiny even if the goal is to prevent minors' access so long as the restriction impedes adults' access. And they fail strict scrutiny if less restrictive alternatives are available to accomplish the government's goal.

ii. Ashcroft v. ACLU and COPA

After *Reno*, Congress again tried its hand at protecting minors from sexually-explicit materials online, this time in the form of the Child Online Protection Act (COPA), which "impose[d] criminal penalties . . . for the knowing posting, for 'commercial purposes,' of World Wide Web content that is 'harmful to minors.'"[32] COPA reflected some lessons learned from *Reno*.[33] In contrast to the CDA's prohibitions on indecent and patently offensive content, COPA's prohibition was limited to "harmful to minors" content; it defined "minors" as "any person under 17 [rather than 18] years of age"; and it regulated only posts made for "commercial purposes."[34] As with the CDA, Congress again included a website operator's attempts to verify the age of viewers as an affirmative defense.[35] Thus, the law made it illegal to make available "harmful to minors" content without first verifying the age of the viewer.

The Supreme Court—in an opinion joined by Justice Clarence Thomas, who went on to author *Free Speech Coalition v. Paxton*—held that the law was subject to strict scrutiny because it was "a content-based speech restriction," and found the government's efforts

[31] *Id.* at 881–82.

[32] *Ashcroft*, 542 U.S. at 661 (quoting 47 U.S.C. § 231(a)(1)).

[33] *Id.* at 660 ("In enacting COPA, Congress gave consideration to [the Supreme Court's] earlier decisions on the subject, in particular in the decision *Reno v. ACLU*.").

[34] *Id.* at 661–62 (explaining that "[h]armful to minors" was defined using the *Ginsberg-Miller* standard).

[35] *Id.* at 662 (quoting 47 U.S.C. § 231(c)(1)) (listing three options for age verification: "requiring use of a credit card, debit account, adult access code, or adult personal identification number"; "accepting a digital certificate that verifies age"; or "any other reasonable measures that are feasible under available technology").

lacking under the standard because there were plausible, less restrictive alternatives available to accomplish its goals.[36]

In particular, the Court struck down COPA because "[f]ilters are less restrictive" and "may well be more effective" than COPA. Filters "impose selective restrictions on speech at the receiving end, not universal restrictions at the source,"[37] and they "can prevent minors from seeing all pornography," regardless of where it originates from, "not just pornography posted . . . from America," and not just communications available via the World Wide Web."[38]

Though the government argued that Congress could not mandate the use of filters and so they were not a true alternative, the Court held that "[t]hat argument carries little weight, because Congress undoubtedly may act to encourage the use of filters," whether by "giv[ing] strong incentives to schools and libraries to use them" or "tak[ing] steps to promote their development by industry, and their use by parents."[39] And such encouragement has the added benefit of "not condemn[ing] as criminal any category of speech," such that "the potential chilling effect is eliminated, or at least much diminished."[40]

The Court also highlighted ways in which the promotion of filters would be more tailored and more effective than COPA's age-verification scheme. With filters, the Court explained, adults "may gain access to speech they have a right to see without having to identify themselves or provide their credit card information. Even adults with children may obtain access to the same speech on the same terms simply by turning off the filter on their home computers."[41] Meanwhile, "verification systems may be subject to evasion and circumvention, for example, by minors who have their own credit cards."[42] Again, age verification was both more onerous and less effective than other options.

---

[36] *Id.* at 665.

[37] *Id.* at 667.

[38] *Id.* at 667–68.

[39] *Id.* at 669.

[40] *Id.* at 667.

[41] *Id.*

[42] *Id.* at 668.

"All of these things," the Court explained, "are true . . . regardless of how broadly or narrowly the definitions in COPA are construed," highlighting that its analysis and its holding were not altered by the fact that, unlike the CDA, COPA was limited to "harmful to minors" content.[43]

The upshot? Much like the CDA, a law prohibiting the display of "harmful to minors" content without first verifying a viewer's age is subject to—and fails—strict scrutiny.

C. Texas' HB 1181

Nearly 20 years after *Ashcroft*, legislators—this time at the state, not federal, level—again began enacting laws targeting the distribution of sexually-explicit content to minors online. Texas's HB 1181 is just one of at least 25 such laws now on the books in states around the country.[44]

HB 1181 imposes an age-verification obligation on any "commercial entity that knowingly and intentionally publishes or distributes material on an Internet website, . . . more than one-third of which is sexual material harmful to minors."[45] It defines "sexual material harmful to minors" as "material that: (1) 'is designed to appeal to or pander to the prurient interest' when taken 'as a whole and with respect to minors'; (2) describes, displays, or depicts 'in a manner patently offensive with respect to minors' various sex acts and portions of the human anatomy, including depictions of 'sexual intercourse, masturbation, sodomy, bestiality, oral copulation, flagellation, [and] excretory functions'; and (3) 'lacks serious literary, artistic, political, or scientific value for minors.'"[46] And the age-verification options it offers are: "'a commercial age verification system' that uses 'government-issued identification' or 'a commercially reasonable method that relies on public or private transactional data,'" performed either by the commercial entity itself or through a third-party service.[47]

---

[43] *Id.* at 667.

[44] *State Age Verification Laws*, FREE SPEECH COAL. ACTION CTR. (2025), https://action.freespeechcoalition.com/age-verification-resources/state-avs-laws/.

[45] *Free Speech Coal.*, 145 S. Ct. at 2300 (quoting TEX. CIV. PRAC. & REM. CODE § 129B.002(a)).

[46] *Id.* (quoting TEX. CIV. PRAC. & REM. CODE § 129B.001(6)).

[47] *Id.* (quoting TEX. CIV. PRAC. & REM. CODE § 129B.003(b)).

The prohibition is not criminal, but it comes with stiff civil penalties. The state attorney general can sue to enjoin knowing violations and recover up to $10,000 per day that a website is noncompliant, as well as an additional penalty of up to $250,000 if any minors access "harmful" sexual material as a result of the violation.[48]

The law also requires covered sites to prominently publish "sexual materials health warnings" written by the government, including the statement that "[p]ornography is potentially biologically addictive, is proven to harm human brain development, desensitizes brain reward circuits, increases conditioned responses, and weakens brain function."[49]

II. The Supreme Court Opinion

Before the Supreme Court,[50] the artists and publishers who challenged HB 1181 argued that the law must be subject to strict scrutiny because it imposes a content-based burden on adult speech.[51] The federal government also filed a brief arguing that strict scrutiny applies,[52] while the state maintained that the law is subject to rational basis scrutiny because of the state's authority to restrict minors' access to "harmful to minors" content.[53] The state also offered intermediate scrutiny as a last-ditch alternative.[54]

The Supreme Court concluded that "neither party has it right" and, purporting to "[a]pply[ ] our precedents," held that "intermediate scrutiny applies"—not for the reasons the state offered, but because, in the Court's telling, HB 1181 is a regulation of unprotected speech or conduct (anyone accessing speech that is obscene for minors without first submitting proof of age) with only an incidental effect on protected speech (adults accessing speech that is obscene only for minors).[55]

---

[48] *Id.* (citing Tex. Civ. Prac. & Rem. Code § 129B.006(a), (b)).

[49] Tex. Civ. Prac. & Rem. Code § 129B.004(1).

[50] The ACLU joined the plaintiffs' counsel team at the petition for certiorari stage.

[51] Brief for Petitioners, *Free Speech Coal., Inc. v. Paxton*, 145 S. Ct. 2291 (2025) (No. 23-1122), 2024 WL 4241180, at *24–27.

[52] Brief for the United States as Amicus Curiae Supporting Vacatur, *Free Speech Coal., Inc. v. Paxton*, 145 S. Ct. 2291 (2025) (No. 23-1122), 2024 WL 4336505, at *16–19.

[53] Brief for Respondent, *Free Speech Coal., Inc. v. Paxton*, 145 S. Ct. 2291 (2025) (No. 23-1122), 2024 WL 5399127, at *17–22.

[54] *Id.* at *31–35 ("At most, intermediate scrutiny applies.").

[55] *Free Speech Coal.*, 145 S. Ct. at 2306.

The law "is an exercise of Texas's traditional power to prevent minors from accessing speech that is obscene from their perspective. To the extent that it burdens adults' rights to access such speech, it has only an incidental effect on protected speech, making it subject to intermediate scrutiny."[56]

The Court also rejected Plaintiffs' argument that "regardless of first principles, [the Court's] precedents," including *Reno* and *Ashcroft*, "require [the Court] to apply strict scrutiny" because those cases addressed "outright bans" on adult speech, not mere burdens.[57] And finally, the Court held that HB 1181 "readily satisfies" intermediate scrutiny.[58]

III. The Opinion Breaks New Ground . . .

To reach its ultimate holding—and bypass clearly controlling precedent on the way—the majority opinion appears to break new ground in two ways.

First, it reads a burden on speech—the very thing that typically necessitates First Amendment scrutiny—*out of* the underlying First Amendment right. The Court holds that "no person—adult or child—has a First Amendment right to access speech that is obscene to minors without first submitting proof of age."[59] Put slightly differently, "speech that is obscene to minors" is "unprotected"—not only for minors, but period—"to the extent the State seeks only to verify age."[60]

The decision appears to be outcome driven[61]—if the rights of minors and adults to access sexual content are different, of course a law requiring an age-check before allowing a specific person to access such material has to be okay—and its reasoning suffers as a result.

---

[56] *Id.*

[57] *Id.* at 2311–13.

[58] *Id.* at 2317.

[59] *Id.* at 2306.

[60] *Id.* at 2309.

[61] *See, e.g., id.* at 2309 (explaining that strict scrutiny does not apply in part because "[a]pplying the more demanding strict-scrutiny standard would call into question the validity of *all* age-verification requirements"); *id.* at 2310 ("Strict scrutiny therefore cannot apply to laws, such as in-person age-verification requirements, which are traditional, widespread, and not thought to raise a significant First Amendment issue."); *id.* at 2311 ("The only principled way to give due consideration to both the First Amendment and States' legitimate interests in protecting minors is to employ a less exacting standard.").

What is the reasoning exactly? That the government has a "traditional power to prevent minors from accessing speech that is obscene from their perspective"—and that "[t]hat power necessarily includes the power to require proof of age before an individual can access such speech."[62] If the government can prohibit minors from accessing content that's obscene for them, the logic goes, the government must be able to figure out who is a minor in the first place. "Only an age-verification requirement can ensure compliance with an age-based restriction" because liability could otherwise be avoided simply "by asserting ignorance as to the purchaser's age."[63]

Even if that may have some intuitive appeal, the other necessary aspect of this holding decidedly does not: "Because HB 1181 simply requires proof of age to access content that is obscene to minors, it does not directly regulate the protected speech of adults."[64] In other words, per the Court's opinion, the burdens online age verification imposes on speech through exposing adults to privacy and security risks and robbing them of anonymity—is simply not part of what the First Amendment protects against.[65] Instead, "the right of adults to view the speech has the burden of age verification built right in."[66]

Second, because the Court had to contend with *Reno* and *Ashcroft*, the opinion pretends that First Amendment doctrine treats bans and burdens differently. It disclaims the relevance of *Reno* because the CDA "operated as a ban on speech to adults" and "effectively *suppresse[d]* a large amount of speech that adults have a constitutional right to receive[.]"[67] And the opinion gives *Ashcroft* the same treatment because that opinion "likewise characterized COPA as a ban."[68] "This kind of ban," the Court writes, "is categorically different from HB 1181's age-verification requirement."[69] This holding is wholly

---

[62] *Id.* at 2306. *See also id.* at 2299 ("The power to require age verification is within a State's authority to prevent children from accessing sexually explicit content.").

[63] *Id.* at 2308.

[64] *Id.* at 2309.

[65] *See id.* at 2327 (Kagan, J., dissenting) ("The majority [employs] . . . a maneuver found nowhere in the world of First Amendment doctrine. It turns out, the majority says, that the First Amendment only 'partially protects' the speech in question: . . . the speech is unprotected to the extent that the State is imposing the very burden under review. That is convenient, if altogether circular.").

[66] *Id.*

[67] *Id.* at 2312 (majority opinion) (quoting *Reno*, 521 U.S. at 874).

[68] *Id.* (quoting *Ashcroft*, 542 U.S. at 665).

[69] *Id.*

inconsistent with precedent—including, as the dissent pointed out, *Playboy* in particular, which the *Free Speech Coalition* majority characterizes as a ban even though it was, by the *Playboy* Court's own account, not a "complete prohibition" but rather a "content-based burden."[70]

Both of these results are surprising and disturbing—but, as described in the next section, they should not apply to anything but regulations of "harmful to minors" content.

Moreover, they are also conclusions that the rest of the opinion itself appears to resist, as shown by the fact that the Court ultimately applies intermediate, rather than rational-basis, scrutiny to the age-verification law at issue. Even though adults apparently "have no First Amendment right to avoid age verification," and even though the First Amendment apparently treats burdens and bans differently, HB 1181 does not entirely "escape[ ] all First Amendment scrutiny" because "[a]dults have the right to access speech that is obscene only to minors" and "submitting to age verification is a burden on the exercise of that right."[71] Thus, an adult having to undergo age verification and face the attendant burdens *does* get First Amendment protection.[72] It is hard to square the Court's logic on this—if "accessing material obscene to minors *without verifying one's* age is not constitutionally protected,"[73] how does having to verify one's age trigger any First Amendment scrutiny at all?[74] But, given that age verification chills and restricts speech, there is some comfort in knowing that even the majority could not actually ignore that reality, whatever circuitous path it took to recognize it.

IV. . . . But the Opinion's Reach Is Small

Troubling as these doctrinal moves are, they are ultimately very limited in their reach: by their own terms, they cannot apply beyond laws that target minors' access to "harmful to minors" speech.

[70] United States v. Playboy Entm't Grp., Inc., 529 U.S. 803, 812 (2000).

[71] *Id.* at 2309.

[72] *Id.*

[73] *Id.*

[74] *See id.* at 2325–26 (Kagan, J., dissenting) ("The more puzzling question is how the majority's reasoning fits with the idea that the First Amendment plays any role at all. . . . If the First Amendment does not protect adults in viewing obscene-for-children materials unimpeded by age verification, as the majority argues, then how could there be any constitutional objection to age verification laws like H. B. 1181?").

The first troubling holding—that there simply is no right for adults to access speech that they have the right to receive and access without first having to verify their age—is premised on the idea that, where rights differ by age, the government must have the power to verify age without violating a constitutional right.[75] Because sexually-explicit content is the only category of speech for which minors' and adults' rights differ,[76] it is also the only category of speech to which this logic can apply.

And the opinion explicitly limits the second troubling holding—that the First Amendment may ignore a burden where it would prohibit a ban—to this context in a footnote. In responding to the dissent's (correct) criticism that this is simply wrong as a matter of existing doctrine,[77] the Court concedes that "a burden on obscenity to minors may not trigger strict scrutiny even if a comparable burden on indecent speech would."[78]

Of course, that doesn't make the result any less outcome-driven or any more principled—though it is consistent with the Supreme Court's general treatment of sexual content as a pariah in American law.[79] What it does do, however, is significantly narrow the holdings, making this a quite limited opinion. The rules it establishes only work for "harmful to minors" content—the only category of speech for which adults' and minors' First Amendment rights differ.[80]

Indeed, the opinion leaves the door open to as-applied challenges even to such laws, further highlighting the narrowness of its holdings. One area of dispute between the parties was what role HB 1181's

---

[75] *See supra* Section III.

[76] *See supra* Section I.A.

[77] *See Free Speech Coal.*, 145 S. Ct. at 2329 (Kagan, J., dissenting) ("In *Playboy*, the law did not ban adult cable channels, but instead limited their transmission to hours when children were unlikely to be in the audience.").

[78] *Free Speech Coal*, 145 S. Ct. at 2311 n.9 (majority op.).

[79] *See, e.g.*, Geoffrey R. Stone, *Sex, Violence, and the First Amendment*, 74 U. Chi. L. Rev. 1857, 1863 (2007) (grappling "with the question: why is obscenity of only low First Amendment value?" including as compared to speech about or imagery of violence); Blanca L. Hernández, *The Prurient Investment: How First Amendment Speech Jurisprudence Obstructs the Movement for LGBT Equality*, 22 S. Cal. Rev. L. & Soc. Just. 377, 377–78 (2013) (discussing the ways in which the Supreme Court has "discriminately and unjustifiably afford[ed] sexually related speech minimal constitutional protection," including "the regulation of obscenity, adult entertainment venues, and pornography").

[80] *See supra* Section I.A.

one-third requirement played: did the fact that the law regulates a website where a mere one-third of the content qualifies as "harmful to minors" mean that it is insufficiently tailored (the Plaintiffs's view) or could the law be read to allow a website to segregate its "harmful to minors" material from the rest of its content and only subject the former to the law's requirements (at times, the Defendant's view)? The Court declined to "resolve that question" because it concluded it was not necessary for the facial analysis it was undertaking—but it allowed for the possibility that "the statute requires covered websites to demand age verification for *all* their content" and that "such a requirement would be unconstitutional."[81] It suggested that a site faced with this dilemma could bring a First Amendment challenge. That alone emphasizes how narrow the opinion is: the Court's analysis does not even necessarily govern every regulation of "harmful to minors" speech.

V. Some Additional Silver Linings

Along with the strange but limited holdings, the opinion includes a few additional speech-protective pieces: it emphasizes that when the Court says *strict* scrutiny, that's what it means; as alluded to above, it recognizes that burdens *are* subject to First Amendment scrutiny even as it tries to pretend that some aren't; and it suggests that "harmful to minors" is itself a category that has some teeth, and isn't simply any content that is too sexual and lacking in value for a toddler.

With respect to strict scrutiny, the Court writes that the requirement that "a restriction be the least restrictive means of achieving a compelling governmental interest[ ] is 'the most demanding test known to constitutional law.'"[82] And it bolsters the oft-stated claim that such scrutiny is strict in theory, but fatal in fact, asserting that "[i]n the First Amendment context, we have held only once that a law triggered but satisfied strict scrutiny[.]"[83] Whether those assertions are right or wrong,[84] they will certainly be cited by many litigants

[81] *Free Speech Coal*, 145 S. Ct. at 2308 n.7.

[82] *Id.* at 2310 (quoting City of Boerne v. Flores, 521 U.S. 507, 534 (1997)).

[83] *Id.* (citing Holder v. Humanitarian L. Project, 561 U.S. 1 (2010)).

[84] For example, one might argue that the standard applicable to prior restraints is even more rigorous than strict scrutiny. *See, e.g.*, Smith v. Daily Mail Publ'g Co., 443 U.S. 97, 102 (1979); Landmark Commc'ns, Inc. v. Virginia, 435 U.S. 829, 845 (1978).

challenging content-based laws on First Amendment grounds going forward.

In addition, much as the Court's suggestion that burdens and bans can be subject to different tiers of scrutiny even in the limited "harmful to minors" context is troubling, its necessary walking back of that suggestion even in this context will make it exceedingly difficult to extend to regulations of any other kind of speech. As noted above, even the majority could not fully stomach the suggestion that the burden at issue in this case does not trigger First Amendment review—notwithstanding the centrality of that conclusion to the opinion's entire purported logic.[85] No lower court should accept the proposition that burdens are okay even when bans aren't either.

As for what qualifies as "harmful to minors" under the *Ginsberg-Miller* test, the Court suggested that it should not "be read to cover, say, a PG-13 or R-rated movie" and "question[ed] whether it is coherent to speak of the 'prurient interest' of a very young child with no concept of sexuality," meaning that any reading of a regulation of such speech "may well call for assessing obscenity from the perspective of an adolescent."[86] Though the opinion couched these limitations as specific to the language of HB 1181, the particular aspects of the statute to which it tethered the conclusions—first, that "the statute only covers *explicit portrayals of nudity or sex acts*" and second that those must "predominantly appeal to the prurient interest"[87]—are in fact required or any constitutional definition of "harmful to minors" content,[88] and should therefore appear in any regulation that passes constitutional muster.[89]

---

[85] *See supra* Section III.

[86] *Free Speech Coal*, 145 S. Ct. at 2308 n.7.

[87] *Id.*

[88] *See supra* Section I.A.

[89] Of course, other courts have gone further, holding that such statutes must be read to require viewing the material not simply from the perspective of an adolescent, but through older minors' (i.e., a seventeen-year-old's) eyes. *See, e.g.*, Am. Booksellers Ass'n, Inc., 882 F.2d 125 (4th Cir. 1989); Commonwealth v. Am. Booksellers Ass'n, Inc., 372 S.E.2d 618 (Va. 1988); Am. Booksellers v. Webb, 919 F.2d 1493 (11th Cir. 1990); Davis-Kidd Booksellers, Inc. v. McWherter, 866 S.W.2d 520 (Tenn. 1993). *See also* Brief of Am. Booksellers for Free Expression, et al. as Amici Curiae in Support of Petitioners, *Free Speech Coal., Inc. v. Paxton*, 145 S. Ct. 2291 (2025) (No. 23-1122), 2024 WL 4388485, at *6. This opinion does not close the door to such a requirement.

So what does this all mean going forward? Ultimately, it shouldn't mean all that much. Prohibitions on adult access to harmful-to-minors speech are still subject to strict scrutiny. The same is true for burdens on other categories of speech, even if they are enacted in the name of protecting children. When it comes to harmful-to-minors speech, some avenues remain open for future challenges—and the harmful-to-minors category of speech is itself narrower than some speakers may otherwise have assumed. The opinion is disappointing, but it should not be the end of the Internet as we know it.

Mahmoud v. Taylor

*Cynthia Crawford**

Introduction

Mahmoud v. Taylor breathed new life into constitutional protections for parents who want to withdraw their children from public school instruction that infringes their religious exercise. Relying on *Wisconsin v. Yoder*[1] and *West Virginia Board of Education v. Barnette*,[2] the Court held that the Free Exercise Clause and the rights of parents to direct the religious upbringing of their children required granting the parents' request that their grade school children be excused from instruction regarding newly introduced books comprising LGBTQ+ issues or characters while litigation is pending. *Mahmoud* held that the interest recognized in *Yoder* is an exception to the rule from *Employment Division, Department of Human Resources of Oregon v. Smith*.[3] *Smith* held that government is generally free to place incidental burdens on religious exercise so long as it does so pursuant to a "neutral policy that is generally applicable" and provides protection for parents' right to direct the religious instruction of their children.

The clarification of the relationship between *Yoder* and *Smith* may open the door to resolving conflicts between state efforts to impose or restrict the availability of otherwise generally available publicly funded education for parents who have religiously motivated constraints on the type of instruction they seek for their children.

* Senior policy counsel, Americans for Prosperity Foundation.

[1] 406 U.S. 205, 221, 236 (1972).

[2] 319 U.S. 624 (1943).

[3] 494 U.S. 872, 878–79 (1990).

I. Background

A. The Question Presented

"Do public schools burden parents' religious exercise when they compel elementary school children to participate in instruction on gender and sexuality against their parents' religious convictions and without notice or opportunity to opt out?"

B. The Positions of the Parties

The plaintiff parents framed *Mahmoud* as a Free Exercise case in which denying parents the ability to remove their children from public school instruction that promoted viewpoints offensive to the parents' religious beliefs imposed an unconstitutional burden on their Free Exercise rights.[4] Accordingly, they argued that when a public school implements a course of study or materials that burden parents' sincerely held religious beliefs, parents must be given notice and the opportunity to opt out of such instruction for their children.[5] This argument relies on *Wisconsin v. Yoder*, which held that the state's interest in its school system was inadequate to override parents' rights to educate their children in accordance with their religious beliefs.

The government, by contrast, argued that coercion was the proper standard—although it actually argued for a coercion-plus-effectiveness standard, in which the Free Exercise Clause would not be violated unless the children were required to participate in the lessons and the mandated participation was effective in changing their religious views or behavior.[6] In support, the government relied largely on precedent relating to parental challenges to curriculum, in which the remedy sought was a change to the curriculum and not, like *Yoder*, the ability to withdraw children without penalty.

C. The Facts

For the 2022–2023 school year, as part of its "commitment to providing a culturally responsive curriculum that promotes equity,

---

[4] Brief for Petitioners at 24, Mahmoud v. Taylor, No. 24-297 (U.S. 2025).

[5] *Id.*

[6] Brief in Opposition at 12, Mahmoud v. Taylor, No. 24-297 (U.S. 2025).

respect, and civility,"[7] Montgomery County Public Schools (MCPS) introduced into its pre-kindergarten through 12th grade language arts curriculum storybooks that feature lesbian, gay, bisexual, transgender, and queer characters.[8] At the time the curriculum was implemented, parents were told they would be notified when the storybooks were used, allowed to opt-out their children from the material, and provided a substitute text by the teacher.[9] That process was confirmed by the Montgomery County Board of Education (Board) in a press statement in March 2023.[10] The process was reversed, however, for the 2023–2024 school year.[11] The basis for the reversal was the large number of requests to opt-out from lessons involving those storybooks,[12] which "gave rise to three related concerns: high student absenteeism, the infeasibility of administering opt-outs across classrooms and schools, and the risk of exposing students who believe the storybooks represent them and their families to social stigma and isolation."[13] Thus, the unpopularity of the program led to reversal of the ability to opt-out, notwithstanding the opt-out's consistency with the Board's "Guidelines for Respecting Religious Diversity."[14] Opt-outs remained available for the sex education unit of state-mandated health classes as well as any other instruction that violated the parents' religious beliefs.[15]

The conflict in viewpoint regarding the new storybooks is not surprising given the multiplicity of backgrounds represented within the MCPS. Montgomery County, Maryland, is the state's most populous county and the "most religiously diverse county" in the nation.[16] It is

[7] *Id.* at 4.

[8] *Id.*

[9] Brief for Petitioners, *supra* note 4, at 1, 14.

[10] *Id.*

[11] *Id.*

[12] *Id.* at 6–7.

[13] Petitioners' App. at 96a–99a, 606a-608a, Mahmoud v. Taylor, No. 24-297 (U.S. 2025).

[14] Mahmoud v. Taylor, No. 24-297, slip op. at 14 (U.S. June 27, 2025).

[15] Brief for Petitioners, *supra* note 4, at 1, 15.

[16] *Mahmoud*, slip op. at 2 (citing Aleja Hertzler-McCain, *Montgomery County, Maryland, Was Most Religiously Diverse US County in 2023*, Relig. News Serv. (Aug. 30, 2024), https://religionnews.com/2024/08/30/montgomery-county-maryland-was-most-religiously-diverse-u-s-county-in-2023/).

home to a mix of Christian denominations and ranks in the top five in the nation in per-capita population of Jews, Muslims, Hindus, and Buddhists, as well as having one of the largest Ethiopian communities in the country.[17] Maryland law requires resident children ages 5 to 18 to attend a public school, private school, or home school.[18] Parents who fail to ensure their children attend can be fined, required to perform community service, or imprisoned.[19]

Maryland statutory law recognizes and provides for parents to opt-out their children from instruction in human sexuality; it places the burden on the school system to facilitate opt-outs and provide "appropriate alternative learning activities and/or assessments in health education" and the "opportunity for parents/guardians to view instructional materials to be used in the teaching of family life and human sexuality objectives."[20] This practice is consistent with 37 other states, as well as 4 states that require a parental opt-in before children receive such instruction and 6 states that have a combination of opt-in and opt-out rights.[21] It is also not unusual for public schools to require an additional degree of consent from parents to deviate from expected practices. Montgomery County, for example, requires express authority from parents before children may be taken to other locations outside the typical school premises by

---

[17] *Id.* (citing PUB. RELIG. RSCH. INST., 2023 PRRI CENSUS OF AMERICAN RELIGION: COUNTY-LEVEL DATA ON RELIGIOUS IDENTITY AND DIVERSITY 19, 28, 42–49 (Aug. 29, 2024); Rosanne Skirble, *Silver Spring Is the Epicenter of a Thriving Ethiopian Diaspora*, MONTGOMERY MAG. (Oct. 19, 2022), https://www.montgomerymag.com/silver-spring-is-the-epicenter-of-a-thriving-ethiopian-diaspora/).

[18] *Id.* at 2–3 (citing MD. CODE ANN., EDUC. § 7-301(a-1)(1) (2025); § 7-301(a)(3)).

[19] *Id.*; MD. CODE ANN. EDUC. § 7-301(e).

[20] MD. CODE REGS. 13A.04.18.01(e) ("Student Opt-Out: (i) The local school system shall establish policies, guidelines, and/or procedures for student opt-out regarding instruction related to family life and human sexuality objectives; (ii) For students opting out of family life and human sexuality instruction, each school shall establish a procedure for providing a student with appropriate alternative learning activities and/or assessments in health education; (iii) Each school shall make arrangements to permit students opting out of the objectives related to family life and human sexuality to receive instruction concerning menstruation; (iv) The local school system shall provide an opportunity for parents/guardians to view instructional materials to be used in the teaching of family life and human sexuality objectives.").

[21] Brief for Petitioners, *supra* note 4, at 6–7, 6 n.3 (collecting citations to state codes).

school personnel, including for field trips,[22] and before medication may be administered to a child.[23] There are thus multiple circumstances in which express parental authority is required and honored.

In response to the Board's reversal of the ability to opt-out, more than 1,100 parents signed a petition asking the Board to restore notice and opt-out rights.[24] Hundreds of people, "largely . . . Muslim and Ethiopian Orthodox parents" claimed that the schools were violating their First Amendment religious rights.[25] Some members of the Board responded by accusing the parents of "hate" and comparing them to "white supremacists" and "xenophobes."[26] The manner in which the books were to be used and the guidance provided by MCPS to teachers on how to use the storybooks in the classroom were subject to conflicting interpretations. On the one hand, proposed responses to student questions focused on "tolerance, empathy, and respect for different views."[27] On the other hand, guidance directed teachers to "disrupt the either/or thinking of students" and to characterize disagreement with nonbinary gender views as "hurtful."[28]

---

[22] Off. Sch. Support & Improvement, *Parent/Guardian Approval for Trips MCPS Transportation Is Provided*, MONTGOMERY CNTY. PUB. SCHS. (July 2018), https://ww2.montgomeryschoolsmd.org/departments/forms/pdf/555-6.pdf; Off. Sch. Support & Improvement, *Parent/Guardian Approval for Trips MCPS Transportation is NOT Provided*, MONTGOMERY CNTY. PUB. SCHS. (July 2018), https://ww2.montgomeryschoolsmd.org/departments/forms/pdf/560-31.pdf; Off. Sch. Support & Improvement, *Parent/Guardian Approval MCPS Virtual Field Trip/Program Addendum*, MONTGOMERY CNTY. PUB. SCHS. (Nov. 2020), https://ww2.montgomeryschoolsmd.org/departments/forms/pdf/210-7.pdf; Off. Sch. Support & Improvement, *Approval for Extended Day, Out-of-Area, and Overnight Field Trips*, MONTGOMERY CNTY. PUB. SCHS. (Sept. 2019), https://ww2.montgomeryschoolsmd.org/departments/forms/pdf/210-4.pdf.

[23] *Authorization to Administer Prescribed Medication*, MONTGOMERY CNTY. PUB. SCHS. & MONTGOMERY CNTY. DEP'T HEALTH & HUM. SERVS. (Feb. 2019), https://www.montgomeryschoolsmd.org/siteassets/schools/elementary-schools/a-c/burningtreees/uploadedfiles/authorization-to-administer-prescribed-medication.pdf.

[24] Brief for Petitioners, *supra* note 4, at 14.

[25] *Id.* at 15.

[26] *Id.*

[27] Brief in Opposition, *supra* note 7, at 6.

[28] Brief for Petitioners, *supra* note 4, at 13 (cleaned up).

II. The State of the Law

The important element in analyzing *Mahmoud* is clarifying what was at stake and what was not. The issue was whether the schools could deny parents the ability to opt-out their children from lessons that burdened their religion.[29] The issue was not whether the schools could include the storybooks in the schools' book collections, nor whether the schools could include lessons based on the storybooks in their curriculum. It was also not about asking the Court to manage MCPS's curriculum choices, but rather who decides—the parents or the schools—what a child's religious instruction should be.

Accordingly, the case was governed by *Wisconsin v. Yoder* and *West Virginia Board of Education v. Barnette*. In *Yoder*, "Amish parents . . . wished to withdraw their children from conventional schooling after the eighth grade, in direct contravention of a Wisconsin law requiring children to attend school until the age of 16." In *Yoder*, "[the Court] recognized that parents have a right 'to direct the religious upbringing of their children,' and that this right can be infringed by laws that pose 'a very real threat of undermining' the religious beliefs and practices that parents wish to instill in their children."[30] Similarly, in *Barnette*, the Court "considered a resolution adopted by the West Virginia State Board of Education that required students 'to participate in the salute honoring the Nation represented by the flag.'"[31] "A group of plaintiffs sued to prevent the enforcement of this policy against Jehovah's Witnesses who considered the flag to be a 'graven image' and refused to salute it."[32] The challengers asserted that the policy was, among other things, "an unconstitutional denial of religious freedom."[33] The Court agreed that the mandatory salute policy could not be squared with the First Amendment.[34]

Interestingly, the forms of compulsion used in *Yoder* and *Barnette* were opposites—although both approaches were represented in *Mahmoud*.

---

[29] Plaintiffs sought "a preliminary and permanent injunction 'prohibiting the School Board from forcing [their] children and other students—over the objection of their parents—to read, listen to, or discuss' the storybooks." *Mahmoud*, slip op. at 14.

[30] *Mahmoud*, slip op. at 14–15 (quoting *Yoder*, 406 U.S. at 218, 233).

[31] *Id.* at 19 (citing *Barnette*, 319 U.S. at 626).

[32] *Id.* (internal quotation marks omitted).

[33] *Id.* (citing *Barnette*, 319 U.S. at 630).

[34] *Id.*

In *Yoder,* the compulsory attendance law was used to threaten parents to make their children attend school.[35] In *Barnette,* the Board threatened exclusion from school for failing to comply.[36] Both approaches are relevant here because MCPS made keeping children out of the instruction an unexcused absence, thus invoking the power of the state to make children attend school, while simultaneously announcing that if parents didn't want their children to participate in the instruction they would have to take their children out of school.[37] Compulsion and exclusion.

Recently, in *Espinoza v. Montana Department of Revenue,* the Court reiterated that it has "long recognized the rights of parents to direct 'the religious upbringing' of their children."[38] However, the bulk of legal development regarding parents' right to educate their children was a series of cases from the first half of the 20th century that relied on an array of constitutional rights.

Some relied on the Fifth and Fourteenth Amendments' due process protection against deprivation of liberty. In *Meyer v. Nebraska,* for example, the issue was whether a Nebraska law that prohibited the teaching of students, who had not completed eighth grade, in any modern language other than English, "unreasonably infringe[d] the liberty guaranteed . . . by the Fourteenth Amendment."[39] The plaintiff was a teacher who taught parochial school in the German language and had been convicted under the challenged statute.[40] The Court, while acknowledging that the exact forms of liberty protected by the Fourteenth Amendment have not been defined, provided an assortment of example freedoms that "without doubt" it includes, such as "freedom from bodily restraint but also the right of the individual to contract, to engage in any of the common occupations of life, to acquire useful knowledge, to marry, establish

[35] *Yoder,* 406 U.S. at 218.

[36] *Mahmoud,* slip op. at 19 (citing *Barnette,* 319 U.S. at 629) ("If students failed to comply, they faced expulsion and could not be readmitted until they yielded to the State's command.").

[37] *Id.* at 8 (citing Petitioners' App., *supra* note 13, at 640a) ("Parents always have the choice to keep their student(s) home while using these texts; however, it will not be an excused absence.").

[38] *Id.* at 17 (citing Espinoza v. Mont. Dept. of Rev., 591 U.S. 464, 486 (2020)).

[39] Meyer v. Nebraska, 262 U.S. 390, 399 (1923).

[40] *Id.* at 396–97.

a home and bring up children, to worship God according to the dictates of his own conscience, and generally to enjoy those privileges long recognized at common law as essential to the orderly pursuit of happiness by free men."[41] While acknowledging the interest of the government in encouraging education and fostering "a homogeneous people with American ideals," that interest was not enough to overcome the liberty interests of the parents, children, and teacher.[42]

Farrington v. Tokushige[43] presented a similar issue when Hawaii attempted to regulate "foreign language schools" to such a degree that it threatened to squeeze them out of existence.[44] Like in *Meyer*, the plaintiffs were educators whose services were subject to the regulations. But instead of prohibiting the schools altogether, the state burdened them with regulations requiring annual permits, payment of headcount-based fees, disclosure of student lists, and permits for all teachers—which were prohibited unless the applicant was "possessed of the ideals of democracy, knowledge of American history and institutions, and [knew] how to read, write, and speak the English language" and signed a pledge to "direct the minds and studies of pupils in such schools as will tend to make them good and loyal American citizens."[45]

The Supreme Court found constitutional violations because the law gave "affirmative direction concerning the intimate and essential details of such schools, intrust[ed] their control to public officers, and den[ied] both owners and patrons reasonable choice and discretion in respect of teachers, curriculum and text-books."[46] Moreover, "[e]nforcement of the act probably would [have] destroy[ed] most, if not all, of them; and, certainly, it would [have] deprive[d] parents of fair opportunity to procure for their children instruction which they think important."[47]

---

[41] *Id.* at 399 (collecting cases).

[42] *Id.* at 396–97, 399–400.

[43] *Id.* at 291.

[44] 273 U.S. 284 (1927).

[45] *Id.* at 291–94.

[46] *Id.* at 298.

[47] *Id.*

Similarly, in *Pierce v. Society of the Sisters of the Holy Names of Jesus and Mary*, plaintiff, the Society of Sisters, was a provider of primary and high schools, junior colleges, and orphanages for children between the ages of 8 and 16.[48] When Oregon passed a law requiring children to attend public school, the compelled withdrawal of children from parochial schools threatened the schools' existence.[49] The Society of Sisters challenged the law asserting three constitutional violations: (1) the "right of parents to choose schools where their children will receive appropriate mental and religious training"; (2) "the right of the child to influence the parents' choice of a school"; and (3) "the right of schools and teachers therein to engage in a useful business or profession."[50] Hill Military Academy, a private for-profit provider of elementary, college preparatory, and military training school for boys between the ages of 5 and 21 years also challenged the law under the Fourteenth Amendment claiming deprivation of property without due process.[51] The Court resolved the case by holding that "the Act of 1922 unreasonably interferes with the liberty of parents and guardians to direct the upbringing and education of children under their control."[52] Further, the Court rejected "any general power of the state to standardize its children by forcing them to accept instruction from public teachers only," holding that the "child is not the mere creature of the state; those who nurture him and direct his destiny have the right, coupled with the high duty, to recognize and prepare him for additional obligations."[53]

Caselaw following *Yoder* was mixed. One analyst suggested that the "*Yoder* Court's ambiguous messaging about the robustness of parenting rights is reflected in the later caselaw."[54] Another predicted, "Whatever side wins in *Mahmoud*, it won't win because of *Yoder*."[55]

---

[48] Pierce v. Soc'y of Sisters, 268 U.S. 510, 532 (1925).

[49] *Id.* at 531.

[50] *Id.* at 532.

[51] *Id.* at 532–33.

[52] *Id.* at 534–35.

[53] *Id.* at 535.

[54] Mark Strasser, Yoder's Legacy, 47 Hofstra L. Rev. 1335, 1349 (2020).

[55] Chad Flanders, *Is* Yoder v. Wisconsin *Limited to Its Facts?*, 16 ConLawNOW 23, 23 (2024-2025).

A. State Policy Has Long Supported Parental Control over Instruction that Implicates Religion and Human Sexuality

Despite those mixed reviews, the Court's reliance on *Yoder* should come as no surprise: integral to *Mahmoud* is commonplace parental control over exposure to instruction in human sexuality or other topics that may have religious overtones. This concern is not new; it has been central to parents' efforts to uphold their authority over their children while navigating exposure to public schools that may have different goals. The atmospherics were thus on par with *Yoder*, in which the Amish parents simply sought to maintain the existing way of life of their community. In each case, the parents were not demanding exotic relief for an obscure dispute but rather to maintain the boundaries of the delegation of authority they had made to the school regarding their children's instruction.

Among the variety of topics over which delegation of parental authority is presumed to be limited, subject to withdrawal, or required to be explicit, the teaching of human sexuality is widespread.[56] As described in Part I, Maryland statutory law recognizes and provides for parents to opt-out of such instruction for their children and places the burden on the school system to facilitate opt-outs and provide "appropriate alternative learning activities and/or assessments in health education" and the "opportunity for parents/guardians to view instructional materials to be used in the teaching of family life and human sexuality objectives."[57] Other states have similar provisions covering a variety of topics in addition to religion and sexuality, including rights of conscience and controversial

---

[56] *See* Brief for Petitioners, *supra* note 4, at 6–7, 6 n.5 (collecting state laws).

[57] Md. Code Regs. 13A.04.18.01(e) ("Student Opt-Out: (i) The local school system shall establish policies, guidelines, and/or procedures for student opt-out regarding instruction related to family life and human sexuality objectives; (ii) For students opting out of family life and human sexuality instruction, each school shall establish a procedure for providing a student with appropriate alternative learning activities and/or assessments in health education; (iii) Each school shall make arrangements to permit students opting out of the objectives related to family life and human sexuality to receive instruction concerning menstruation; (iv) The local school system shall provide an opportunity for parents/guardians to view instructional materials to be used in the teaching of family life and human sexuality objectives.").

issues.[58] And federal law even provides notice and opt-out options for any surveys that concern political affiliations, psychological problems, sex, self-incriminating behavior, privileged relationships (lawyers, physicians, and ministers), religious beliefs, or income, without the prior written consent of the parent.[59]

B. Attempts to Use the Courts to Control Curriculum Have Been Largely Unsuccessful

Plaintiffs were explicit that the remedy they sought was the ability to opt out of material they found objectionable—not to have that material excluded from the curriculum.[60] The limited relief sought distinguishes this case from numerous cases in which plaintiffs challenged school curricula seeking to have certain material excluded and were unsuccessful.

School boards are generally empowered to determine what the curriculum will be, and that authority has been upheld by courts across the country against challenges from parents and teachers. In *Boring v. Buncombe County Board of Education*, the Fourth Circuit held, "We agree with Plato and Burke and Justice Frankfurter that the school, not the teacher, has the right to fix the curriculum."[61]

"Any discussion of the constitutionality of a state's decision to reject a textbook for its public schools must begin with the recognition that the states enjoy broad discretionary powers in the field of public education. Central among these discretionary powers is the authority to establish public school curricula which accomplishes the states' educational objectives."[62]

---

[58] *See* Brief for Amici Curiae Def. of Freedom Inst. for Pol'y Stud. et al. in Support of Petitioners at 15–16, Mahmoud v. Taylor, No. 24-297 (U.S. 2025) (collecting state statutes); Brief for Protect Our Kids (Cal.) et al. as Amici Curiae in Support of Petitioners at 7–11, Mahmoud v. Taylor, No. 24-297 (U.S. 2025) (table summarizing 47 states and the District of Columbia that provide parental opt-outs or opt-ins).

[59] 20 U.S.C. § 1232(h).

[60] Brief for Petitioners, *supra* note 4, at 1 ("Petitioners filed suit not challenging the curriculum . . . ."); Mahmoud v. Taylor, 102 F.4th 191, 201 (4th Cir. 2024) ("The Parents do not challenge the Board's adoption of the Storybooks or seek to ban their use in Montgomery County Public Schools.").

[61] Boring v. Buncombe Cnty. Bd. of Educ., 136 F.3d 364, 370 (4th Cir. 1998).

[62] Chiras v. Miller, 432 F.3d 606, 611 (5th Cir. 2005) (citing Bd. of Educ. v. Pico, 457 U.S. 853, 864 (1982); Ambach v. Norwick, 441 U.S. 68, 76–77 (1979)).

Likewise, in *Fleischfresser v. Directors of School District 200*, the court denied an injunction to prevent the school from using a supplemental reading program to which the parents objected. The court emphasized "the broad discretion vested in the school board to select its public school curriculum."[63] The Eighth Circuit agreed, holding that "[t]he public schools are not required to delete from the curriculum all materials that may offend any religious sensibility."[64] And, the Ninth Circuit rebuffed an attempt to exclude *Huckleberry Finn* and *A Rose for Emily* from the curriculum based on accusations that the works are "racist in whole or in part."[65]

But even though parents have limited power to exclude material from a school curriculum, any perceived violation of rights from the inclusion or use of material in instruction may be cured by providing the ability to opt-out the children from the perceived violation. In *Florey v. Sioux Falls School District*, for example, the school board recognized that, while not required to eliminate activities that may conflict with the individual beliefs of some students and their parents, "forcing any person to participate in an activity that offends his religious or nonreligious beliefs will generally contravene the Free Exercise Clause, even without an Establishment Clause violation."[66] The school board, however "recognized that problem and expressly provided that students may be excused from activities authorized by the rules if they so choose."[67] The court accordingly upheld the school's programming.[68]

III. The Holding

Against this background, Justice Samuel Alito, writing for a 6–3 majority, delivered the opinion in *Mahmoud* holding: "A government burdens the religious exercise of parents when it requires them to submit their children to instruction that poses 'a very real threat of

[63] Fleischfresser v. Dirs. of Sch. Dist. 200, 15 F.3d 680, 688 (7th Cir. 1994).

[64] Florey v. Sioux Falls Sch. Dist., 619 F.2d 1311, 1318 (8th Cir. 1980).

[65] Monteiro v. Tempe Union High Sch. Dist., 158 F.3d 1022, 1027–28 (9th Cir. 1998); *see also* Cal. Parents for the Equalization of Educ. Materials v. Torlakson, 267 F. Supp. 3d 1218, 1222 (N.D. Cal. 2017), *aff'd*, 973 F.3d 1010 (9th Cir. 2020) (rejecting attempt to modify school curriculum to more accurately portray the Hindu religion in California public schools under an assortment of constitutional theories).

[66] *Florey*, 619 F.2d at 1318–19 (citing *Yoder*, 406 U.S. at 218).

[67] *Id.* at 1319.

[68] *Id.*

undermining' the religious beliefs and practices that the parents wish to instill. . . . And a government cannot condition the benefit of free public education on parents' acceptance of such instruction."[69] The Court thus held that Petitioners should receive preliminary relief and remanded with instruction that while this lawsuit proceeds, the Board should be ordered to notify the parents in advance whenever one of the books in question or any other similar book is to be used in any way and to allow them to have their children excused from that instruction.[70]

Although the challenged policy had two elements—withholding notice and forbidding opt-outs—the opinion treated them together, relying largely on *Yoder* and *Barnette*. Regarding *Yoder*, the Court rejected the lower courts' narrow reading of *Yoder* as *"sui generis"* and "inexorably linked to the Amish community's unique religious beliefs and practices."[71] The Court put a final nail in the coffin on attempts to interpret *Yoder* as applying only if the parents are Amish, stating, "We have never confined *Yoder* to its facts. To the contrary, we have treated it like any other precedent. We have at times relied on it as a statement of general principles. . . . And we have distinguished it when appropriate."[72] "*Yoder* is an important precedent of this Court, and it cannot be breezily dismissed as a special exception granted to one particular religious minority."[73]

It is fair to say that after *Mahmoud*, *Yoder* is not only alive and well but provides robust support for parents' free exercise rights in analogous circumstances. The Court did recognize, however, that any such inquiry is fact-specific, explaining, "As our decision in *Yoder* reflects, the question whether a law 'substantially interfer[es]' with the religious development' of a child will always be fact-intensive.[74] It will depend on the specific religious beliefs and practices asserted, as well as the specific nature of the educational requirement or curricular feature at issue."[75] The facts the Court found relevant here

---

[69] *Mahmoud*, slip op. at 1–2 (quoting *Yoder*, 406 U.S. at 218).

[70] *Id.* at 41.

[71] *Id.* at 15 (citing Mahmoud v. Taylor, 688 F. Supp. 3d 265, 294, 301 (D. Md. 2024)).

[72] *Id.* at 29 (citations omitted).

[73] *Mahmoud*, slip op. at 29–30.

[74] *Yoder*, 406 U.S. at 218.

[75] *Mahmoud*, slip op. at 21.

included these: (1) like many books targeted at young children, the books were unmistakably normative;[76] (2) the students were young, roughly 5 to 11 years old;[77] (3) the Board "encourage[d] the teachers to correct the children and accuse them of being 'hurtful' when they express a degree of religious confusion";[78] (4) the parents only requested to opt-out of the instruction;[79] and (5) the Board allowed for opt-outs for nonreligious reasons or for religious reasons for other parts of the curriculum or schedule.[80]

In applying *Yoder* and *Barnette*, the Court rejected the government's argument that "coercion" is the proper standard and that a necessary element of coercion is whether the activity was successful in getting the students to abandon their religious tenets. Although the Court found a level of compulsion in *Barnette* that did not appear in *Yoder*, in neither case was the child required to adopt "any contrary convictions of their own and become unwilling converts."[81] The Court thus rejected the dissent's efforts to limit the Free Exercise Clause's guarantee to "nothing more than protection against compulsion or coercion to renounce or abandon one's religion," and it rebuffed the proposal that "[w]hether or not a requirement or curriculum could be characterized as 'exposure'" is "the touchstone for determining whether that line is crossed."[82]

The Court also relied on *Barnette* to reject the argument that parents could cure their own injury by simply withdrawing their children from public school and providing private or home schooling for them. That alleged defense is already foreclosed by *Barnette* because it conditions access to a public benefit on capitulating to the government's constitutional demands.[83] Like here, although the policy in *Barnette* did not clearly require students to "forego any contrary

[76] *Id.* at 22.
[77] *Id.* at 4, 26.
[78] *Id.* at 26.
[79] *Id.* at 14.
[80] *Id.* at 38.
[81] *Id.* at 19 (citing *Barnette*, 319 U.S. at 633).
[82] *Id.* at 28, 30.
[83] *Id.* at 19 (citing *Barnette*, 319 U.S. at 630–31) ("The effect of the State's policy, we observed, was to 'condition access to public education on making a prescribed sign and profession and at the same time to coerce attendance by punishing both parent and child.'").

convictions of their own and become unwilling converts," it none-theless required a particular "affirmation of a belief and an attitude of mind."[84] "Public education is a public benefit, and the government cannot 'condition' its 'availability' on parents' willingness to accept a burden on their religious exercise."[85]

Moreover, as the Court pointed out, the claim that parents can simply walk away from the infringing demands is impractical, because "[d]ue to financial and other constraints, . . . many parents 'have no choice but to send their children to a public school.' As a result, the right of par-ents 'to direct the religious upbringing of their' children would be an empty promise if it did not follow those children into the public school classroom. We have thus recognized limits on the government's abil-ity to interfere with a student's religious upbringing in a public school setting."[86] "Moreover, since education is compulsory in Maryland, . . . the parents are not being asked simply to forgo a public benefit. They have an obligation—enforceable by fine or imprisonment—to send their children to public school unless they find an adequate substi-tute. . . . And many parents cannot afford such a substitute."[87] Thus, "It is both insulting and legally unsound to tell parents that they must abstain from public education in order to raise their children in their religious faiths, when alternatives can be prohibitively expensive and they already contribute to financing the public schools."[88]

IV. What's *Smith* Got to Do with It?

Smith has long presented an obstacle to Free Exercise claims. But, as *Mahmoud* reiterated, *Yoder* presents a different legal framework from the sometimes troubling two-part test from *Smith* that may doom religious exercise claims. Under *Smith*, the government is gen-erally free to place incidental burdens on religious exercise so long as it does so pursuant to a "neutral policy that is generally applicable."[89]

---

[84] *Id.; Barnette,* 319 U.S. at 633.

[85] *Mahmoud,* slip op. at 32–33 (citing Trinity Lutheran Church of Columbia, Inc. v. Comer, 582 U.S. 449, 462 (2017)).

[86] *Id.* slip op. at 19 (quoting Morse v. Frederick, 551 U.S. 393, 424 (2007) (Alito, J., concurring)).

[87] *Id.* slip op. at 33 (citations omitted).

[88] *Id.* at 34.

[89] *Smith,* 494 U.S. at 878–79.

There is, however, an exception derived from *Yoder* that is applicable in cases like this one and bypasses *Smith* altogether.

The Court here relied on a *Yoder* exception, stating, "Here, the character of the burden requires us to proceed differently. When the burden imposed is of the same character as that imposed in *Yoder*, we need not ask whether the law at issue is neutral or generally applicable before proceeding to strict scrutiny. That much is clear from our decisions in *Yoder* and *Smith*."[90]

But what does it mean to say the "burden imposed is of the same character"? The basis for the *Yoder* exception in *Smith* was the Court's speculation that the hybrid rights at issue made the *Smith* rule inapplicable.[91] Here, the Court did not do a hybrid-rights analysis because "the burden imposed here is of the exact same character as that in *Yoder*," and thus strict scrutiny applies.[92] An assortment of elements may make the burden here the same as the burden in *Yoder*. For example, in both cases the defendants were public schools, the plaintiffs were parents who wanted to withdraw their children from instruction, and the Free Exercise infringement was instruction that contradicted the parents' religious beliefs. But are all of those elements necessary to invoke the *Yoder* exception? Would two elements, such as public school plus Free Exercise or public school plus refusal to allow opt-out, suffice? Or would *Smith* apply in those lesser scenarios? Leaving those questions for another day, here, the Court held that once *Yoder* applies, then strict scrutiny is the appropriate standard—and the program failed on two prongs.

First the Court acknowledged that the Board has a "compelling interest in having an undisrupted school session conducive to the students' learning."[93] But that interest is undermined when the Board allows opt-outs for reasons other than for religious exercise.[94] Likewise, the Board's "asserted interest in protecting students from 'social stigma and isolation'" is undermined by shifting stigma to another group of students.[95] In addition, the requisite link between the government's

---

[90] *Mahmoud*, slip op. at 36.

[91] *Smith*, 494 U.S. at 881.

[92] *Mahmoud*, slip op. at 36 n.14.

[93] *Id.* (citing Grayned v. City of Rockford, 408 U.S. 104, 119 (1972)).

[94] *Id.* (citing Fulton v. City of Philadelphia, 593 U.S. 522, 542 (2021)).

[95] *Id.* at 39.

interest and its proposed course of action breaks down when, as here, it relies on self-inflicted challenges, such as how it structures its curriculum and school schedule, to justify its infringing policies.

V. Justice Thomas's Concurrence

In his concurrence, Justice Clarence Thomas highlighted some themes that may be relevant to future cases, such as the inadequacy of conformity-driven rationales to overcome the individual rights of the students, the inappropriateness of efforts by the state to position itself as the savior of the child, and the impropriety of creative efforts by the government to create burdens on itself to pump up its "compelling interest."

The "conformity-driven rationale" refers to an approach in which schools argue that they have a compelling interest in driving uniformity among school children. But the Court has rejected that approach before.[96] The shortcomings of the related "savior" approach were identified in *Yoder*, in which "the Court observed that if a State were 'empowered, as *parens patriae*, to "save" a child' from the supposed 'ignorance' of his religious upbringing, then 'the State will in large measure influence, if not determine, the religious future of the child.'"[97] "Such an arrangement would upend the 'enduring American tradition' of parents occupying the 'primary role . . . in the upbringing of their children'—a role that includes the 'inculcation of . . . religious beliefs.'"[98]

These approaches are not new. As Justice Thomas pointed out, "The arguments that Oregon pressed in defense of its compulsory-education law [in *Pierce*] make clear that the State sought ideological conformity among its citizens, and viewed immigrants and their religious schools as standing in the way."[99] "The State even asserted an interest in 'a greater equality' to justify its attempt at state-enforced uniformity."[100]

The second approach relates to the apparently deliberate practice of dispersing controversial material within curriculum to make

---

[96] *Mahmoud*, slip op. at 6 (Thomas, J., concurring) (citing Pierce v. Soc'y of Sisters, 268 U.S. 510 (1925)).

[97] *Id.* (citing *Yoder*, 406 U.S. at 222, 232).

[98] *Id.*

[99] *Id.* (citing *Pierce*, 268 U.S. at 526).

[100] *Id.* (citing *Pierce*, 268 U.S. at 526).

opting-out logistically challenging.[101] The moral hazard of reducing First Amendment protections wherever the government may creatively introduce complexity is clear. Thus, "[i]nsofar as schools or boards attempt to employ their curricula to interfere with religious exercise, courts should carefully police such 'ingenious defiance of the Constitution' no less than they do in other contexts."[102]

VI. The Dissent

The dissent asserted that the "ruling threatens the very essence of public education" by focusing largely on issues that were not before the Court, such as whether parents may use the courts to impose changes on curricula.[103] The well-established precedent that demands for changes to curriculum are unlikely to prevail highlights the dichotomy between remedies that require freedom from state demands versus remedies that demand the state to perform specific acts.

VII. What's Next

A variety of doctrinal issues that are not addressed in *Mahmoud* are logical next steps in determining the boundaries between parents rights to guide the education of their children and efforts of public schools to use their curriculum to influence the opinions of students on potentially provocative topics.

---

[101] *Id.* at 12 ("But these alleged logistical challenges are attributable to the Board's deliberate decision to 'weave' the storybooks into its broader curriculum.").

[102] *Id.* (citing South Carolina v. Katzenbach, 383 U.S. 301, 309 (1966)).

[103] *Id.* at 2 (Sotomayor, J., dissenting) (claiming that "[t]he Court's ruling, in effect, thus hands a subset of parents the right to veto curricular choices long left to locally elected school boards."); *id.* at 14 (flipping the burden of the First Amendment to require limits on the limits that are applied to government by arguing that the majority "imposes no meaningful limits on the types of school decisions subject to strict scrutiny"); *id.* at 24 (conflating one child calling another child a sinner with a school instructing children on whether behavior is a sin: "If a student calls a classmate a 'sinner' for not wearing a head covering or coming out as gay, how can a teacher respond without 'undermining' that child's religious beliefs?"); *id.* at 27 ("At present, States and localities across the Nation have adopted a patchwork of different policies governing school material related to gender and sexuality and parental opt-out rights."); *id.* at 28 (subjugating minority constitutional rights to the democratic process by claiming the majority "subverts Maryland's functioning democratic process, whistling past decades of precedent that recognizes the primacy and importance of local decision making in this area of law.").

The majority opinion relied largely on *Yoder*, which involved two rights: Free Exercise and the right of parents to direct the education of their children. This so-called "hybrid rights" precedent leaves open the issue to whether one or the other of those rights would be sufficient to require the government to allow parents to opt-out their children from certain topics. The reasoning here, as well as the abundance of Free Exercise precedent, make it likely that Free Exercise alone would be sufficient. But whether nonreligious matters—even matters of conscience—would prevail seems less likely.

A second question turns on whether an argument similar to the one made here could rely on a different clause of the First Amendment, either as one of two hybrid rights or on a stand-alone basis, such as arguing for Free Speech or Freedom of Association to shield children from topics that parents do not want presented to their children. Under the doctrine that the right to speak includes the right not to speak and the right not to listen (likewise for association), it does not seem a stretch to imagine that other clauses may provide an approach to securing nonreligious opt-out programs.

Another question is whether other topical areas may drive parental interest in opting their children out of instruction—with or without a religious element. For example, in Maryland, as well as in the majority of other states, public schools provide opt-out or opt-in programs for instruction regarding human sexuality.[104] These programs have been implemented via the political process, not via constitutional litigation. So for nonreligious parents, or for parents who choose not to rely on religion to support their choices, it is an open question whether instruction on human sexuality could be made mandatory as a condition of attending public school. But the prevalence of this form of opt-out illustrates that, for some topics, parental choice is generally expected and respected. And, there is some precedent for the notion that courts may be open to arguments regarding parental choice for topics other than sex.[105]

---

[104] MD. CODE REGS., *supra* note 58.

[105] *See, e.g., Torlakson*, 267 F. Supp. 3d at 1224 (quoting Fields v. Palmdale Sch. Dist., 427 F.3d 1197 (9th Cir. 2005), *amended by* 447 F.3d 1187 (9th Cir. 2006)) ("[T]here is no constitutional reason to distinguish [concerns regarding sex education] from any of the countless moral, religious, or philosophical objections that parents might have to other decisions of the School District.").

Regarding live litigation, other educational freedom cases in the pipeline may be affected by *Mahmoud*. For example, various cases pending in Maine and Vermont challenge the states' exclusion of religious schools from their state tuition programs by invoking state law prohibitions against participants discriminating on the basis of religion. The potential effect of *Mahmoud* on those cases would work as follows. First, under *Carson v. Makin*, if a state is required to provide tuition funding for a group of students under state law, it may not exclude otherwise qualified religious schools from the list of schools at which students may use their tuition dollars on the basis that the schools are religious actors. Following *Carson*, some states have taken another bite at the apple by invoking state law that prohibits discrimination on the basis of gender identity to exclude religious schools that would not agree to adopt the state's viewpoint on gender-based issues. The effect of *Mahmoud* on these cases remains to be seen. But it seems plausible that if a public school must allow a parent to opt-out a child from gender-based instruction where there is a religious conflict—and likewise cannot condition receipt of the benefit of publicly funded education on accepting the government's viewpoint, then the state cannot condition receipt of the benefit of publicly funded education on parents sending their children to only those schools that present gender-based issues from the state's favored viewpoint. Requiring parents to forgo the entire publicly funded educational benefit would seem to be more severe than the proposal that parents could be required to forgo attendance at a particular school that was rejected here.

Relevant to such an approach would be the extent to which "acceptable" schools teach such issues from a normative perspective that aligns with the state's preferred viewpoint. The likelihood that this factor would weigh in favor of the parents seems high where the state has deliberately determined which schools may participate on the very normative basis that's in dispute.

Similarly, for states that have compulsory education laws, forcing parents to choose between their religious views and complying with state law would tend to favor parents as extending well beyond the authority of the government to conduct its own affairs.

Longer term doctrinal issues may include whether a curriculum may be so burdensome to religion that a parent must be allowed to opt-out of having their children attend the public school altogether without forfeiting the benefit of a publicly funded education. Remedies in such circumstances could be broad, including allowing the child to transfer to an otherwise inaccessible public school with a different curriculum or allowing the child to take the funding to another educational source.

Or, for states that have state constitutions with Blaine Amendments (prohibiting the use of public funds for sectarian schools) or broader amendments that prohibit the use of public funds for any private educational entity, if the conflict between the school program and the First Amendment becomes irreconcilably severe, state constitutions may need to yield to a remedy that would cure the federal constitutional injury.

Finally, what is left of *Smith* when it comes to material taught in public schools? Does it retain vigor wherever there is no hybrid Free Exercise/parental rights issue in play? Or has it been narrowed to the extent that schools simply cannot infringe a religious viewpoint even if the pedagogy is neutral and generally applicable?

Conclusion

Mahmoud presents an affirmation that parental rights to guide the religious upbringing of their children are not narrow rights that apply only where the religious community requires total, or near-total, withdrawal from the public schooling system. Rather, they extend to discrete conflicts within the public school from which the parents seek to have their children excused. This case did not raise issues regarding control of public school curriculum. But its holding may extend to other types of educational choice disputes where the state's position relies on *Smith* to either impose instruction that conflicts with the parents' religious exercise or to force parents to forgo a public benefit if they will not conform to the state's preferred viewpoint.

Skrmetti's Mistake

*Ezra Ishmael Young**

Introduction

Can the government define who you are and, having labeled you, prohibit you from accessing medically necessary care simply because of that label? Should the answer be any different if you are a minor?

Does it matter whether the rule is guaranteed to deprive some individuals who, but for the law, are capable of evaluating the pros and cons of treatment and whose judgment to decide for themselves is attested to by both their doctors and parents? Should the rarity of the ailment for which treatment is sought factor into the scheme?

These are some of the questions that the United States Supreme Court wrestles with in *Skrmetti v. United States*,[1] a recent equal protection challenge to Tennessee's SB1.[2] But they are not the only ones.

SB1 regulates minors' access to hormone blockers, masculinizing and feminizing exogenous hormones, and reconstructive surgeries of primary and secondary sexual characteristics.

SB1 does not presumptively ban care for all minors. Instead, all minors are further classified as either trans, nontrans (without an intersex condition), and intersex. Trans and nontrans kids (but not intersex kids) are further tautologically classed as either male or female. Males are only those assigned male at birth, and females are only those assigned female at birth. The overarching classificatory

*Thanks to Kylar Broadus, Jessica Clarke, Kimberlé Crenshaw, Michael Dorf, Sheri Johnson, Chan Tov McNammarah, Sloan Manning, Sawyer Nash, Victoria Rodriguéz-Roldán, Katavia Sloan, and Brittany Stewart for helpful conversations and comments. All mistakes are my own.

1 145 S. Ct. 1816 (2025).

2 TENN. CODE ANN. § 68-33-101 *et seq.*

scheme is not premised on any individual's chosen identity. Nor is it informed by medicine or science.

In *Skrmetti*, before assessing whether Tennessee has the specific power to impose SB1, the Supreme Court asks what degree of judicial scrutiny should be afforded to trans minors diagnosed with gender dysphoria who medically need the prohibited care. If heightened scrutiny applies, SB1 is presumptively unconstitutional. If instead rational basis applies, SB1 is presumptively constitutional.

This means that to determine whether discrimination hurting a particular individual violates equal protection, the Supreme Court first must pick which groups deserve more protection than others. This is despite the fact that choosing at the threshold *which* groups to protect more than others is itself a violation of equal protection.

This Article uses *Skrmetti v. United States* to illustrate how the Court's analytic mistake unconstitutionally deprives members of targeted groups of the guarantee of equal protection.

Part I explains an analytic mistake that plagues the Supreme Court's equal protection jurisprudence. From there it explains SB1's design and uplifts the faulty rationales Tennessee lawmakers proffered in support of the law's enactment.

Part II evaluates Chief Justice John Roberts's majority opinion and Justice Amy Coney Barrett's concurrence in *Skrmetti v. United States*. It goes on to dissect how both Chief Justice Roberts's and Justice Barrett's opinions fail to apprehend how SB1 functions as per its text and misevaluate the evidence of irrationality and bias presented to the Court.

I. Contextualizing Tennessee's SB1

In the last several years, lawmakers across the nation have enacted a slew of anti-trans bills. All are premised on the notion that government has the power to idiosyncratically define sex to single out trans persons for burdens and deny them benefits otherwise due them but for being trans. Tennessee's SB1 is one example.

Unfortunately, the Supreme Court is ill-equipped to ascertain whether anti-trans laws like SB1 are unconstitutional. This is because the Court insists, in violation of equal protection itself, that it has the judicial power to pick and choose what degree of judicial scrutiny should be afforded equal protection challenges solely premised on the identity of persons who allege discrimination.

A. The Court's Equal Protection Mistake

The notion that all persons are equal before the law is not a lofty ideal. It is a legal reality that is constitutionally mandated. The equal protection clause of the Fourteenth Amendment is not ambiguous. Government is without power to "deny any person within its jurisdiction the equal protection of the laws."[3]

There are no textual exceptions to equal protection.[4] Equal protection is an absolute limit on governmental power.[5] With respect to the branches of government, the express powers conferred to them by the Constitution are constrained by rights expressly conferred to the people[6] (in addition to those impliedly conferred by reservation

---

[3] U. S. Const. amend. XIV, § 1, cl. 1 (equal protection clause) *constitutionally rejecting* Barron v. Baltimore, 32 U.S. 243 (1833) (holding individuals' rights guaranteed by Constitution are solely limitation on federal, not state government). *See also* U.S. Const. amend. IX ("The enumeration in the Constitution, of certain rights, shall not be construed to deny or disparage others retained by the people.") *and* U.S. Const. art. IV, § 2 ("The Citizens of each State shall be entitled to all Privileges and Immunities of Citizens in the several States.").

[4] *See, e.g.,* Plyler v. Doe, 457 U.S. 202, 212 (1982) (quoting Yick Wo v. Hopkins, 118 US 356, 369 (1886) (provisions of the Fourteenth Amendment "are universal in their application, to all persons within the territorial jurisdiction")); Craig v. Boren, 429 U.S. 190, 211 (1976) (Stevens, J., concurring) ("There is only one Equal Protection Clause").

[5] *See, e.g.,* W. Va. State Bd. of Educ. v. Barnette, 319 U.S. 624, 638 (1943) (Jackson, J.) ("The very purpose of the Bill of Rights was to withdraw certain subjects from the vicissitudes of political controversy, to place them beyond the reach of majorities and officials and to establish them as legal principles to be applied by the courts. One's right to life, liberty, and property, to free speech, a free press, freedom of worship and assembly, and other fundamental rights may not be submitted to vote; they depend on the outcome of no elections.").

[6] *Cf.* Bond v. United States, 564 U.S. 211, 221 (2011) (the Constitution allocates powers "between the National Government and the States [to enhance freedom] first by protecting the integrity of the governments themselves, and second by protecting the people, from whom all governmental powers are derived"); New York v. United States, 505 U.S. 144, 181 (1992) ("federalism secures to citizens the liberties that derive from the diffusion of sovereign power") (cleaned up).

through the Ninth[7] and Tenth[8] Amendments). This means that even where the Constitution gives Congress, the Executive, and the Judiciary general and specific powers, none contains within that delegation the power to violate equal protection.[9]

There are some seminal Supreme Court opinions that call out and condemn equal protection violations committed by judicial officers.[10] Taken together, they teach that equal protection bars the

[7] *See, e.g.,* Griswold v. Connecticut, 381 U.S. 479, 482 (1965) ("We do not sit as a super-legislature to determine the wisdom, need, and propriety of laws that touch economic problems, business affairs, or social conditions. This law, however, operates directly on an intimate relation of husband and wife and their physician's role in one aspect of that relation.").

See also generally DANIEL FARBER, RETAINED BY THE PEOPLE: THE 'SILENT' NINTH AMENDMENT AND THE CONSTITUTIONAL RIGHTS AMERICANS DON'T KNOW THEY HAVE (Basic Books 2007) (arguing that originalism illustrates that conservatives are hypocritically refusing to apply their commitment to text and history when it comes to the Ninth Amendment); Thomas B. McAffee, *The Original Meaning of the Ninth Amendment,* 90 COLUM. L. REV. 1215 (1990) (presenting an originalist account of the Ninth Amendment as securing residual rights as opposed to affirmative rights).

[8] District of Columbia v. Heller, 554 U.S. 570, 580 (2008) (quoting United States v. Verdugo-Urquidez, 494 U.S. 259, 265 (1990)) ("'The people' seems to have been a term of art employed in select parts of the Constitution[. Its uses suggest] that 'the people' protected by the Fourth Amendment, and by the First and Second Amendments, and to whom rights and powers are reserved in the Ninth and Tenth Amendments, refers to a class of persons who are part of a national community or who have otherwise developed sufficient connection with this country to be considered part of that community.") (cleaned up).

[9] Valley Forge Christian Coll. v. Ams. United for Separation of Church & State, 454 U.S. 464, 471 (1982) ("The judicial power of the United States defined by Art. III is not an unconditioned authority to determine the constitutionality of legislative or executive acts. The power to declare the rights of individuals and to measure the authority of governments . . . is legitimate only in the last resort, and as a necessity in the determination of real, earnest and vital controversy.").*Cf.* Am. K-9 Detection Servs., LLC v. Freeman, 556 S.W.3d 246, 252 (Tex. 2018) (Hecht, C.J.) ("limits on judicial power are as important as its reach").

See also Adarand Constructors, Inc. v. Pena, 515 U.S. 200, 231–32 (1995) ("the Constitution imposes upon federal, state, and local government actors the same obligation to respect the personal right to equal protection") (citing Charles Fried, *Metro Broadcasting, Inc. v. FCC: Two Concepts of Equality,* 104 HARV. L. REV. 107, 113–17 (1990) (arguing "adoption of different standards of review for federal and state classifications placed the law in an 'unstable condition' and advocating for strict scrutiny across the board")).

[10] *See, e.g.,* Palmore v. Sidoti, 466 U.S. 429, 432 n.1 (1984) ("The actions of state courts and judicial officers in their official capacity have long been held to be state action governed by the Fourteenth Amendment.") (citing Shelley v. Kraemer, 334 US 1 (1948); Ex parte Virginia, 100 U.S. 339, 346–47 (1880)).

judiciary from employing the judicial power to authorize, enforce, or give effect to discriminatory schemes. This rule holds true even where the government, litigants, or third parties insist that they prefer discrimination for extra-constitutional reasons.

Nevertheless, the Supreme Court's equal protection jurisprudence allows and facilitates the judiciary meting out equal protection unequally, which itself is an equal protection violation. Since the mid-twentieth century, the Court has employed the tiers of scrutiny, a framework used to justify different degrees of judicial scrutiny afforded to equal protection challenges. Under the tiers of scrutiny, race and sex classifications are afforded heightened scrutiny and thus presumed unconstitutional. And virtually all other classifications are given only rational basis review and thus presumed constitutional. The net result is again that the Court is picking and choosing which classifications get more equal protection than others.[11]

The Court occasionally explains away the discrimination built into the judicial decision-making process that the tiers of scrutiny mandate as a kind of institutional reparations. On this logic, race and sex classifications merit heightened scrutiny because of the Court's historic failure to realize both are inherently suspect.[12] Conversely, all other classifications are not inherently suspect because they are neither race nor sex.

Ultimately, the tiers of scrutiny framework simply redound to whether the Supreme Court wishes to give certain groups more or less equal protection. This is not analytically different from the

---

[11] *Cf.* Romer v. Evans, 517 U.S. 620, 633 (1996) (Kennedy, J.) ("[L]aws singling out a certain class of citizens for disfavored legal status or general hardships are rare. A law declaring that in general it shall be more difficult for one group of citizens than for all others to seek aid from government is itself a denial of equal protection of the laws in the most literal sense."); Sweatt v. Painter, 339 U.S. 629, 635 (1950) ("Equal protection of the laws is not achieved through indiscriminate imposition of inequalities.") (citing *Shelley*, 334 U.S. at 22); Skinner v. Oklahoma ex rel. Williamson, 316 U.S. 535, 541 (1942) ("The guarantee of equal protection of the laws is a pledge of the protection of equal laws.") (cleaned up).

[12] For examples of race cases, see for example Hernandez v. Texas, 347 U.S. 475 (1954); Brown v. Bd. of Educ., 347 U.S. 483 (1954); Bolling v. Sharpe, 347 U.S. 497 (1954); Loving v. Virginia, 388 U.S. 1 (1967). For sex cases, see, for example, Frontiero v. Richardson, 411 U.S. 677 (1973); Orr v. Orr, 440 U.S. 268 (1979); Miss. Univ. for Women v. Hogan, 458 U.S. 718, 723 (1982); United States v. Virginia, 518 U.S. 515, 533 (1996); J.E.B. v. Alabama ex rel. T.B., 511 U.S. 127 (1994).

Court's holdings in *Plessy v. Ferguson*[13] and *Bradwell v. Illinois*,[14] which respectively reasoned that race and sex-based rules are not inherently suspect and thus do not merit searching judicial scrutiny.

B. SB1's Design

SB1 is designed to do one thing—bar only trans kids from accessing puberty blockers, hormones, and surgical treatment.[15] The law does not have a safety-valve to permit the small number of children who indisputably require those treatments for gender dysphoria in youth.[16]

Trans kids are categorically barred from hormone blockers, hormones, and reconstructive surgeries where treatment is indicated by a gender dysphoria diagnosis.[17] (Gender dysphoria is today highly associated with trans persons, but intersex and nontrans persons can also be diagnosed with the condition.[18]) This categorical ban

---

[13] 163 U.S. 537 (1896).

[14] 83 U.S. 130 (1973).

[15] *Accord* Romer v. Evans, 517 U.S. 620, 635 (1996) (Kennedy, J.) ("It is a status-based enactment divorced from any factual context from which we could discern a relationship to legitimate state interests; it is a classification of persons undertaken for its own sake, something the Equal Protection Clause does not permit.").

[16] This is achieved by reading together § 68-33-102(9), which tautologically defines sex as that which is assigned at birth, with § 68-33-102(1)'s provision that creates a carve out for intersex kids (those with a "congenital defect") and § 68-33-102(1)'s exclusion of "gender dysphoria, gender identity, [and] gender incongruence" from the definition of congenital defect.

[17] Even the UK's Hillary Cass agrees that there are a small number of trans kids who need treatment for gender dysphoria in youth. *See generally* HILLARY CASS, INDEPENDENT REVIEW OF GENDER IDENTITY SERVICES FOR CHILDREN AND YOUNG PEOPLE (2024), https://cass.independent-review.uk/home/publications/final-report/.

[18] *See, e.g.*, Paulo Sampaio Furtado et al., *Gender Dysphoria Associated with Disorders of Sex Development*, 9 NATURE REVIEWS UROLOGY 620 (2012) (elevating that rates of gender dysphoria in patients with disorders of sex development ranging somewhere between 8.5–20%); Cynthia Kraus, *Classifying Intersex in DSM-5: Critical Reflections on Gender Dysphoria*, 44 ARCHIVES SEX BEHAVIOR 1147 (2015) (addressing shift from intersex conditions being an exclusion criteria for gender dysphoria in past versions of the DSM to the DSM-5's embrace of intersex conditions being a specifier of gender dysphoria); Lih-Mei Liao et al., *Determinant Factors of Gender Identity: A Commentary*, 8 J. PEDIATRIC UROLOGY 597 (2012) (observing that gender assignment of newborn infants diagnosed with a disorder of sexual development does not predict long-term gender outcome with certainty); Yuqi Li & Lijun Zheng, *Validation of Two Measures of Gender Dysphoria/Incongruence in Transgender and Cisgender Populations in China*, 52 ARCHIVES SEXUAL BEHAVIOR 1019 (2023) (measuring relative rates of gender dysphoria in trans and nontrans populations).

is imposed despite decades of evidence-based research concluding medical transition is the only viable treatment for gender dysphoria.[19] The ban also flies in the face of more than 150 years of research evidencing that it is impossible to change any person's (trans, nontrans, or intersex) innermost sense of sex.[20]

Nontrans kids without intersex conditions face no restrictions on access to hormone blockers, hormones, and reconstructive surgeries.[21] This is so even though this population seeks the same care

---

[19] *See, e.g.*, Kellan E. Baker et al., *Hormone Therapy, Mental Health, and Quality of Life Among Transgender People: A Systematic Review*, 5 J. Endocrine Soc'y 1 (2021); Tim C. van de Grift et al., *A Longitudinal Study of Motivations Before and Psychosexual Outcomes After Genital Gender-Confirming Surgery in Transmen*, 12 J. Sexual Medicine 1621 (2017); Dogu Aydin et al., *Transgender Surgery in Denmark from 1994 to 2015: 20-Year Follow-Up Study*, 13 J. Sexual Medicine 720 (2016); Sofia Pavenello Decaro et al., *It Might Take Time: A Study on the Evolution of Quality of Life in Individuals with Gender Incongruence During Gender-Affirming Care*, 12 J. Sexual Medicine 2045 (2021).

[20] *See, e.g.*, Richard von Krafft-Ebing, Psychopathia Sexualis, with Especial Reference to Contrary Sexual Instinct: A Medico-Legal Study (1870) (employing the term androgyny to refer to FtM persons and gyandry to refer to MtF patients, and concluding both conditions are "congenital" and "incurable" where cross-sex identity established in early childhood); Havelock Ellis, *The Study of Sexual Inversion*, 12 Medico-Legal J. 148 (1894) (discussing Dr. Westphal of Berlin's 1870 study of an FtM transsexual whose gender identity was deemed congenital and could not be altered); Magnus Hirschfeld, Die Transvestiten (1910) (articulating a grand theory to explain trans persons as a natural variation of human sex); J. Allen Gilbert, *Homo-sexuality and its Treatment*, 52 J. Nervous & Mental Disease 297 (1920) (observing that FtM transsexual's male identity could not be altered by psychoanalytic treatment); Harry Benjamin, *Transsexualism and Transvestism as Psychosomantic and Somato-Psychic Syndromes*, 8 Am. J. Psychotherapy 219 (1954) (refining framework proposed by Hirschfeld); Robert Stoller, Sex and Gender (1968) (observing impossibility of changing gender identity of MtF and FtM patients); Milton T. Edgerton, Norman J. Knorr, & James R. Callison, *The Surgical Treatment of Transsexual Patients: Limitations and Indications*, 45 Plastic & Reconstructive Surgery 38, 38 (1970) ("Since antiquity some men have shown evidence of conflict, arising from feelings of inappropriateness of the sex assigned to them on the basis of their external anatomical development."); Lawrence Newman, *Transsexualism in Adolescence: Problems in Evaluation and Treatment*, 23 Archives Gen. Psychiatry 112 (1970) ("There are no reports of older children responding to psychological treatment aimed at reversing their cross-gender orientation.").

[21] Tenn. Code Ann. § 68-33-102(9) defines male and female tautologically to always be that which corresponds with sex assigned at birth. Consequently, male and female are defined in such a way that only nontrans kids' innermost sense of sex—because it is not discordant with that assigned at birth—is recognized. Tennessee Code Section 68-33-103(b)(1)(A) goes on to specify that nontrans kids may undergo treatment if sought "to treat a minor's congenital defect, precocious puberty, disease, or physical injury" without any limitations.

denied to trans kids for similar reasons—to pause puberty, or to induce permanent masculinization or feminization of the body while natural puberty is still in process.[22]

Intersex kids fall into their own sex category under SB1.[23] These children may access puberty blockers, hormone therapy, and reconstructive surgeries at any age, even if the sole impetus for care is that the child's parents' wish her to undergo treatments as young as possible for social, not medical reasons.[24]

---

[22] Nontrans children diagnosed with cancer or precocious puberty are also routinely prescribed hormone blockers. Louis J. Gooren, *Care of Transsexual Persons*, 364 NEW ENG. J. MED. 1251, 1253 (2011) (noting similarity between cancer treatment and GD); *id.* at 1255 (noting similarity between precocious puberty treatment and GD).

Exogenous masculinizing and feminizing hormones are used to treat both trans and nontrans patient populations. *See, e.g.*, Eva Moore et al., *Endocrine Treatment of Transsexual People: A Review of Treatment Regimens, Outcomes, and Adverse Effects*, 88 J. CLINICAL ENDOCRINOLOGY & METABOLISM 3467, 3470 (2003) (describing similarities in testosterone regimens for transgender men and nontrans men with hypogonadism); *id.* at 3472 (comparing estrogen regimens for transgender women and nontrans women with hypogonadism).

Surgery is also a last resort for both trans and nontrans patient populations where other interventions fail to alleviate symptoms of distress or meet the aesthetic preferences of the specific patient. Take as one example double mastectomies, a surgery that can be medically indicated in both trans and nontrans males during adolescence. *See, e.g.*, Kotb Metwalley & Hekma Saad Farghaly, *Gynecomastia in Adolescent Males: Current Understanding of its Etiology, Pathophysiology, Diagnosis, and Treatment*, 29 ANNALS PEDIATRIC ENDOCRINOLOGY & METABOLISM 75 (2024). Today double mastectomy is the most popular surgery regularly performed on both adolescent trans and nontrans males. It is estimated that by today's metrics, upwards of one-third of non-trans males qualify for double-mastectomy in adolescence. *See, e.g.*, Trine Koch, et. al., *Marked Increase in Incident Gynecomastia: A 20-Year National Registry Study, 1998 to 2017*, 105 J. CLINICAL ENDOCRINOLOGY & METABOLISM 3134 (2020). *See also* Annie Tang et al., *Gender-Affirming Mastectomy Trends and Surgical Outcomes In Adolescents*, 88 ANNALS PLASTIC SURGERY S325 (2022) (observing similar increase of treatment performed in trans male population between 2013 and 2020).

[23] This is achieved by Tennessee Code Paragraph 68-33-102(1) tautologically defining congenital defects as those which are "inconsistent with the normal development of a human being of the minor's sex," as including "abnormalities caused by a medically verifiable disorder of sex development," but absolutely excluding from disorders of sex development "gender dysphoria, gender identity disorder, [and] gender incongruence." Read in conjunction with Tennessee Code Section 68-33-103(b)(1)(A), which does not prohibit the "performance or administration of the medical procedure [if it] is to treat a minor's congenital defect."

[24] For discussion of how intersex children are harmed by laws that allow parents and doctors to change their sex in youth without consent, *see generally* Ido Katri & Maayan Sudai, *Intersex, Trans, and the Irrationality of Gender Affirming-Care-Bans*, 134 YALE L.J. 1521 (2025).

C. SB1's Irrationality

Tennessee's rationales for treating trans, nontrans, and intersex minors differently under SB1 are not premised on medical or scientific truths. In fact, some of the rationales for drawing class lines under SB1 are false or merely stereotypes. And some aspects of SB1 conflict with federal law that already regulates the same pharmaceuticals and medical devices and state law that already regulates medical licensure, punishes malpractice, and restricts when genital surgery may be performed on minors.

1. SB1 causes the very harm it purports to prevent

At the threshold, SB1 is a solution in search of a problem. Take, as one example, the legislative finding that SB1 is needed to protect all minor children from permanent alteration by surgery of a minor's genitals that they may, upon adulthood, regret.[25]

SB1's legislative findings insist that it is inherently evil for doctors and parents to make decisions that permanently alter kids' genitals.[26] This is so because kids cannot make decisions about preferred reproductive capacities or sexual function before adulthood.[27]

---

[25] TENN. CODE ANN. § 68-33-101(a) ("The legislature declares that it must take action to protect the health and welfare of minors."); *Id.* at (b) ("The legislature determines that medical procedures that alter a minor's hormonal balance, remove a minor's sex organs, or otherwise change a minor's physical appearance are harmful to a minor when these medical procedures are performed for the purpose of enabling a minor to identify with, or live as, a purported identity inconsistent with the minor's sex or treating purported discomfort or distress from a discordance between the minor's sex and asserted identity. These procedures can lead to the minor becoming irreversibly sterile, having increased risk of disease and illness, or suffering from adverse and sometimes fatal psychological consequences. Moreover, the legislature finds it likely that not all harmful effects associated with these types of medical procedures when performed on a minor are yet fully known, as many of these procedures, when performed on a minor for such purposes, are experimental in nature and not supported by high-quality, long-term studies.").

[26] TENN. CODE ANN. § 68-33-101(d) ("The legislature finds that medical procedures are being performed on and administered to minors in this state for such purposes, notwithstanding the risks and harms to the minors.").

[27] TENN. CODE ANN. § 68-33-101(h) ("The legislature finds that minors lack the maturity to fully understand and appreciate the life-altering consequences of such procedures and that many individuals have expressed regret for medical procedures that were performed on or administered to them for such purposes when they were minors.").

SB1 does not solve this problem. It causes the very harm it is supposed to guard against.

Intersex minors are worse off under SB1 than before it was adopted.[28] Prior to SB1, some genital surgeries with respect to minors were already restricted, even if recommended by medical providers and approved by parents. The only exceptions were procedures that were approved and deemed medically efficacious by the American College of Obstetrics and Gynecology.[29] Under that rule, a small fraction of trans and intersex minors may qualify for pharmaceutical interventions and, in exceedingly rare cases, surgery prior to majority.

But SB1 turns the old rule on its ear. Rather than defer to what medical experts think is best and allow individual minors and their parents to opt into treatment in light of the pros and cons of care, SB1 prohibits both trans and intersex kids from having a say one way or another. The restraints SB1 places on trans and intersex kids' capacity to consent to medical treatment helps neither group. This is because, by design, SB1's intent is to coerce minors to accept the label SB1 applies to them.[30] Consequently, under SB1 trans children who

---

[28] Intersex treatment protocols for the last seven decades are inhumane in the most basic sense. Their primary concern is sexing a child's body as young as possible, despite the interventions being permanent and initiated long before the child is capable of consent. *See* Julie A. Greenberg, *Intersex and Intrasex Debates: Building Alliances to Challenge Sex Discrimination*, 12 CARDOZO J. L. & GENDER 99, 104–05 (2005).

[29] *Compare* TENN. CODE ANN. § 39-13-101(e)(3) (allowing surgery that conforms with standards of the American College of Obstetrics and Gynecology) *with* American College of Obstetricians and Gynecologists, Committee Opinion, Care for Transgender Individuals 1 (December 2011) ("The American College of Obstetricians and Gynecologists opposes discrimination on the basis of gender identity and urges public and private health insurance plans to cover the treatment of gender identity disorder."). *See also* American College of Obstetricians and Gynecologists, Committee Opinion, Healthcare for Transgender and Gender Diverse Individuals (Policy No. 823, Mar. 2021), https://www.acog.org/clinical/clinical-guidance/committee-opinion/articles/2021/03/health-care-for-transgender-and-gender-diverse-individuals.

[30] Medical treatment is only prohibited where provision enables "a minor to identify with, or live as, a purported identity inconsistent with the minor's sex." Tenn. Code §68-33-103(a)(1)(A).

See also id. at (c) (characterizing trans kids' identities as "purported" and insisting that any measurable "discordance can be resolved by less invasive approaches that are likely to result in better outcomes for the minor"); *id.* at (m) ("This state has a legitimate, substantial, and compelling interest in encouraging minors to appreciate their sex, particularly as they undergo puberty.").

medically need care cannot access it, and intersex children who do not need medical care are forced to undergo it anyways.[31]

2. SB1 Imposes a Sex Classification

While SB1 might look a bit different than sex classification schemes that discriminate between males and females, it operates the same. The sex any given individual is labeled operates to impose different benefits and burdens upon otherwise similarly situated persons.

Taking a closer look, SB1 insists that girls and boys as defined by statute should only ever be legally permitted to undergo medical treatments that permanently alter their bodies during minority if treatment accords with the girl and boy labels as defined by SB1 itself. This is tautological. It imagines sex as only intelligible by parameters that deny the existence of trans persons.[32]

At bottom, SB1's animating purpose is to restrict some groups, but not others, from access to generally available medical care based solely on group membership. This is so because Tennessee presumes that the same treatments, which pose the same chance of permanently altering the body during minority because the group label itself bespeaks a greater hazard incurred but for the law. But that premise defies the evidence we have about the pros and cons of treatment for all three groups.

For as long as hormone blockers, masculinizing and feminizing hormones, and reconstructive surgery have existed, all three groups

---

[31] For a thoughtful approach to treatment of intersex conditions in minors, *see generally* Kevin G. Behrens, *A Principled Ethical Approach to Intersex Pediatric Surgeries*, 21 BMC MED. ETHICS 108 (2020) (proposing five principles for intersex surgeries: (1) they should only be performed when there is strong evidence that they are beneficial and not harmful, (2) they should only be performed in cases of true medical necessity, (3) they should normally only be performed in cases of true medical necessity; (4) conventional ethical requirements regarding truth telling apply equally to intersex children as to anyone else; (5) where physicians or parents think that surgery is in the best interests of the child, the burden of proof lies with them).

[32] *See, e.g.*, Catherine A. MacKinnon, *Reflections on Sex Equality Under Law*, 100 YALE L. J. 1281, 1292–93 (1991) ("[T]he law of discrimination, to the extent it centers on empirical accuracy of classification and categorization, has targeted inequality's failures of perception such that full human variety is not recognized, above inequality's imposition of commonalities, such that full human variety is not permitted to exist."); Courtney Megan Cahill, *Sex Equality's Irreconcilable Differences*, 132 YALE L.J. 1065 (2023) (biologically rationalized sex distinctions have always been sex stereotypes); Katherine M. Franke, *The Central Mistake of Sex Discrimination Law: The Disaggregation of Sex from Gender*, 144 U. PA. L. REV. 1, 2 (1995) ("By accepting . . . biological differences, equality jurisprudence reifies as a foundational fact that which is really an effect of normative gender ideology.").

in SB1's scheme have had access and utilized those treatments. SB1 sidesteps that historical fact by simply insisting the use-case is so recent for trans minors as to be experimental and inherently dangerous. This is false.

The problem with the lack of medical evidence justification is that it is tautological. SB1 simply insists there is insufficient evidence of efficacy of treatment in trans youth, and presumes there must be considerably better evidence of the efficacy of care in nontrans and intersex youth.[33] But that is not true either.[34] Prior to this moment in

---

[33] *Compare* TENN. CODE ANN. § 68-33-101(a) ("The legislature declares that it must take action to protect the health and welfare of minors.") *with id.* at (b) ("The legislature determines that medical procedures that alter a minor's hormonal balance, remove a minor's sex organs, or otherwise change a minor's physical appearance are harmful to a minor when these medical procedures are performed for the purpose of enabling a minor to identify with, or live as, a purported identity inconsistent with the minor's sex or treating purported discomfort or distress from a discordance between the minor's sex and asserted identity. These procedures can lead to the minor becoming irreversibly sterile, having increased risk of disease and illness, or suffering from adverse and sometimes fatal psychological consequences. Moreover, the legislature finds it likely that not all harmful effects associated with these types of medical procedures when performed on a minor are yet fully known, as many of these procedures, when performed on a minor for such purposes, are experimental in nature and not supported by high-quality, long-term studies.").

See also id. at (c) ("The legislature determines that there is evidence that medical procedures that alter a minor's hormonal balance, remove a minor's sex organs, or otherwise change a minor's physical appearance are not consistent with professional medical standards when the medical procedures are performed for the purpose of enabling a minor to identity with, or live as, a purported identity inconsistent with the minor's sex or treating purported discomfort or distress from a discordance between the minor's sex and asserted identity because a minor's discordance can be resolved by less invasive approaches that are likely to result in better outcomes for the minor.").

[34] *See generally* JULIAN GILL-PETERSON, HISTORIES OF THE TRANSGENDER CHILD (2018); Simona Giordano & Søren Holm, *Is Puberty Delaying Treatment 'Experimental Treatment'?*, 21 INT'L J. TRANSGENDER HEALTH 113 (2020); Michael Biggs, *The Dutch Protocol for Juvenile Transsexuals: Origins and Evidence*, 49 J. SEX & MARITAL THERAPY 348 (2023). *See also* Beth A. Clark & Alice Virani, *This Wasn't a Split-Second Decision": An Empirical Ethical Analysis of Transgender Youth Capacity, Rights, and Authority to Consent to Hormone Therapy*, 18 BIOETHICAL INQUIRY 151 (2021); Lieke JJJ Vrouenraets et al., *Assessing Medical Decision-Making Competence in Transgender Youth*, 148 Pediatrics e2020049643 (2021); O. Ravindranath et al., *Adolescent Neurocognitive Development and Decision-Making Abilities Regarding Gender-Affirming Care*, 67 DEVELOPMENTAL COGNITIVE NEUROSCIENCE 67 (2024); Luk Gijs & Anne Brewaeys, *Surgical Treatment of Gender Dysphoria in Adults & Adolescents: Recent Developments, Effectiveness, and Challenges*, 18 ANNUAL REV. SEX RESEARCH 178 (2012); Yolanda Smith et al., *Sex Reassignment: Outcomes and Predictors of Treatment for Adolescent and Adult Transsexuals*, 35 PSYCH. MED. 89 (2005).

time, neither providers nor the government insisted that medical care be investigated on the basis of trans, nontrans, or intersex status.[35] Additionally, in light of evidence already accumulated in peer review medical literature over the last century, it is unethical to deny trans kids with gender dysphoria medical care in a double-blind study simply to reaffirm what previous studies already conclude.[36]

Take as one example hormone blockers. These drugs were first studied to treat trans and nontrans children in the 1980s.[37] Nevertheless, Tennessee insists that the use-case for treating trans minors is not well evidenced because the first peer review medical studies were not published until the 1990s. Properly contextualized, it is not alarming that medical researchers did not start writing about the use-case for trans minors in longitudinal studies until the 1990s. The same is true for all minor patient populations.

---

[35] Drugs and devices that have obtained FDA approval are always allowed to be prescribed off-label—meaning administered to a patient population not studied in the clinical trials required for initial approval and/or for a disease different than that for which it was originally approved. *See* Buckman v. Plaintiff's Legal Committee, 531 U.S. 341, 350 (2001) (Rehnquist, J.) (holding that off-label use is an accepted and necessary corollary to the FDA's mission to regulate in this area without directly interfering with the practice of medicine and has long been recognized as such by courts, states, and the FDA its self) (citing James Beck & Elizabeth Azari, *FDA, Off-Label Use, and Informed Consent: Debunking Myths and Misconceptions*, 53 Food & Drug L.J. 71, 76–77 (1998)).

[36] *See* Florence Ashley et al., *Randomized-Controlled Trials Are Inappropriate in Adolescent Transgender Healthcare*, 25 Int'l J. Transgender Health 407 (2024) (explaining evidence supporting care and explaining why randomized-controlled trials would be unethical in this context).

[37] *See, e.g.*, P. Feuillan et al., *Use of Aromatase Inhibitors in Precocious Puberty*, 6 Endocrine-Related Cancer 303, 304 (1999) (observing that earliest case study of single minor nontrans patient published in 1985 with follow up pilot study of five nontrans youth published in 1986); Peggy T. Cohen-Kettenis et al., *The Treatment of Adolescent Transsexuals: Changing Insights*, 5 J. Sex. Med. 1892, 1893 (2008) (observing that Dutch gender clinics had at that point already been treating trans youth for about 20 years, meaning earliest clinical studies began sometime in the mid 1980s). *See also* Yolanda L.S. Smith et al., *Adolescents with Gender Identity Disorder Who Were Accepted or Rejected for Sex Reassignment Surgery: A Prospective Follow-Up Study*, 40 J. Am. Acad. Child Adolescent. Psychiatry 472 (2001) (longitudinal assessment of psychological and social functioning); P.T. Cohen-Kettenis & S.H.M. van Goozen, *Pubertal Delay as an Aid in Diagnosis and Treatment of a Transsexual Adolescent*, 7 Euro. Child & Adolescent Psych. 246 (1998) (observing minors treated at gender clinics); Peggy T. Cohen-Kettenis & Stephanie H.M. van Goozen, *Sex Reassignment of Adolescent Transsexuals: A Follow Up Study*, 36 J. Am. Acad. Child Adolescent. Psychiatry 263 (1997).

3. Detransitioner Regret is a Red Herring

Other legislative findings also undermine, rather than support, the need for SB1. For instance, SB1 says it is trying to prevent today's kids from being driven to suicide by gender medicine initiated in youth that patients come to regret later in life. It points to two different examples of kids the law is supposedly trying to protect.

The first are detransitioners—persons who were incorrectly diagnosed with gender dysphoria in youth, underwent treatments indicated by that diagnosis even after being apprised of the permanent consequences of treatment, and later came to regret it.[38] While detransitioners, like all persons, deserve empathy and compassion, a law like SB1 does nothing to strike at the problem detransitioners actually experience.

The detransitioner's brief filed in *Skrmetti* proves this point.[39] All detransitioner signatories attest that they repeatedly lied to health providers (some also lied to their parents) leading up to obtaining a gender dysphoria diagnosis and thereafter.[40] They all also withheld doubts they experienced once medical interventions began, and they continued to do so for years. All three admit that they repeatedly threatened to kill themselves; some specifically threatened suicide if

---

[38] TENN. CODE ANN. § 68-33-103(h) ("The legislature finds that minors lack the maturity to fully understand and appreciate the life-altering consequences of such procedures and that many individuals have expressed regret for medical procedures that were performed on or administered to them for such purposes when they were minors.").

[39] Brief of Amici Curiae Isabelle Ayala, Jill Doe, Soren Aldaco, and Jane Smith, *Skrmetti v. United States*, 145 S. Ct. 1816 (2025) (No. 23-477), https://www.supremecourt.gov/DocketPDF/23/23-477/328202/20241015112933955_23-477bsacIsabelleAyala.pdf [Detransitioner Brief].

[40] Detransitioner Brief at 4 ("Isabelle's determination to pursue the path of medicalization grew to the point that she was ready to do or say whatever she needed to get what she thought would help her."); *id.* at 9–14 (blaming medical providers for Jill Doe's failure to divulge history of "prolonged sexual abuse" which, in hindsight Doe surmises explains why she found female puberty psychologically distressing; going on to reveal that Doe divulged her history of sexual abuse only at age 17 at which point she got mental health treatment and detransitioned); *id.* at 16–20 (contending Soren Aldaco at age 16, while in a manic episode told mental health providers that she identified as male and she did not correct providers despite being given plenty of opportunity to do so until age 19); *id.* at 20 (insisting that Jane Smith's self-diagnosis with gender dysphoria before seeking therapy at age 16 was the fault of her medical providers to whom she did not disclose her suicidal tendencies stemmed not from gender dysphoria but a history of sexual abuse and a "traumatic upbringing" for which she did seek care until after more than six years of treatment for gender dysphoria).

they were denied treatment for gender dysphoria. And all also admit they spent considerable time isolating themselves from others trying to come up with schemes to obtain the diagnosis and care they knew would be denied if they told the truth.

The detransitioners' candor should be taken at face value, but the legal conclusion they demand does not follow from what their experiences evidence. A child hellbent on lying to obtain a medical diagnosis by fraud and medical interventions they do not need even when repeatedly admonished there will be permanent consequences will not be stopped by a law like SB1. The hazard these children face is that of their own making.

Some people, irrespective of age, will engage in deceit for long periods of time during which they harm themselves irreversibly.[41] Even if in hindsight society prefers that the detransitioners did not, as adults, profoundly regret the medical decisions they made as children, such empathy does not constitutionally justify a law drawn like SB1. It is wildly arbitrary to insist state law be designed in such a way that children who absolutely need care are prohibited from getting it for the chance that children who do not need it will lie about symptoms and deceive providers and parents.

If we instead consider a less politically fraught form of medical care, SB1's error is easier to see. Open heart surgery is a go-to treatment for certain heart conditions. It is invasive, leaves permanent scars, and entails a lengthy recovery period. The surgery is also inherently dangerous. That is why the treatment is only available to patients with medical diagnoses that justify the risks of the intervention.

---

[41] *See, e.g.*, Joanne Turner & Steven Reid, *Munchausen's Syndrome*, 359 Lancet 346, 346 (2002) ("Munchausen's syndrome is a disorder characterized by a triad of features: simulated illness; pathological lying (psuedologia fantastica); and wandering from place to place (peregrination). It is an extreme variant of factitious disorder, and despite being the most widely reported in published work, Munchausen's syndrome probably accounts for less than 10% of all factitious disorders seen in the hospital. The main feature of factitious disorder is the simulation or fabrication of physical symptoms and signs, psychiatric symptoms and signs, or both, with no apparent motivation other than to adopt the role of being a patient."); Peggy Cadet & Marc D. Feldman, *Pretense of a Paradox: Factitious Intersex Conditions on the Internet*, 24 Int'l J. Sexual Health 91, 91 (2012) ("Persons with factitious intersex conditions may interfere with peer-group support and spread misinformation. While acknowledging the reality of intersex conditions in some people, we advise a high index of suspicion and, as needed, verification of claims."); Peggy Cadet, *Intersex Pretenders*, 53 Archives Sexual Behavior 1667 (2024) (similar).

If an adult, hellbent on having open heart surgery, were to engage in a protracted scheme to deceive her health care providers into mistakenly diagnosing her with a condition that is treatable with open heart surgery, who is at fault? At the very least, the patient is not an innocent so in need of protection that the law should forbid persons who do not lie about their need for treatment from receiving it.

4. SB1 Could Not Have Saved David Reimer

SB1 cites the suicides of David and Brian Reimer as evidence that hormone blockers, hormones, and surgery pose a special danger to trans minors.[42] There are several reasons why this premise is faulty.

Among them are that neither David nor Brian Reimer were trans, and both died in their late 30s. Another is that while David did commit suicide,[43] his twin brother Brian died from an accidental drug overdose two years prior.[44] But the bigger problem with even invoking David Reimer as proof of why SB1 is needed is that that real bad things that were done to him are perfectly licit under the law.

David Reimer's ordeal started with what was supposed to be a routine male circumcision.[45] When David and Brian were six months old, both were diagnosed with phimosis—a condition in which the foreskin cannot retract behind the glans of the penis. Phimosis is normal in young children; most of the time it resolves on its own. Unfortunately, David's surgeon imprudently used an electrocauterization tool to burn the flesh apart rather than a scalpel to cut. David's penis was catastrophically burned. (Brian was spared surgery—and his phimosis resolved without intervention later.) David's doctors and parents decided it would be better, because the penile injury was severe and reconstruction would be difficult, to create labia and castrate David while still a baby. And so, David was raised female until, at age 14, he was told the truth. Thereafter, David transitioned back to male, took testosterone, and eventually as an adult underwent phalloplasty.

---

[42] TENN. CODE ANN. § 68-33-101(f).

[43] *David Reimer, 38, Subject of John/Joan Case*, N.Y. TIMES (May 12, 2004), https://www.nytimes.com/2004/05/12/us/david-reimer-38-subject-of-the-john-joan-case.html.

[44] John Calapinto, *What Were the Real Reasons Behind David Reimer's Suicide*, SLATE (June 3, 2004), https://slate.com/technology/2004/06/why-did-david-reimer-commit-suicide.html.

[45] *See generally* JOHN COLAPINTO, AS NATURE MADE HIM: THE BOY WHO WAS RAISED AS A GIRL (Harper Perennial 2006).

The unnecessary circumcision David Reimer underwent is perfectly licit in Tennessee.[46] The State prohibits only female circumcision, not male circumcision.[47] Male circumcision can be performed at any age.[48] The minor's consent is unnecessary. And even a nonmedical professional may perform the procedure.[49] There is no medical diagnosis required.[50] If a child is injured like David was, SB1 does not prohibit his parents and doctors from choosing to change his sex without his consent.[51]

David Reimer's suicide at age 38 is a tragedy. But we do not know if he took his life because of his harrowing medical ordeal, or something else altogether. We know David struggled with his brother's death. We also know that he lost his job, separated from his wife, and had recently incurred a major financial loss all close in time to his suicide.[52]

What we do know for certain is that David wanted the world to know about his medical ordeal. He wanted the truth to be told about what damage can be done if a child's genitals are operated

---

[46] The same is true in every American jurisdiction. For a thoughtful critique of why male circumcision is presumptively licit in the United States and exploration of how this illustrates social norms' influence on behavior and law, *see generally* Sarah E. Waldeck, *Using Male Circumcision to Understand Social Norms as Multipliers*, 72 UNIV. CIN. L. REV. 455 (2003).

See also Shea Lita Bond, *State Laws Criminalizing Female Circumcision: A Violation of the Equal Protection Clause of the Fourteenth Amendment?*, 32 J. MARSHALL L. REV. 353 (1999) (arguing that all minors be protected from circumcision).

[47] TENN. CODE ANN. § 39-13-110 (categorically prohibiting female circumcision, there termed "female genital mutilation").

[48] *See, e.g.*, Thompson v. Thomas, 12 Tenn. App. 484 (1930) (holding doctor liable for death induced by drug administered during surgery—Infant's male circumcision should have been performed without pain relief).

[49] *See In re* EZ, 2019 WL 1380110, at *13 (Tenn. App. Mar. 26, 2019) (characterizing other tearing of penis, but not unrecorded circumcision likely performed by parents to be child abuse).

[50] *But see* J. Steven Svoboda et al., *Circumcision is Unethical and Unlawful*, 44 J. L. MED. & ETHICS 263 (2016) (arguing that non-therapeutic minor male circumcision is not medically justified and unethical).

[51] The only bar on sex changes imposed by SB1 are those pursued to affirm the child's innermost sense of sex. There are no limitations placed on parents or doctors if care is instigated by them to "treat" an injury. *See* TENN. CODE ANN. § 68-33-103(a)(1)(A)–(B) (treatment is forbidden if it enables "a minor to identify with, or live as, a purported identity inconsistent with the minor's sex" or is intended to treat "purported discomfort or distress from a discordance between the minor's sex and asserted identity").

[52] See sources cited *supra* notes 44–46.

on unnecessarily and without their consent.[53] For obvious reasons, David thought even circumcision should require consent. But David did not blame trans people, or intersex people for his plight. He blamed the adults who insisted they knew what was best for him before he was capable of telling them what he wanted for himself. Things only got better for David once his parents and doctors finally started listening to what he wanted and needed.

II. *Skrmetti*'s Mistake

The primary analytic mistake made by the *Skrmetti* Court is that the judiciary, when confronted with an equal protection challenge, has the power to apply more or less scrutiny purely premised on how the law or the Court itself classifies the individual challenger. Equal protection allows no such thing. Once the Court made this mistake, *Skrmetti*'s result is a foregone conclusion. Trans kids get only rational basis scrutiny, and in affording as much deference as possible to Tennessee, the Court refuses to confront SB1's irrationality, let alone the real hazards it creates to solve a problem that does not exist.

A. Chief Justice Roberts's Majority Opinion

Chief Justice Roberts's opinion turns on SB1 being a diagnosis-based, not sex-based, classification scheme. Through that lens SB1 is cast as a valiant, neutral effort[54] by state lawmakers to help vulnerable children

---

[53] *See* BBC, *Transcript: Dr. Money and the Boy with No Penis*, https://www.bbc.co.uk/sn/tvradio/programmes/horizon/dr_money_trans.shtml (David Reimer: "You're always going to see people that are going to say well the Dave Reimer case could have been successful. I'm living proof, and if you're not going to take my word as gospel, because I have lived through it, who else are you going to listen to? Who else is there? I've lived through it. Like, is it going to take somebody to wind up killing themselves, shooting themselves in the head for people to listen?"); PBS, *Transcript: Sex Unknown*, Oct. 30, 2011, https://www.pbs.org/wgbh/nova/transcripts/2813gender.html (David Reimer: "I was never happy as Brenda. Never. I'd slit my throat before I'd go back to that. I'd never go back to that. It didn't work because that's life, because you're human and you're not stupid and eventually you wind up being who you are.").

[54] *But see* Patricia Williams, *The Obliging Shell: An Informal Essay on Formal Equal Opportunity*, 87 MICH. L. REV. 2128, 2140 (1989) ("Neutrality is from this perspective a suppression, an institutionalization of psychic taboos as much as segregation was the institutionalization of physical boundaries."); Reva Siegel, *Why Equal Protection No Longer Protects: The Evolving Forms of Status-Enforcing State Action*, 49 STAN. L. REV. 1111 (1997) (recognizing that the rules and reasons the legal system employees to enforce status relations evolve as they are contested, we should scrutinize justifications for racially neutral state action with skepticism, knowing that we may be rationalizing practices that perpetuate historic forms of stratification).

navigate a world with a new disease and little evidence supporting a specific treatment recently developed.[55] And given Tennessee's general police power, it seems sensible enough for state lawmakers to be afforded some leeway to figure out what is best for trans kids.[56]

At the threshold, supporters of Chief Justice Roberts's majority opinion in *Loper Bright Enterprise v. Raimondo*[57] should be dismayed that his opinion afforded such extreme deference to the Tennessee legislature in *Skrmetti*. After all, it was Roberts who insisted in *Loper Bright* that "judges have always been expected to apply their judgment independent of the political branches when interpreting the laws those branches enact."[58]

There are a few additional problems with Roberts's characterization of SB1 as a diagnosis-based instead of sex-based classification scheme. The most astounding is Roberts's insistence that SB1 does not discriminate on the basis of sex. His logic is that because all children are assigned a sex by the law—male or female—all are restricted to only care that corresponds to that sex stereotypically.[59]

---

[55] *But see* Roman Catholic Diocese of Brooklyn v. Cuomo, 592 U.S. 14, 30 (2020) (Kavanaugh, J., concurring) ("[J]udicial deference in an emergency or a crisis does not mean wholesale judicial abdication, especially when important questions of religious discrimination, racial discrimination, free speech, or the like are raised.").

[56] *But see* South Bay United Pentecostal Church v. Newsom, 141 S. Ct. 716 (Mem.), 717 (2021) (quoting South Bay United Pentecostal Church v. Newsom, 140 S. Ct. 1613, 1613 (2020) (Roberts, C.J., concurring)) ("I adhere to the view that the 'Constitution principally entrusts the safety and health of the people to the politically accountable officials of the States.' But the constitution also entrusts the protection of the people's rights to the Judiciary—not despite judges being shielded by life tenure, but because they are. Deference, though broad, has its limits.").

See also Gamble v. United States, 139 S. Ct. 1960, 1985 (2019) (Thomas, J., concurring) ("The judicial power must be understood in light of the Constitution's status as the supreme legal document over other sources of law. . . . Put differently, because the Constitution is supreme over other sources of law, it requires us to privilege its text over our own precedents when the two are in conflict.").

[57] 603 U.S. 369 (2024).

[58] *Loper Bright*, 603 U.S. at 412 (cleaned up).

[59] *Contra Loving*, 388 U.S. at 8 (rejecting the "notion that the mere 'equal application' of a statute containing racial classifications is enough to remove the classifications from the Fourteenth Amendment's proscription of all invidious racial discriminations"); *id.* at 11 (where laws "rest upon distinctions drawn according to race . . . the Equal Protection Clause demands that the classifications be subjected to the most rigid scrutiny") (cleaned up). *See also* Cruzan by Cruzan v. Missouri, 497 U.S. 261, 350 (1990) (Stevens, J., dissenting) ("It is not within the province of secular government to circumscribe the liberties of the people by regulations designed wholly for the purposes of establishing a sectarian definition of life.").

Therefore, all are regulated equally. This is why Roberts reasons that the same limit—prohibiting all children from accessing medical interventions to treat gender dysphoria—is imposed on both trans and nontrans kids.[60] But this is incorrect. As previously discussed, SB1 imposes male and female labels on all but intersex kids.

Roberts insists that in a compounded discrimination scheme, the lowest degree of scrutiny applicable to one of the several classifications at play should govern. That is illogical, and does not make sense even under the tiers of scrutiny. If a scheme like SB1 imposes a compounded classification, there is no way to distinguish between the parts that touch on sex from those that touch on disability. Any attempt at disentanglement misses how part of the scheme operates.[61]

Another flaw is that Roberts minimizes SB1's devastating consequences for trans kids.[62] Gender dysphoria is not a new

---

[60] *But see* Miller v. Johnson, 515 U.S. 900, 911 (1995) ("[A]t the heart of the Constitution's guarantee of equal protection lies the simple command that the Government must treat citizens as individuals, not as simply components of racial, religious, sexual or national class.").

[61] Devon W. Carbado & Kimberlé W. Crenshaw, *An Intersectional Critique of Tiers of Scrutiny: Beyond "Either/Or" Approaches to Equal Protection*, 129 YALE L.J. F. 108, 127 (2019) ("Our worry is that the tiers-of-scrutiny approach legitimizes the existential predicament about which Audre Lorde so powerfully wrote: 'As a Black lesbian feminist comfortable with the many different ingredients of my identity, and a woman committed to racial and social freedom from oppression, I find I am constantly being encouraged to pluck out some one aspect of myself and present this as the meaningful whole, eclipsing or denying the other parts of self'.").

[62] *See, e.g.*, Katherine L. Kraschel et al., *Legislation Restricting Gender-Affirming Care for Transgender Youth: Politics Eclipse Healthcare*, 3 CELL REPORTS MED. 100719 (2022); Landon D. Hughes et al., *"These Laws Will Be Devastating": Pediatric Provider Perspectives on Laws and Policies Impacting Sports Participation for Transgender Youth*, 9 LGBT HEALTH 247 (2022) (surveying transition care specialists concerns re exclusion of trans youth from sport); Ellis Barrera et al., Opinion, *The Medical Implications of Banning Transgender Youth from Sport Participation*, JAMA PEDIATRICS (2021); Harry Barbee et al., Viewpoint, *Anti-Transgender Legislation—A Public Health Concern for Transgender Youth*, 176 JAMA PEDIATRICS 125 (2022) (cautioning legislation could exacerbate existing health disparities, facilitate risky behaviors, and lead to preventable deaths); George B. Cunningham et al., *Anti-Transgender Rights Legislation and Internet Searches Pertaining to Depression and Suicide*, PLOS One, Dec. 22, 2022, https://journals.plos.org/plosone/article?id=10.1371/journal.pone.0279420 (observing defeat of anti-trans bills linked with fewer depression-related internet searches, and a strong association between anti-trans bills being passed with suicide-related searches where state has high LGBT population density); Jaclyn M.W. Hughto et al., *Uncertainty and Confusion Regarding Transgender Non-discrimination Policies: Implications for the Mental Health of Transgender*

phenomenon—medical providers have acknowledged it since antiquity.[63] Moreover, gender dysphoria is not a fleeting bad feeling about one's body. Experiencing it feels like torture until medical intervention resolves the disconnect between mind and body. When properly contextualized, Tennessee's suggestion that trans kids simply "wait and see" whether gender dysphoria endures to majority before treatment is accessible is cruel. It is simply an impermissible government preference for trans kids to be subject to conversion attempts until majority (colloquially called conversion therapy)[64] that have no chance of working because once gender identity is formed it cannot be changed.[65]

Americans, 19 SEXUALITY RES. & SOC. POL'Y 1069 (2022) (study participants who were concerned about the enactment of state anti-trans laws had greater odds of depression, anxiety, and PTSD). *See also* Sharon G. Horne, *The Stench of Bathroom Bills and Anti-Transgender Legislation: Anxiety and Depression Among Transgender, Nonbinary, and Cisgender LGBQ People During a State Referendum*, 69 J. COUNSELING PSYCH. 1 (2022) (suggesting increased anxiety in the face of anti-LGBTQ ballot bills that is lessened after the bill is defeated).

There is also an emerging literature on supportive parental figures' fears about these laws. *See, e.g.*, Kacie M. Kidd et al., *"This Could Mean Death for My Child": Parent Perspectives on Laws Banning Gender-Affirming Care for Transgender Adolescents*, 68 J. ADOLESCENT HEALTH 1082 (2021) (finding in survey of 273 parents and guardians of trans youth most feared that anti-trans laws would lead to worsening mental health and suicide for trans youth); Roberto L. Abreu et al., *"I Am Afraid for Those Kids Who Might Find Death Preferable": Parental Figures' Reactions and Coping Strategies to Bans on Gender Affirming Care for Transgender and Gender Diverse Youth*, 9 PSYCH. SEXUAL ORIENTATION & GENDER DIVERSITY 500 (2022).

[63] Nicholas S. Literski, *Defacing Dionysus: The Fabrication of an Anti-Transgender Myth*, 64 PSYCH. PERSPECTIVES 360 (2021); Milton T. Edgerton, Norman J. Knorr, & James R. Callison, *The Surgical Treatment of Transsexual Patients: Limitations and Indications*, 45 PLASTIC & RECONSTRUCTIVE SURGERY 38, 38 (1970) ("Since antiquity some men have shown evidence of conflict, arising from feelings of inappropriateness of the sex assigned to them on the basis of their external anatomical development.").

[64] Even if conversion therapy were evidence based, it still would not be within the public health power to force persons to pick that treatment over puberty blockers, exogenous hormones, or surgery. *Accord* Nat'l Inst. of Fam. & Life Advocs. v. Becerra, 585 U.S. 755, 771 (2019) (Thomas, J.) (quoting Abrams v. United States, 250 U.S. 616, 630 (1919) (Holmes, J., dissenting) ("[T]he best test of truth is the power of the thought to get itself accepted in the competition of the market," and people lose when the government is the one deciding which ideas should prevail.).

[65] *See generally* FLORENCE ASHLEY, BANNING TRANSGENDER CONVERSION PRACTICES: A LEGAL AND POLICY ANALYSIS (Univ. B.C. 2022).

Roberts's opinion also fails to respect that the public health power conferred to states by our Constitution is not plenary.[66] Government cannot force even minors to undergo treatment against their wishes.[67] Nor does government have the power to categorically substitute its judgment for that of parents with respect to minor's treatment options.[68] Rather than mind the limits of the public health power, Roberts's opinion affords extreme deference to Tennessee lawmakers.

---

[66] Jacobson v. Commonwealth of Massachusetts, 197 U.S. 11, 39 (1905) ("The police power of a state may be exerted in such circumstances, or by regulations so arbitrary and oppressive in particular cases, as to justify the interference of the courts to prevent wrong and oppression.").

I agree with Daniel Rodriguez that the metes and bounds of government police powers has been undertheorized in the last several decades. While in earlier generations the Court tended to focus on whether government had the power to act in the first instance, the shift towards fundamental rights has distorted constitutional thinking into myopically only considering whether a fundamental right has been violated or the appropriate tier of scrutiny is applied. *See generally* DANIEL B. RODRIGUEZ, GOOD GOVERNING: THE POLICE POWER IN THE AMERICAN STATES (Cambridge Univ. Press 2024).

[67] The Constitution does not afford government special leeway with respect to incursions on children's liberty interest in picking what medical care they wish to undergo. Cruzan v. Dir., Mo. Dep't of Health, 497 U.S. 261, 278 (1990) (declaring that "the principle that a competent person has a constitutionally protected liberty interest in refusing unwanted medical treatment may be inferred from our prior decisions"); Planned Parenthood of Central Mo. v. Danforth, 428 U.S. 52, 74 (1976) (Blackmun, J.) ("Minors, as well as adults, are protected by the Constitution and possess constitutional rights."); Parham v. JR, 442 U.S. 584, 602 (1979) (citing Pierce v. Society of Sisters, 268 U.S. 510, 535 (1925); 1 Blackstone, Commentaries 447; 2 J. Kent, Commentaries on American Law 190) ("Our constitutional system long ago rejected any notion that a child is the mere creature of the State[.]"). *Cf.* Weber v. Aetna Cas. & Sur. Co., 406 U.S. 164, 175-76 (1972) (in context of illegitimate children, "Courts are powerless to prevent the social opprobrium suffered by these hapless children, but the Equal Protection Clause does enable us to strike down discriminatory laws relating to status of birth where—as in this case—the classification is justified by no legitimate state interest, compelling or otherwise.").

[68] Family bonds are usually respected by the government. Absent exceptional circumstances, minor children are not mere creatures of the State. *Parham*, 442 U.S. at 602 (citing *Pierce*, 268 U.S. at 535; 1 WILLIAM BLACKSTONE, COMMENTARIES 447; 2 JAMES KENT, COMMENTARIES ON AMERICAN LAW 190) ("Our constitutional system long ago rejected any notion that a child is the mere creature of the State and, on the contrary, asserted that parents generally have the right, coupled with the high duty, to recognize and prepare their children for additional obligations. Surely, this includes a high duty to recognize symptoms of illness and to seek and follow medical advice. The law's concept of the family rests on a presumption that parents possess what a child lacks in maturity, experience, and capacity for judgment required for making life's difficult decisions. More important, historically it has recognized that natural bonds of affection lead parents to act in the best interests of their children.").

Roberts's majority opinion also improperly relies upon *Geduldig v. Aiello*,[69] a decision so bad that Congress immediately rebuked it decades ago, but which the Court in *Dobbs v. Jackson Women's Health Organization*[70] and again in *Skrmetti* insists remains good law today. Briefly, *Geduldig* holds that a disability insurance scheme which covers all disabilities except those connected to pregnancy discriminates on the basis of diagnosis, not sex. At the time, the Court reasoned that even though only women can get pregnant, not all women do in fact get pregnant, which in turn means that the scheme does not discriminate against all women, and therefore it does not discriminate on the basis of sex.

In *Skrmetti*, Roberts cites *Geduldig* for the proposition that a classificatory scheme does not discriminate on the basis of sex unless it treats all males worse than all females, or vice versa. Applying that rule to SB1, Roberts reasons if all female minors are prohibited from accessing treatments for the purpose of masculinizing the body, and all male minors are barred from treatments that feminize the body, there is no sex discrimination because all sexes are treated equally.[71] This point, Justice Sonia Sotomayor notes in dissent, is nonsensical and also defies *Loving v. Virginia*'s condemnation of equal application as a test for equal protection violations.[72]

Ironically enough, *Skrmetti* should have been a launch point for the Court to reassess the correctness of *Geduldig*. The *Geduldig* Court presumed at the time that only women can get pregnant. But Roberts's majority opinion, to its credit, acknowledges that some people at least in adulthood change sex. Consequently, even if statistically rare, there are some trans men who can be pregnant. (Some intersex persons can also get pregnant.) This possibility could retroactively justify the bizarre line drawing in *Geduldig*.

One reason the *Skrmetti* Court may have stopped short of shoring up *Geduldig* is SB1's unstated premise that trans people do not legitimately exist. Chief Justice Roberts seemingly did not wish to go that far. Roberts's opinion goes out of the way to call trans boys

---

[69] 417 U.S. 484 (1974).

[70] 597 U.S. 215, 236 (2022) (Alito, J.) (citing *Geduldig v. Aiello*, 417 U.S. 484, 496 n. 20 (1974)).

[71] *Skrmetti*, 145 S. Ct. at 1833–84 (Roberts, C.J.).

[72] *Skrmetti*, 145 S. Ct. at 1877 (Sotomayor, J., dissenting) (citing *Loving*, 388 U.S. at 9).

and trans girls boys and girls respectively throughout. However, the courtesy Justice Roberts extends trans youth misses that SB1 itself declares trans boys are not boys, and trans girls are not girls.[73]

Roberts's good manners may also have made it harder to discern the other ways that SB1 insists, by implication, that there is no such thing as trans kids. It is on that premise real trans kids are prohibited from medically treating gender dysphoria.[74] SB1's hyper fixation on the detransitioner problem, combined with its false insistence that trans people are new to our society and treatments for gender dysphoria are inherently dangerous, implies that but for the availability of treatment for gender dysphoria, no one would be trans.

If we step back from the minutiae of SB1's textual scheme and consider the law within the context of our current political moment, its invidious purpose is crystal clear. Trans people are not new. Nor are treatments for gender dysphoria. Trans kids with exceptionally severe gender dysphoria have been medically treated in some parts of the United States since at least the early twentieth century. Our predecessors were not idiots. They knew that modern medicine is capable of making permanent changes to the body, and they witnessed over the course of decades the difference that treatment makes in trans persons' lives. Ask any older American about Christine Jorgensen, the Caitlyn Jenner of the Greatest Generation.[75]

---

[73] M. Dru Levasseur, *Gender Identity Defines Sex: Updating the Law to Reflect Modern Medical Science is Key to Transgender Rights*, 39 VT. L. REV. 943, 947 (2015) ("For transgender people to be recognized as full human beings under the law, the legal system must make room for the existence of transgender people—not as boundary-crossers but as people claiming their birthright as part of a natural variation of human sexual development.").

[74] Michael C. Dorf, *The Roberts Court Puts a Velvet Glove on the Iron Fist of Anti-Trans Backlash*, VERDICT, June 23, 2025, https://verdict.justia.com/2025/06/23/the-roberts-court-puts-a-velvet-glove-on-the-iron-fist-of-anti-trans-backlash ("The Chief Justice's opinion is not exactly offensive on its face. It uses terms like "transgender boy" in a matter-of-fact manner. Thus, it does not simply seek to erase or deny the existence of transgender persons[.] [While] the tone of the majority opinion in *Skrmetti* may be civil, its substance is highly problematic. Indeed, by treating the Tennessee legislature as having carefully attended to the medical evidence regarding the benefits and risks of puberty blockers and hormone therapy, the Court sanitizes the wave of transphobia washing over the United States.").

[75] Christine Jorgensen, a transgender woman who honorably served in World War II, made national headlines in 1952 when news of her sex reassignment surgery broke. *See* Joanne Meyerwotiz, *Sex Change and the Popular Press: Historical Notes on Transsexuality in the United States, 1930–50*, 4 GLQ 159 (1998) (exploring media coverage of Jorgensen's transition).

The only thing that changed in the 2020s is that it is now politically advantageous to discriminate against trans persons.[76] The tsunami of anti-trans bills lawmakers considered (let alone enacted) in the last five years alone illustrates just how quickly a group can go from experiencing sporadic *de facto* discrimination to being pummeled with *de jure* discrimination at every turn.[77] Even the executive branch has been captured by anti-trans animus that is unprecedented.[78]

The Supreme Court's failure to consider that, all of a sudden, there is an unmistakable sea change with respect to trans people in this nation is inexplicable. Even if the Court were only to consider *Skrmetti*'s docket, it is impossible to miss the shift. The case is titled *Skrmetti v. United States* because it is the federal government that sued

---

[76] *See, e.g.*, Andrew Demillo & John Hanna, *Some States Are Trying to Make Sex Binary. Transgender People See Their Existence Denied*, Assoc. Press, Feb. 27, 2024, https://apnews.com/article/states-define-sex-transgender-dc8c48669aef760c68d2fb7abde10e8c; Joe Killian, *"They Assume We Don't Exist,"* NC Newsline, Apr. 18, 2023, https://ncnewsline.com/2023/04/18/they-assume-we-dont-exist/; John Janna, *States' Push to Define Sex Decried as Erasing Trans People*, Assoc. Press, Feb. 15, 2023, https://apnews.com/article/politics-kansas-state-government-arkansas-health-8f2edaa40b962e5642e108b83bc14246.

[77] *See* Reva Siegel, *Why Equal Protection No Longer Protects: The Evolving Forms of Status-Enforcing State Action*, 49 Stan. L. Rev. 1111 (1997) (observing that the rules and reasons the legal system employs to enforce status relationships evolve as they are contested).

[78] *See, e.g.*, Christopher Wiggins, *Donald Trump's Government Declares that Transgender and Nonbinary People Don't Exist*, The Advocate, Jan. 20, 2025, https://www.advocate.com/politics/donald-trump-invalidates-transgender-identities; Talya Minsberg, *What We Know About Trump's New Executive Order on Trans Athletes*, N.Y. Times, Feb. 5, 2025, https://www.nytimes.com/2025/02/05/us/politics/trump-trans-athletes-executive-order.html; Juliet Macur, N.Y. Times, Feb. 6, 2025, https://www.nytimes.com/2025/02/06/us/politics/ncaa-transgender-athletes-ban.html; Jeré Longman, *A Fencing Match, a Viral Video and a Hearing Before Congress*, N.Y. Times, May 6, 2025, https://www.nytimes.com/2025/05/06/us/trump-transgender-athletes-fencing-olympics.html; Juliet Macur, *US Olympic Officials Bar Transgender Women From Women's Competitions*, N.Y. Times, July 24, 2025, https://www.nytimes.com/2025/07/22/us/politics/us-olympics-trans-women-athletes-ban-trump.html.

The absolute bar on trans women competing in the Olympic games is a historical aberration. This appears to be the first ever historical bar on trans athletes in any modern Olympic Games. *See, e.g.*, Michael Waters, The Other Olympians: Fascism, Queerness, and the Making of Modern Sports (Farrar, Straus, and Giroux 2024) (reporting open participation of trans and intersex athletes at 1936 Olympic Games hosted by Adolf Hitler's Nazi Germany). *See also* Tariq Panja & Ken Belson, *Olympics First Openly Transgender Woman Stokes Debate on Fairness*, N.Y. Times (July 31, 2021), https://www.nytimes.com/2021/07/31/sports/laurel-hubbard-trans-weight-lifting.html (misreporting Ms. Laurel Hubbard, a weight lifter from New Zealand, is first trans women to compete in any sport at the Olympics).

Tennessee for violating the equal protection rights of trans minors in the first instance. Nevertheless, once Trump came into office, his Department of Justice notified the Court that the federal government concedes the constitutionality of SB1. No explanation was offered, let alone briefing explaining why the constitution requires the opposite of what it did on January 19, 2025.[79]

Taken together, the Court's opinion in *Skrmetti* is nothing more than judicial gaslighting. It is as if the Court is riding on top of a tsunami wave that is about to hit the shore, but nevertheless insists there is zero chance a tsunami will strike. The Court cannot see any tsunami wave if it looks only at shore, but if it looked down or behind it the tsunami would be impossible to miss.[80]

B. Justice Barrett's Concurrence

It is a classic horror movie trope for an innocent to get a terrifying phone call from a killer, only to realize after it is too late that the call is coming from inside the house.[81] This is how Justice Barrett's very sympathetic sounding concurrence comes across.[82]

The main premise of Barrett's concurrence is that trans kids may some day in the future qualify for heightened scrutiny. But she points out that this can only happen if there is proof of a long history of *de jure* discrimination targeting trans persons as such.[83] In the alternative, Justice Barrett commits that if trans kids one day have

---

[79] Amy Howe, *Trump Changes Government's Position in Pending Trans Healthcare Case at Supreme Court*, SCOTUSblog (Feb. 7, 2025), https://www.scotusblog.com/2025/02/trump-changes-governments-position-in-pending-trans-healthcare-case-at-supreme-court/.

[80] *Cf.* DON'T LOOK UP (Paramount Pictures 2021).

[81] *See, e.g.*., WHEN A STRANGER CALLS (Columbia Pictures 1979); SCREAM (Dimension Films 1996). *But see* GET OUT (Universal Pictures 2017) (protagonist realizes threat is within house with just enough time to escape).

[82] *See* MLADEN DOLAR, A VOICE AND NOTHING MORE 60–61 (MIT Press 2006) ("A voice whose source one cannot see, a voice whose origin cannot be identified, a voice one cannot place. It is a voice in search of an origin, in search of a body, but even when it finds its body, it turns out that this doesn't quite work, the voice doesn't stick to the body, it is an excrescence which doesn't match the body.").

[83] *Skrmetti*, 145 S. Ct. at 1854 (Barrett, J., concurring) (arguing that required showing of history of *de jure* discrimination "is consistent with the Fourteenth Amendment's text and purpose" and "is judicially manageable" given that courts "are ill suited to conduct an open-ended inquiry into whether the volume of private discrimination exceeds some indeterminate threshold.").

proof that a law like SB1 was enacted because of animus, anti-trans laws could be deemed unconstitutional.[84]

Justice Barrett misses entirely that the invidiousness of any given equal protection violation should not turn on whether there is a long history of similar *de jure* discrimination. It is perfectly possible, as has been trans Americans' experience recently, that our nation's politics devolve to inventing new kinds of bias not shared by our predecessors. Discrimination is, after all, neither rational nor evidence based. Bigotry does not concern itself with facts; it trades in myths, stereotypes, and untruths.

Justice Barrett's further suggestion that proof of animus was wanting in *Skrmetti* rings hollow.[85] Tennessee, along with many of the *amici* who filed briefs in support of SB1, do not think SB1 is good because it helps trans kids. SB1's entire purpose is to bar trans minors from obtaining safe and efficacious treatments. Tennessee does not want trans kids to exist. That is why it insists it is a good thing for trans kids to go without treatment in the first instance. That is also why all the supposed evidence of harm that will occur without SB1 suggests the Court not worry about trans kids and instead focus on whether nontrans kids will be harmed if trans kids are allowed medical care.[86]

The additional suggestion that if the Court misses some trans discrimination for a time, this might help trans people in the future make the case for heightened scrutiny also misses the mark. Even if the Court made good on that promise, being forced to endure *de jure* discrimination for a long period of time *before* heightened scrutiny is available is the very evil equal protection prohibits.

---

[84] *Id.* at 1855 ("Because the litigants assumed that evidence of private discrimination could suffice for the suspect-class inquiry, they did not thoroughly discuss whether transgender individuals have suffered a history of *de jure* discrimination as a class. And because the group of transgender individuals is an insufficiently discrete and insular minority, the question is largely academic. In future cases, however, I would not recognize a new suspect class absent a demonstrated history of *de jure* discrimination.").

[85] *Id.* at 1855 n.5 ("The evidence that is before this Court is sparse but suggestive of relatively little *de jure* discrimination.")

[86] *Contra id.* at 1853 ("If laws that classify based on transgender status necessarily trigger heightened scrutiny, then courts will inevitably be in the business of closely scrutinizing legislative choices in all these domains. To be sure, an individual law inexplicable by anything but animus is unconstitutional. But legislatures have many valid reasons to make policy in these areas, and so long as a statute is a rational means of pursuing a legitimate end, the Equal Protection Clause is satisfied.").

Justice Barrett's other point, that trans people should do their best to engage in the political process to defeat laws that target them, is also misguided.[87] Trans people have always participated in our political processes. The problem is not lack of engagement with politics. The problem is that the democratic process can be perverted by bias.

This takes me to the most troubling aspect of Justice Barrett's concurrence. She suggests in good faith that states should be afforded wide latitude to consider what the best legal solutions are to reckon with the existence of trans persons.[88] She goes on to hold that it is a good thing for states to be laboratories of democracy in times like these, and the judicial branch must allow the states some period of trial and error.

What Justice Barrett misses about laws like SB1 is they are not produced by laboratories of democracy. They are forged by laboratories of discrimination. The entire point of equal protection is that it deprives government, the political and judicial branches alike, from taking steps that cast some groups to the gutters. Lawmaking, like voting, is an awesome power. But neither lawmakers nor voters are permitted by our Constitution to deny others equal protection of the law.

Returning to the horror trope that begins this subsection, Justice Barrett is the innocent in the trope, but the phone call is coming from inside the house. Once the political branches have failed to abide by equal protection, it is the judiciary's solemn duty to call out and rebuke violations. Insisting that groups of victims suffer now, in hopes that the judiciary may one day decide to come to their rescue misses that the judiciary is not constitutionally permitted to wait this problem out in hopes it fixes itself down the line.

Conclusion

The Supreme Court's refusal to apply the same degree of judicial scrutiny to all classifications challenged under equal protection continues to wreak havoc on our nation.

In the months since *Skrmetti* issued, some commentators have fixated on what sets the opinion apart from others. Most conclude it is unique because the Court decides in *Skrmetti* for the first time

---

[87] *Id.* at 1851 (construing the Court's failure up to present to recognize any new suspect classes justifies that "when social or economic legislation is at issue, the Equal Protection Clause allows the States wide latitude, and the Constitution presumes that even improvident decisions will be eventually rectified by the democratic processes") (cleaned up).

[88] *Id.* at 1852.

that laws that target trans persons for being trans are not sex classification schemes but instead discriminate because of disability.[89] Consequently, because as a class disabilities are distinct from sex, even where sex and disability are compounded within the discriminatory scheme, only rational basis review applies.

While I agree that SB1 is by all measures a sex classification scheme, that error appears to me to be incidental to the overarching mistake that still plagues the Court's equal protection jurisprudence. As in the past, today the Court insists different types of classification merit different degrees of judicial scrutiny. And where a classification scheme is compounded, the Court will ratchet down scrutiny.

The key problem with *Skrmetti* is not that trans persons' equal protection challenges are afforded only rational basis review. That is the symptom, not the disease. The overarching mistake is the Court's insistence that it is within the judicial power to pick and choose which groups of persons enjoy more equal protection than others.

Today the Court insists that the tiers of scrutiny are the right framework to guide judicial review of all equal protection challenges. The Court is unconcerned that so few classifications are afforded heightened scrutiny because, it reasons, nothing stands in the way of later in time challengers proving their classification should be afforded heightened scrutiny. This is tautological. It is also judicial gaslighting. The actual obstacle in the way is the Court itself. Unless the Court wishes to ratchet up scrutiny for all equal protection challenges, nothing changes.

In sum, this Article is mostly about an analytic mistake that has long plagued the Supreme Court's equal protection jurisprudence. It is also a critique of *Skrmetti v. United States*. It discusses trans rights at some length but does not contend that trans people merit special treatment under equal protection. Instead, it insists that all similarly situated individuals should be treated the same, and the judiciary has no constitutional power to declare, let alone allow, otherwise.

---

[89] *See, e.g.,* Leah Litman, *The Archaic Sex-Discrimination Case the Supreme Court is Reviving,* THE ATLANTIC (June 24, 2025), https://www.theatlantic.com/ideas/archive/2025/06/supreme-court-sex-discrimination-skrmetti/683296/; Mark Joseph Stern, *John Roberts' Anti-Trans Opinion Is a Gabled Mess. It's Easy to See Why.,* SLATE (June 18, 2025), https://slate.com/news-and-politics/2025/06/skrmetti-john-roberts-anti-trans-supreme-court.html; Elie Mystal, *The Supreme Court's Anti-Trans Decision Will Live in Infamy,* THE NATION (June 18, 2025), https://www.thenation.com/article/politics/us-vs-skrmetti-ruling-analysis/.

Looking Ahead: October Term 2025

John J. Vecchione*

"It's tough to make predictions, especially about the future," a Yankee skipper informed us.[1] And more apt for this journal, the greatest lawyer of the ancient world relates "Vetus autem illud Catonis admodum scitum est, qui mirari se aiebat quod non rideret haruspex haruspicem cum vidisset."[2] And if we to are follow the elder Cato's admonition, all predictions and forecasts are in some sense folly. Having acknowledged the wisdom of sages, ancient and modern, it still behooves us to peer into the upcoming Supreme Court Term on a somewhat firmer basis of already accepted cases, as well as reading the entrails of the emergency docket.

As in recent Terms, the past may be prologue to what the Court takes up.[3] *Garland v. Cargill*[4] two Terms ago was mirrored, albeit with different results, in *Bondi v. Vanderstok*.[5] Last term the Court took up transgender issues in *United States v. Skrmetti*,[6] finding Tennessee's law against hormonal therapy and sex reassignment surgery for

---

* Senior Litigation Counsel, New Civil Liberties Alliance. The author thanks NCLA summer clerks Ian Baumer and Henry Dai without whom this note would not have been timely completed.

[1] This quote is often attributed to Yogi Berra. Alex R. Piquero, *It's Tough to Make Predictions, Especially About the Future*, Vital City (March 12, 2024), https://www.vitalcitynyc.org/articles/the-perils-and-necessity-of-jail-population-forecasting.

[2] Cicero, De Divinatione II 51 ("Old Cato always wondered how two fortune-tellers could look at each other without laughing.").

[3] William Shakespeare, The Tempest act 2, sc. 1, l. 253.

[4] 602 U.S. 406 (2024) (holding ATF had no authority to prohibit the use of bumpstocks).

[5] 145 S. Ct. 857 (2025) (holding ATF could regulate easily completed "ghost gun" kits) Both *Cargill* and *Vanderstok* are better understood as administrative law cases than "gun cases." The other big "gun case" of the term, which proved Smith & Wesson not only beats four aces but also Mexico, was a statutory interpretation case rather than a Second Amendment case which the Court still seems chary of taking. Smith & Wesson Brands, Inc. v. Estados Unidos Mexicanos, 145 S. Ct. 1556 (2025).

[6] 145 S. Ct. 1816 (2025).

minors constitutional. This Term, legal questions surrounding those whose genders do not conform to their biological sex have come up in three separate cases.[7] The question of where transgender status stands on the tiers of scrutiny will be front and center: strict, intermediate or rational basis?

Similarly, it is highly unlikely that we have seen the last of *Trump v. CASA, Inc.*[8] or the issues lurking within it. Billed as "the birthright citizenship" case by the press, it was actually the "nationwide injunctions" case. Not only was the question of birthright citizenship and whether it can be changed by executive order, if at all, unaddressed by the Court, but the decision also left loopholes in its "no nationwide injunctions" ruling that a plaintiff's attorney should be able to run a defectively designed truck through.

The Court also rejected the effort of *Learning Resources* to expedite consideration of the petition for writ of certiorari before judgment.[9] But it is still pending as a petition for cert. There may yet be an early adjudication of whether the tariffs imposed willy-nilly by the executive branch, relying on the International Emergency Economic Powers Act (IEEPA) are lawful or a usurpation of congressional prerogatives without statutory or constitutional warrant.[10] It is highly likely this issue will be before the Court before the 2025 Term is out.

It should be noted that the solid originalist-textualist majority, heralded in these pages for the October 2022 Term, has continued into last Term and can expected to continue into the Term ahead.[11] The mighty

---

[7] Hecox v. Little, 104 F.4th 1061 (9th Cir. 2024), *cert. granted*, Little v. Hecox, No. 24-38, 2025 WL 1829165 (U.S. July 3, 2025) (whether laws limiting participation in girls' sports to biological females violates the Equal Protection Clause of the 14th Amendment); B.P.J. v. W. Va. State Bd. of Educ., 98 F.4th 542 (4th Cir. 2024), *cert. granted sub nom.*, West Virginia v. B. P.J., No. 24-43, 2025 WL 1829164 (U.S. July 3, 2025) (same with additional question of whether Title IX prohibits such limitations on the participation in girls' sports); United States v. Shilling, 221 L. Ed. 2d 962 (May 6, 2025) (from the emergency docket whether transgender individuals can be excluded from military service).

[8] 145 S. Ct. 2540 (2025).

[9] Learning Res., Inc. v. Trump, No. 24-1287, 2025 WL 1717468 (U.S. June 20, 2025).

[10] In the interests of full disclosure, the author is counsel to several plaintiffs in similar litigation around the country and has filed amicus briefs in the *Learning Resources* litigation. *See* Complaint, Emily Ley Paper Inc. v. Trump, No. 3:25-cv-00464 (N.D. Fla. Apr. 3, 2025); Complaint, FIREDISC, Inc. v. Trump, No. 1:25-cv-01134 (W.D. Tex. July 21, 2025).

[11] Ilya Shapiro, *Looking Ahead: October Term 2022*, 2021–2022 CATO SUP. CT. REV. 335 (2022).

SCOTUSblog Stat Pack crunches the numbers for us.[12] Forty-two percent of the cases from last term were unanimous, down slightly from last year's 44 percent but including the sometimes contentious areas of free speech and religious rights. The 6-3 splits between Republican and Democrat appointments to the Court were reduced to nine percent of opinions, where they averaged 13.75 percent between the October 2020 and 2024 Terms. Chief Justice John Roberts was not only in the majority in 95 percent of the cases but issued no separate opinions—that's dissents or concurrences—this Term. Justice Ketanji Brown Jackson was in the majority the least of any of her colleagues at 72 percent. This statistic is a good measure of where the Court is and—with no personnel changes—where it is likely to be in October 2025: "Conservative" in a Roberts rather than Thomas direction but uncongenial to those looking to restore or maintain the progressive methods of analysis of the Burger-era Court. For instance, conservative Justices were in the minority in 28 percent of the cases, which is far more cases than the 6-3 ideological splits (nine percent) that so alarm the *New York Times* Court watchers. That same 6-3 split with only Justices Clarence Thomas, Samuel Alito, and Neil Gorsuch dissenting was six percent of cases. Yet these ideological splits gather no opprobrium or concern from the spectating commentariat. To emphasize the point, Justice Elena Kagan was in the majority 83 percent of the time, which surpassed the majority percentages of Justices Thomas, Gorsuch, or Alito. Which is to say it's John Robert's judicial world and we're all living in it now.

Part of that world is the practice of not taking a lot of cases. There were only 67 cases with written opinions before the October 2024 Term ended. As of July 3, 2025, shortly after the October 2024 Term ended, the Court has only granted *certiorari* in 30 cases.[13] This is pretty thin gruel, even though some of the cases on voting rights and transgender issues may be "blockbusters" by the end of the Term.

---

[12] Jake S. Truscott & Adam Feldman, *SCOTUSblog Stat Pack for the 2024-25 Term*, SCOTUSBLOG, https://www.scotusblog.com/stat-pack-2025/ (last visited Aug. 26, 2025).

[13] *Supreme Court of the United States Granted & Noted List October Term 2025 Cases for Argument*, SUPREMECOURT.GOV (July 3, 2025), https://web.archive.org/web/20250701140519/https://www.supremecourt.gov/orders/25grantednotedlist.pdf. Two others have been set for reargument or to resume merits briefing.

Which brings us to the "known unknowns" of the Supreme Court term.[14] Who knows what surprises lurk in the heart of the Supreme Court? The shadow docket knows.[15] While the Court takes few cases in the current era, it has (particularly this Term and into the summer) been bombarded by emergency petitions to grant or lift stays in contentious litigation. The Justices have had a busy time on the emergency docket. On such things as voting rights, they have stayed the effect of rulings of the appellate courts until *certiorari*, if any, can be considered. The Eight Circuit's momentous decision that the civil rights laws don't allow private parties to sue to enforce Section 2 of the Voting Rights Act has been stayed:

> The issuance of the mandate of the United States Court of Appeals for the Eighth Circuit, case No. 23-3655, is stayed pending the filing and disposition of the petition for a writ of certiorari, if such writ is timely sought. Should the petition for a writ of certiorari be denied, this stay shall terminate automatically. In the event the petition for a writ of certiorari is granted, the stay shall terminate upon the sending down of the judgment of this Court.[16]

Those words portend a return to the Supreme Court in this and many other cases where lower court stays or injunctions have been dissolved for now.

These orders are designated with a non-scarlet "A" on the Court's Orders list. But they might as well bear that color, since they stand out as issues the Court will likely have to address in the coming Term. These "A" orders point to some very consequential cases in the making. These include: (1) the extent of the President's power to dismiss federal employees when an agency is mandated by Congress to exist;[17] (2) whether the Secretary of Homeland Security can revoke the categorical grant of parole to over a half a million noncitizens without

---

[14] News Briefing, Sec. Def. Donald Rumsfeld (Feb. 2, 2002).

[15] With apologies to "the Shadow." *See The Shadow*, RADIOHALLOFFAME.COM, https://www.radiohalloffame.com/the-shadow (last visited Aug. 26, 2025); *see also* STEVE VLADECK, THE SHADOW DOCKET (2023).

[16] Turtle Mountain Band v. Howe, No. 25A62, 2025 WL 2078664 (U.S. July 24, 2025).

[17] McMahon v. New York, No. 24A1203, 2025 WL 1922626 (U.S. July 14, 2025) (granting stay of district court order of reinstatement of Department of Education employees).

providing individual case-by-case adjudication for each person;[18] (3) the continued vitality of *Humphrey's Executor* and the extent of the President's power to terminate federal employees protected by congressional statute;[19] and (4) whether the Department of Defense can enforce its policy of disqualifying individuals with gender dysphoria or who have undergone medical interventions for gender dysphoria.[20] By late July of 2025, the administration had petitioned the Supreme Court 21 times, surpassing the 19 petitions that the Biden administration filed in the entire four years of that presidency.[21] This is a function of either: (1) activist anti-Trump judges, (2) the record number of executive orders issued (over 180, the most since F.D.R.), (3) the aggressive nature of the actions under current law, or (4) as former Cato Supreme Court Review author Kannon Shanmugam postulates "the disappearance of Congress from the scene."[22] Take your pick or mix and match. But an emergency docket that active six months into a presidential term is bound to cause controversy. That is particularly so because, in the teeth of criticisms of the lack of explanation in some of these orders, the Court has stated explicitly that "although [its] interim orders are not conclusive as to the merits, they inform how a court should exercise its equitable discretion in like cases."[23]

With the cases already granted *certiorari* and those waiting for further development after emergency application to the Supreme Court, we have a term poised to address some of the most divisive social issues of the present: transgender legal status, the extent of executive power against the concomitant powers of Congress and the judiciary, and cases that could upend longstanding practices and understandings of voting rights. The questions of free speech and campaign donations and donor privacy are also front and center and promise to make the October 2025 Term one for the books.

---

[18] Noem v. Doe, 145 S. Ct. 1524 (2025) (granting stay).

[19] Trump v. Wilcox, 145 S. Ct. 1415 (2025) (granting stay).

[20] United States v. Schilling, No. 24A1030, 2025 WL 1300282 (U.S. May 6, 2025) (granting stay of district court injunction).

[21] Zach Schonfeld, *Trump Notches Winning Streak in Supreme Court Emergency Docket Deluge*, THE HILL (July 28, 2025), https://thehill.com/regulation/court-battles/5420857-trump-winning-streak-supreme-court/.

[22] *Id.*

[23] Trump v. Boyle, 145 S. Ct. 2653 (2025) (staying an order reinstating NLRB Commissioners terminated by the Trump administration).

I. Is *Humphrey's Executor* as Dead as Humphrey?

The ruling authority of *Humphrey's Executor* has been in the sights of constitutional conservatives for many years.[24] Finally, 90 years after the anti-New Deal Court disposed of *Myers v. United States*[25] to hand F.D.R. a loss by ruling that the firing of the FTC commissioner was unlawful, *Humphrey's* appears to be on its last legs. The Trump administration's efforts to ensure that the entire administrative apparatus is under White House control without "deep state Fifth columnists" undermining the stated goals of the administration, combined with an effort to "defund the left" and perhaps even challenge the constitutionality of the civil service laws, has set up an incredibly rich environment of Article II cases on executive power. The lower courts, all bound by *Humphrey's*, have been saying just that for some time and did so again in the *Wilcox* and *Boyle* cases. It was this clash of precedent binding the lower courts with the likely direction of the current Supreme Court on the matter that drove the dueling concurrence and dissents in *Trump v. Boyle*. The Court, in a *per curiam* order likely written by Roberts, stayed the ruling of the Maryland district court reinstating the terminated NLRB commissioners.[26] Justice Brett Kavanaugh, a staunch defender of minimalism on the emergency docket, urged the Court to grant the stay and grant *certiorari* before judgment both in *Boyle* and in *Wilcox*.[27] Justice Kagan, joining Justices Sonia Sotomayor and Jackson, dissented and chastised the Court for "all but overturn[ing]" *Humphrey's* and doing so, as in *Wilcox*, without a thorough opinion.[28] What was not explained is why the three dissenters did not just join Kavanaugh in granting *certiorari* before judgment? It only takes four to grant *certiorari*, and if your problem is that something important is being overruled *sub silencio* why not vote for full briefing and consideration of the issue?

Another question about all these cases is why no Supreme Court Justice, so prickly on the remedy of universal injunctions, has not simply stayed or recommended staying the dismissal cases, since the

[24] Humphrey's Ex'r v. United States, 295 U.S. 602 (1935).

[25] 272 U.S. 52 (1926).

[26] Who upon receiving the order went back to the agency and countermanded everything done in their absence, generally creating good facts to overrule *Humphrey's*.

[27] *Boyle*, 145 S. Ct. at 2655 (2025) (Kavanaugh, J., concurring).

[28] *Id.* (Kagan, J., dissenting).

remedy is unlikely to be lawful. *Humphrey's Executor* is named that because Humphrey was dead. His estate sought back pay.[29] Where do the district courts get the power to reinstate presidential appointees when they have been terminated and may have successors, acting or confirmed, in their place?

The facts of the cases likely to come before the Court are instructive. In *Wilcox* the two terminated officers were from the National Labor Relations Board (NLRB) and the Merit Systems Protection Board (MSPB).[30] Both organizations are multi-member independent agencies with terms of years. By statute "The President is prohibited . . . from removing these officers except for cause, and no qualifying cause was given."[31] The district court had granted an injunction against their termination. The Court cited *Seila Law LLC* for the proposition that the executive may dismiss any officer "subject to narrow exceptions recognized by our precedents."[32] The Court posited that the officers were unlikely to demonstrate that they did not wield executive power and so would not succeed on the merits. But they also submitted that the harm to the Executive of having to endure a removed officer continuing to wield its executive power exceeds the harm done to the officer from not exercising his statutory duty.[33]

Trump v. Boyle is of a piece. There, three Democratic commissioners of the Consumer Products Safety Commission (CPSC) were terminated with no reason given. The Court, citing *Wilcox* as already explained, stayed the district court order reinstating them. The Fourth Circuit had refused to do so even after *Wilcox*, claiming it was bound by *Humphrey's Executor* and that the case was distinguishable. The Court gave its powerful statement that emergency docket orders "inform

---

[29] *Humphrey's Ex'r*, 295 U.S. at 612.

[30] *Wilcox*, 145 S. Ct. at 1416.

[31] *Id.*

[32] *Id.* (citing Seila Law LLC v. Consumer Fin. Prot. Bureau, 591 U.S. 197, 215–18 (2020)).

[33] *Id.* The case also curiously reached out to exclude the Federal Reserve from the likely effect of these logical conclusions about executive power by citing the history of the First and Second Banks of the United States. *Id.* at 1417. This comports with the author's long-held view that if the independence of the Federal Reserve was ever threatened the Chief Justice would find that it was a tax and within Congress's power to levy. *See* Nat'l Fed'n Indep. Bus. v. Sebelius, 567 U.S. 519 (2012). The President promptly fired Federal Reserve Governor Lisa Cook for cause setting up yet anothjer lawsuit.

how a court should exercise its equitable discretion in like cases."[34] Justice Kagan is right that it would be hard for a court to more strongly signal the abandonment of prior precedent than the Court has here. It is not without interest that the administration has also terminated an FTC commissioner, and one of the fired commissioners has been granted summary judgment (citing *Humphrey's*) on her claim that the firing was illegal.[35] That case is already at summary judgment, not a preliminary ruling, and could be on all fours with *Humphrey's*. Barring an argument that the powers granted to the FTC now are much different than the powers granted to the FTC in 1935, it would be hard to see how *Humphrey's* survives even in vestigial form.[36]

A related issue foreshadowed by the shadow docket is the executive branch termination of over 1,300 employees of the Department of Education. In *McMahon v. New York*, the government undertook a reduction in force (RIF) involving 1,378 employees.[37] Secretary of Education Linda McMahon said in a press release that the RIF "reflects the Department of Education's commitment to efficiency, accountability, and ensuring that resources are directed where they matter most: to students, parents, and teachers."[38]

In an executive order issued nine days later, President Donald Trump instructed McMahon to "take all necessary steps to facilitate the closure" of the department.[39] On March 21, he announced that programs for students with special needs and the federal student loan portfolio would be transferred from the Department of Education to the Department of Health and Human Services and the Small Business Administration, respectively. The plaintiffs—a group of 19 states led by New York, as well as the District of Columbia, two public school districts, and teachers' unions—went to federal court in Massachusetts, arguing that the RIF violated both the Constitution

[34] *Boyle*, 145 S. Ct. at 2653.

[35] Slaughter v. Trump, No. 25-909 (LLA), 2025 WL 1984396 (D.D.C. July 17, 2025).

[36] *See* Eli Nachmany, *The Original FTC*, 77 ALA. L. REV. (forthcoming 2025) (arguing powers of the FTC far exceed those originally granted and commissioners can now be fired without overruling *Humphrey's Executor*).

[37] *McMahon*, 145 S. Ct. at 2643.

[38] Press Release, Dep't Educ., Department of Education Initiates Reduction in Force (Mar. 11, 2025).

[39] Exec. Order No. 14242, 90 Fed. Reg. 13679 (Mar. 20, 2025).

and the federal laws governing administrative agencies. That court granted an injunction against this administrative action.

The Supreme Court stayed that injunction. It allowed the administration to continue its dismantling of the Department of Education. As the dissent by Justice Sotomayor, joined by Justice Kagan and Justice Jackson, pointed out, the Department of Education was created by Congress by statute and is funded by appropriations. They decried the President's "unilateral efforts to eliminate a Cabinet-level agency established by Congress[.]"[40] The dissent also raised the "take care" clause as being violated, which is rare in the Supreme Court context. The dissent also used Secretary McMahon's own words that her termination of half the staff of the agency was a downpayment on the Executive Order to take all steps to close the agency.[41] This case probably requires further work in the district and appellate courts. It is replete with issues around congressional statutory authorizations, control of the executive-created agencies and even the civil service laws. After all, the employees terminated have resorted to the OPMA and the procedures for wrongful termination. But the concerns of the dissent are not going to go away. It is not clear whether those concerns, unless raised in an emergency context, would garner more than three votes.

Finally, on this issue, while there are no cases on the constitutionality of civil service protections likely to reach the Court this term, it does appear that the first shots have been fired against that system—started by Republican administrations to curtail corruption that had emerged from Jacksonian process—by a Republican administration with great admiration for Jackson.[42]

II. Tariffs of Abominations and Executive Power.

The second cessation crisis this nation faced was over the Tariff of Abominations.[43] This sop to mostly Northern manufacturers included 50 percent tariffs and provoked the nullification crisis,

---

[40] *McMahon*, 145 S. Ct. at 2643 (Sotomayor, J., dissenting).

[41] *Id.* at 2643–44.

[42] Leif Emery, *Echoes of Andrew Jackson: Donald Trump and the Legacy of Populism*, THE SCI. SURV. (Mar. 11, 2025), https://thesciencesurvey.com/editorial/2025/03/11/echoes-of-andrew-jackson-donald-trump-and-the-legacy-of-populism/.

[43] The first was caused by New England's being embargoed and cut off from British Trade and the formation of the Hartford convention. *See generally* Jeremy D. Baily,

which had to be put down by President Jackson with the carrot and stick of reduced tariff legislation and the Force Bill to drive South Carolina into line.[44] The tariff of abominations at least had the virtue of being passed by Congress. And then reduced by Congress. This was done using that now nearly obsolete measure of the nineteenth century—legislation.

The Administration has invoked, by executive orders, the International Emergency Economic Powers Act (IEEPA) to claim that the President can declare a trade deficit and its effects an "emergency" to set tariff rates that conflict with previous international agreements, congressionally set tariff rates, and economic reality. IEEPA authorizes the President to take certain actions after declaring a national emergency and allows certain actions to address that emergency. That statute identifies the permitted actions. It authorizes the President to "investigate, block during the pendency of an investigation, regulate, direct and compel, nullify, void, prevent or prohibit" certain transactions and property.[45] It then identifies the categories of transactions and property the authorized actions may address. Conspicuously absent from this detailed subparagraph is any reference to tariffs, imposts, duties, or taxes. That absence should defeat the President's assertions that IEEPA authorizes tariffs because, since after *Loper Bright* silence cannot be construed as a delegation of authority to the executive.[46]

Nonetheless, the Administration, again by executive order, imposed billions of dollars in tariffs on American companies that ship goods from foreign countries into the United States. First on February 1, 2025, using executive orders and declaring various "emergencies" over opioids, near-zero tariffs were increased to 25 percent on Canada, China, and Mexico.[47] On April 2, 2025, no doubt delayed to avoid the conclusion that it was an April Fool's joke, the administration declared "Liberation Day" and immediately

---

The Hartford Convention, BILL OF RTS. INST., https://billofrightsinstitute.org/essays/the-hartford-convention (last visited Aug. 26, 2025).

[44] Michele Metych, *Tariff of 1828*, BRITANNICA, https://www.britannica.com/topic/Tariff-of-1828 (last visited Aug. 26, 2025).

[45] 50 U.S.C. § 1702(a)(1)(B).

[46] Loper Bright Enters. v. Raimondo, 603 U.S. 369 (2024).

[47] The reader may be forgiven for missing the great opioid crisis emanating from the Great White North.

imposed the shackles of 10 percent "reciprocal" tariffs on all Americans importing from abroad with higher tariffs on 57 other countries' goods. These tariffs were sometimes paused and sometimes not in a bewildering series of moves, confusing all Americans trying to plan imports and make a business plan for the year.

Large corporations were strangely quiet, as were large law firms. With one exception, big firms and businesses stayed out. The first case to be filed against the unlawful tariffs was *Emily Ley* in the Northern District of Florida. Initially challenging the original tariffs but amended to cover "Liberation Day" tariffs, this case was followed in short order by two cases filed in the Court of International Trade (CIT) by V.O.S. Selections and a coalition of states lead by Oregon, represented by the Liberty Justice Center and the Oregon Solicitor General.[48] A small single practitioner filed on behalf of some Black Feet Indians in Montana.[49] PLF filed a case representing four small businesses in the CIT titled *Princess Awesome, LLC v. United States Customs and Border Protection*, which, like Emily Ley Paper, was subsequently stayed pending V.O.S. and Oregon.[50]

And California sued in California.[51] In the exception that proves the rule, Akin Gump filed in the D.C. district court for its client *Learning Resources*.[52] It quickly became apparent that the Justice Department preferred the CIT as the exclusive venue for its case largely because of a 1970s case from a court that doesn't exist anymore.[53] It moved to transfer all cases filed anywhere but the CIT to that court.

The Administration suffered losses in both the CIT and in D.C. In a textbook originalist and textualist opinion, Judge Rudolph Contreras

---

[48] Complaint, V.O.S. Selections, Inc. v. United States, 772 F. Supp. 3d 1350 (Ct. Int'l Trade 2025); Complaint, Oregon v. United States, 772 F. Supp. 3d 1350 (Ct. Int'l Trade 2025).

[49] Webber v. U.S. Dep't of Homeland Sec., No. 25-26-GF-DLC, 2025 WL 1207587 (D. Mont. Apr. 25, 2025).

[50] Princess Awesome, LLC v. U.S. Customs and Border Prot., 1:25-cv-00078 (Ct. Int'l Trade filed Apr. 24, 2025).

[51] California v. Trump, No. 25-CV-03372-JSC, 2025 WL 1569334, at *1 (N.D. Cal. June 2, 2025).

[52] NCLA has recently filed another case in the Western District of Texas on behalf of Texas importers and board game association. Complaint, FIREDISC, Inc. v. Trump, *supra* note 10.

[53] Yoshida Int'l, Inc. v. United States, 378 F. Supp. 1155 (Cust. Ct. 1974) (upholding President Nixon's temporary tariffs under the Trading With the Enemies Act (TWEA)).

found that IEEPA is not a tariff statute, and so district courts, not the CIT, had jurisdiction. While he granted plaintiffs summary judgment and an injunction, which halted the collection of tariffs from those plaintiffs, he stayed the order while the D.C. Circuit could address it.[54] The CIT found exclusive jurisdiction in itself but ruled against all of the tariffs as failing to "deal with an unusual and extraordinary threat" and thus not allowed by the language of IEEPA, striking the tariffs down *in toto*.[55]

The only tariff case to make it in any way shape or form to the Supreme Court thus far is that of *Learning Resources*.[56] The Question Presented is whether "IEEPA authorizes the President to impose tariffs." Learning Resources and hand2mind are companies that import materials from China and turn them into educational toys. The Plaintiffs were affected by these EOs, so they challenged the tariffs. The district court granted Plaintiffs' motion for a preliminary injunction that prevented the collection of the tariffs against the Plaintiffs, but then the District Court stayed its order in light of a more sweeping injunction against the tariffs ordered by the CIT in *V.O.S. Selections v. Trump*.

One of these tariff cases and maybe more are bound for the Supreme Court this Term. Whether or not the *Learning Resources* petition is granted, another will be. That is because the government is highly unlikely to win anywhere. The importance of tariffs to the administration and its going to the CIT, which has in its first order struck down every tariff in the country, means that the Solicitor General must petition for *certiorari*.

Not only are these decisions important to the administration, but they also affect nearly every American and the economy in such a massive way that it is virtually impossible for the Court to duck the issue. If, as is probable, the D.C. Circuit and other circuits differ from the Federal Circuit on who has jurisdiction, that will provide another powerful reason to take the case. One way or another the case will be before the Supreme Court this Term.

[54] *Learning Res., Inc.*, 2025 WL 1525376 at *15–16, *appeal filed*, No. 25-5202 (D.C. Cir. 2025).

[55] *V.O.S. Selections*, 772 F. Supp. 3d at 1382-83.

[56] Petition for Writ of Certiorari, Learning Res., Inc. v. Trump, No. 24-1287 (June 17, 2025).

The Court is almost certainly going to strike the tariffs down as unlawful. Not only have four different lower court judges from wildly different backgrounds and outlooks found them so, but an originalist and textualist Court is not going to toss out a method of statutory analysis painstakingly built over decades to affirm these tariffs. The government will lean hard on national security and foreign policy interests. So did the Truman administration in the Steel Seizure cases.[57] It did not work then and it will not work now, when the emergency is not Communists pouring into South Korea but Koreans pouring too many affordable goods into America.

III. Transgender, Equal Protection, and the First Amendment.

"Girls will be boys and boys will be girls. It's a mixed up, muddled up, shook up world" except perhaps for the Supreme Court on a host of gender issues. There are at least four cases on the horizon where the Supreme Court will wade into the area it touched on in last term's *United States v. Skrmetti*.[58]

In *Little v. Hecox*, the question presented is "Whether laws that seek to protect women's and girls' sports by limiting participation to women and girls based on sex violate the Equal Protection Clause of the Fourteenth Amendment."[59] But the facts paint a far more vivid picture of what is involved. In March 2020, Idaho enacted a categorical ban on the participation of transgender women and girls in women's student athletics. The ban also included a sex-verification process whereby any individual can dispute the sex of any student athlete and require the athlete to undergo gynecological exams to confirm the athlete's sex. No such process exists for male sports. Transgender and cisgender athletes challenged the ban and the sex verification as a violation of the Equal Protection Clause. The Ninth Circuit held that heightened scrutiny was triggered on the bases of sex *and* transgender status, leaving the plaintiffs likely to succeed on the merits of their equal protection claims for the purposes of a preliminary injunction.[60]

---

[57] Youngstown Sheet & Tube Co. v. Sawyer, 343 U.S. 579, 584 (1952).

[58] 145 S. Ct. 1816 (2025).

[59] Petition for Writ of Certiorari at i, Litte v. Hecox, No. 24-38 (July 11, 2024), *cert. granted*, No. 24-38, 2025 WL 1829165 (U.S. July 3, 2025).

[60] *Hecox*, 104 F.4th at 1068 (9th Cir. 2024).

This is one of the most politically contentious cases of the Term since it will involve determining whether transgender people are a discrete and insular minority for the purposes of the tiers of scrutiny. This will determine the permissible degree of latitude Congress and the states may undertake on the basis of this status. Even if transgender people are not a discrete and insular minority, the Court will have to determine a way to analyze how laws against transgender athletes changes the metes and bounds of suspect discrimination on the basis of sex. The inspection of young women or girls' sex organs on the accusation of a teammate is likely to raise objections on a host of grounds. Some Justices have already signaled they are in no mood to create new protected classes, but the Court as a whole has not weighed in on the matter.[61]

West Virginia v. B.P.J. addresses gender identity in the context of Title IX. The QPs here are: "Whether Title IX prevents a state from consistently designating girls' and boys' sports teams based on biological sex determined at birth," and "Whether the Equal Protection Clause prevents a state from offering separate boys' and girls' sports teams based on biological sex determined at birth."[62] The facts are that B.P.J. is a 14-year-old biological male who has publicly identified as a girl since the third grade and takes medicine to stave off the onset of male puberty. B.P.J. has also begun to receive hormone therapy with estrogen. B.P.J.'s mother, Heather Jackson, went to federal court when the principal at B.P.J.'s middle school told the family that her daughter would not be allowed to participate on the girls' sports teams because of a West Virginia law "banning girls who are transgender from participating on all girls' sports teams from middle school through college." The Fourth Circuit held that the statute's definition of a person's sex was a facial classification based on gender identity subject to intermediate scrutiny under the Equal Protection Clause and violated Title IX as applied to the student-plaintiff.[63] Even if transgender people are not a discrete and insular minority, the Court will have to determine how to determine how

---

[61] *Skrmetti*, 145 S. Ct. at 1850 (Barrett, J., concurring).

[62] Petition for Writ of Certiorari at i, West Virginia v. B.P.J., No. 24-43 (July 11, 2024), *cert. granted* No. 24-43, 2025 WL 1829164 (U.S. July 3, 2025).

[63] *B.P.J.*, 98 F.4th at 550.

laws against transgender athletes changes the metes and bounds of suspect discrimination on the basis of sex.

It seems unlikely that the current court is going to create a "discrete and insular" minority comprising people who actually claim sex is *not* an immutable characteristic. The specter of *Bostock* haunts these cases, probably unnecessarily.[64] That case, decided under Title VI and involving employment discrimination, did not touch on natural physical differences between men and women or personal spaces. It is likely the Court will decide the cases on rational basis and affirm them, except on different grounds—the intimate inspection of private parts.

In *Chiles v. Salazar* the Court takes up the First Amendment in the medical context. That context, however, involves gender dysphoria. The question presented is "Whether a law that censors certain conversations between counselors and their clients based on the viewpoints expressed regulates conduct or violates the Free Speech Clause."[65] Colorado passed a law called the Minor Conversion Therapy Law (MCTL). The MCTL prevents licensed social workers, therapists, counselors, and psychotherapists from engaging in conversion therapy (defined by the statute as practice or treatment aimed at changing the client's sexual orientation or gender identity) with clients under the age of 18. Chiles, a licensed counselor and practicing Christian, offers services that help her clients, as Chiles claims, "overcome," "reduce," or "eliminate" unwanted sexual attractions or disharmony. She challenged the MCTL. The Tenth Circuit held that Colorado's MCTL regulated professional conduct incidentally involving speech, thus not triggering strict scrutiny.[66]

This case represents an opportunity to strengthen free speech by preventing states from clamping down on it just because the speech comes from a licensed professional. A license should not alter a person's constitutional right to speak their mind according to their conscience. The Tenth Circuit's disposition of this case deepens a circuit split between the Eleventh and Third Circuits, which do not

---

[64] Bostock v. Clayton Cnty., 590 U.S. 644, 656 (2020).

[65] Petition for Writ of Certiorari, Chiles v. Salazar, No. 24-539 (Nov. 8, 2024), *cert. granted*, 145 S. Ct. 1328 (2025).

[66] Chiles v. Salazar, 116 F.4th 1178 (10th Cir. 2024).

treat counseling conversations as conduct, and the Ninth Circuit, which does.[67] It is likely to be highly controversial, as the LGBT community has not only had bad experiences with conversion therapy of this type but also a lot of success in having it criminalized. They may see it not as a free speech issue but one of animus and discrimination. The case may also have an impact on laws that prohibit telehealth or require doctor visits. If medicine is not being prescribed and the treatment is only talk, it may be difficult to defend those laws if *Chiles* turns out to be a strong win for professional free speech.

Finally, the issue of gender dysphoria in the military may come back to the Court this Term. In *United States v. Shilling*, the Court granted a stay against a district court's preliminary injunction against the military's ban on those with gender dysphoria in the military.[68] Seven current transgender members of the armed forces, along with one transgender person who would like to join the military and a nonprofit with similarly situated members, went to federal court to challenge the new policy. The lead plaintiff in the case, Commander Emily Shilling, has been a naval aviator for nearly two decades, and she estimates that the Navy has spent $20 million on her training. Whether this case gets to the Court this term may well turn on how many facts the parties wish to develop in district court as well as expert opinions. Whether or not the Court takes this one, the other three it has taken will be closely watched by the entire civil rights community.

IV. Voting Rights, Political Parties, Redistricting and Spending as Speech

The blockbuster, no holds barred, political and voting case of the year will be *Louisiana v. Catllais*. Not since Elbridge Gerry was redistricting Massachusetts has a district-drawing case been this anticipated. Not only was the case already contentious and portentous, but over the summer the Court asked the parties to brief a new issue. But let's lay the groundwork.

---

[67] NCLA had a case against California for a similar law that prevented doctors from recommending certain treatments for Covid-19 to their patients. After an injunction was entered the law was repealed. Hoeg v. Newsom, 728 F. Supp. 3d 1152, 1155 (E.D. Cal. 2024).

[68] *Shilling*, 221 L. Ed. 2d at 962.

In response to the 2020 census, Louisiana's legislature adopted a congressional map in 2022 that included only one majority-Black district out of the six allotted to the state, even though roughly one-third of the state's population is Black. A group of Black voters went to federal court, where they argued that the 2022 map violated Section 2 of the federal Voting Rights Act (VRA), which prohibits election practices that result in a denial or abridgement of the right to vote based on race, because it diluted the votes of Black residents. A federal district court threw out the 2022 map. It agreed with the voters that the map likely violated Section 2, and, for that reason, barred the state from using the map for congressional elections and instructed it to draw a new map with a second majority-Black district. The U.S. Court of Appeals for the 5th Circuit upheld that ruling and ordered Louisiana to draw a new map by January 15, 2024, or face the prospect of a trial, after which the district court could adopt a new map for the 2024 elections. In response, the Louisiana legislature enacted a new map. That map, known as S.B. 8, created a second majority-Black district—the 6th District—that stretches across Louisiana from Baton Rouge in the southeast corner of the state to Shreveport in the northwest corner. The adoption of S.B. 8 led to the lawsuit in this case, brought by a group of voters who describe themselves as "non-African American." They contended that the map was an unconstitutional racial gerrymander—that is, it sorted voters based primarily on their race. A three-judge federal district court agreed and barred the state from using the map in upcoming elections.[69]

The Supreme Court last year put the lower court's decision on hold, which allowed Louisiana to use the new map during the 2024 elections. Rep. Cleo Fields, who had been a member of Congress for two terms during the 1990s until his district was redrawn, was elected to represent the 6th District. Both the state and the Black voters who had challenged the 2022 map appealed the three-judge district court's ruling to the Supreme Court, which heard oral arguments in the case in March. Now it appears that the Justices will hear oral arguments once again in the fall, with a decision likely to follow sometime in 2026.

[69] Callais v. Landry, 732 F. Supp. 3d 574 (W.D. La. 2024).

The original QPs were: (1) Whether the majority of the three-judge district court in this case erred in finding that race predominated in the Louisiana legislature's enactment of S.B. 8; (2) whether the majority erred in finding that S.B. 8 fails strict scrutiny; (3) whether the majority erred in subjecting S.B. 8 to the preconditions specified in *Thornburg v. Gingles*; and (4) whether this action is non-justiciable. On August 1, 2025, the Supreme Court directed the parties to address a question raised by the Appellees: "Whether the State's intentional creation of a second majority-minority congressional district violates the Fourteenth or Fifteenth Amendments to the U.S. Constitution."[70]

Before addressing the likely outcome, we should return to the Turtle Band of Chippewa Indians in North Dakota mentioned earlier. As noted, a stay of the Eighth Circuit's decision that Title 2 of the VRA does not provide for a private right of action even under 28 U.S.C. 1983. The QP was "[w]hether the Supreme Court should stay an appeals court mandate stating that private plaintiffs cannot rely on 42 U.S.C. § 1983 to file suit under Section 2 of the Voting Rights Act."[71] The Turtle Mountain Band of Chippewa Indians, the Spirit Lake Tribe, and three Native American individuals brought this lawsuit in federal court in North Dakota against North Dakota's Secretary of State. They contended that a state legislative map adopted in 2021 diluted the voting power of Native Americans in violation of Section 2. The 2021 map had eliminated two of the three legislative districts in the northeastern part of North Dakota in which Native American voters had the ability to elect their own candidates. The District Court agreed that the 2021 map violated Section 2. The District Court gave the state just over a month to propose a new map that would correct the violation; when it did not do so, Judge Peter Welte instructed the state to adopt a map created by the plaintiffs. North Dakota used that map in the November 2024 elections, leading to the election of three Native American legislators. North Dakota appealed to the Eighth Circuit, which overturned the District Court's decision. The court of appeals ruled that private plaintiffs, like the tribes and the voters, cannot use federal civil rights laws to bring lawsuits alleging violations of Section 2. And under a 2023 decision by the same

---

[70] Louisiana v. Callais, No. 24-109, 2025 WL 2180226, at *1 (U.S. Aug. 1, 2025).

[71] *See* Application for Stay, Turtle Mountain Band of Chippewa Indians v. Howe, No. 25A62 (July 15, 2025).

court, the majority noted, private plaintiffs cannot bring a lawsuit directly under Section 2. After the full Eighth Circuit declined to reconsider the case, the plaintiffs filed a petition with SCOTUS to stay the Eighth Circuit's ruling. The plaintiffs argued that unless the court intervened, one of the plaintiffs—who was elected to the state's legislature in 2024—could become ineligible to serve because she does not live in the 2021 map's version of her district. Moreover, they added, if the Eighth Circuit's decision is allowed to stand, the plaintiffs will "face irreparable harm if a decidedly unlawful map governs the 2026 election." On July 16, Justice Kavanaugh granted their request for an administrative stay – an order temporarily blocking the implementation of the Eighth Circuit's decision to give the Justices time to consider the plaintiffs' request.

As this case demonstrates, there is a way the Supreme Court could avoid holding that the VRA's requirement of majority-minority districts is unconstitutional because it does not survive strict scrutiny. The Court could hold that neither Section 2 nor Section 1983 allows a private right of action. This would leave the VRA to be enforced by the Attorney General. But that would simply kick the can down the road until the Attorney General decided to bring a case under Section 2.

The conundrum is that the Court has gone very far in excising race as a consideration in legislation, whether it helps racial minorities or not.[72] The Voting Rights Act was passed at a time when nobody thought Whites would elect Blacks or that Blacks would elect Whites to protect their interests. Now, however, there are Black legislators elected by majority-White electorates.[73] And Black districts have elected White men to protect their interests.[74]

The long-term interpretation of this statute, passed when the overwhelming numbers of Americans considered themselves White, Black, or Native American, at a time when Asians, Hispanics, and biracial categories were statistical blips, is in flux. One possible way to brief this issue to preserve congressional intent is to note that the Fourteenth and Fifteenth Amendments were passed to overturn

---

[72] Students for Fair Admissions, Inc. v. President & Fellows of Harvard Coll., 600 U.S. 181 (2023).

[73] See, e.g., Senator Tim Scott.

[74] See, e.g., Representative Steve Cohen.

Supreme Court precedent and put the enforcement of those amendments primarily in the hands of Congress—not the Courts.[75] It is likely that three votes exist, certainly Justice Thomas's, to strike down racial gerrymandering. Whether five exist to do so remains to be seen.

While not as earth shattering as a total rework of the VRA would be on redistricting, another closely watched election case is *National Republican Senatorial Committee v. FEC*, concerning the free speech rights on "coordinated expenditures" between political parties and candidates. The question is whether the limits on coordinated party expenditures under federal law[76] violate the First Amendment, either on their face or as applied to party spending in connection with "party coordinated communications" as defined in the Code of Federal Regulations.[77] This is yet another attempt to loosen the strictures of *Buckley v. Valeo*, the landmark case that allowed certain political spending as free speech and not prone to corruption.[78] The case that is most in the crosshairs is *Colorado II.*[79] The instant dispute was filed by the National Republican Congressional Committee (NRSC), then-Sen. J.D. Vance, and former Rep. Steve Chabot, who represented Ohio in the House of Representatives for more than two decades. The challengers contended that the law violates the First Amendment, and they argued that the *Colorado II* decision should no longer apply because the Supreme Court's later cases have "tightened the free-speech restrictions on campaign-finance regulations" while political fundraising and spending have also changed. The Sixth Circuit did not buy the argument, holding FECA's limits on coordinated campaign expenditures were not unconstitutional, either facially or as applied to plaintiffs' "party coordinated communications."[80] If SCOTUS used this as an

---

[75] RANDY E. BARNETT & EVAN D. BERNICK, THE ORIGINAL MEANING OF THE FOURTEENTH AMENDMENT: ITS LETTER AND SPIRIT (2021).

[76] 52 U.S.C. § 30116.

[77] 11 C.F.R. § 109.37 (2006).

[78] Buckley v. Valeo, 424 U.S. 1, 16 (1976).

[79] Fed. Election Comm'n v. Colo. Republican Fed. Campaign Comm., 533 U.S. 431, 432 (2001).

[80] Nat'l Republican Senatorial Comm. v. Fed. Election Comm'n, 117 F.4th 389, 391 (6th Cir. 2024).

opportunity to overturn *Colorado II*, the face of political advertising would be changed, as political parties would spend as much as they want or can to advertise on candidates' behalf and with the inputs of the candidates. Much of the political world now believes the parties have declined partly as a result of campaign finance laws and the inability to coordinate with the parties' candidates. And moreover, it is difficult to see the corruption that emerges from a party helping candidates running on its platform. For these reasons, the strong free speech bent of this Court may rework campaign finance law in advance of the 2028 election.

An even more minor case may have echoes of the aftermath of the 2016 election that may not sit well with some members of the Court. The perennial issue of standing to challenge election rules is before the Court again. An Illinois law requires the counting of mail-in ballots that arrive up to two weeks after Election Day so long as they are postmarked (or certified) by Election Day. Representative Michael Bost and two former presidential electors sued under the Constitution's elections and electors clauses, arguing that the extended ballot receipt deadline unlawfully extends federal election timing beyond what federal law allows.[81] They also invoked candidate-specific injuries, including campaign resource burdens and the alleged dilution of the "accurate vote tally." The Seventh Circuit held that the allegations in the plaintiffs' complaint were not sufficient to establish the injury necessary to confer them with standing.[82] Bost argues that the Seventh Circuit's decision created a circuit split. In support of this, he points to the Eighth Circuit's decision in *Carson v. Simon* (recognizing candidates' interest in accurate vote tallies) and precedents from the U.S. Court of Appeals for the Fifth Circuit like *Texas Democratic Party v. Benkiser* and *Republican National Committee v. Wetzel* (accepting campaign costs as a cognizable injury).[83] Whatever the outcome, it is probably a good idea to clarify these rules before the next presidential election.

---

[81] 2 U.S.C. § 7; 3 U.S.C. § 1.

[82] Bost v. Ill. State Bd. of Elections, 114 F.4th 634 (7th Cir. 2024).

[83] Carson v. Simon, 978 F.3d 1051 (8th Cir. 2020); Tex. Democratic Party v. Benkiser, 459 F.3d 582 (5th Cir. 2006); Republican Nat'l Comm. v. Wetzel, 120 F.4th 200 (5th Cir. 2024).

V. "Born in the U.S.A.": Birthright Citizenship

Last term in *Trump v. CASA*, the Court made law on the extent of equitable powers in the district courts to impose nationwide injunctions.[84] What it did not do is address whether birthright citizenship can be denied to the children of tourists or illegal aliens born in this country. The President issued an executive order stating that those categories of persons born in the U.S. would no longer be considered American citizens at birth.[85] Seizing on the Fourteenth Amendment's directive that only those persons born to parents in the United States "subject to the jurisdiction thereof" would be citizens, the EO denied citizenship papers to the children of visitors and illegal aliens. The breadth of the judicial hostility to this novel proposition can be measured by the fact that no court anywhere has endorsed the administration's position as lawful. In *Trump v. CASA*, the Supreme Court noted at the outset that three widely dispersed district courts had all enjoined the action.[86] As Justice Amy Coney Barrett relates, every appellate court affirmed the injunctions—all on likelihood of success on the merits.[87]

No wonder. Until the Trump era (2015-?) this was considered a settled question. *United States v. Wong Kim Ark* seemed to hold that the only persons born in the U.S. who are not "subject to the jurisdiction thereof" were foreign diplomats' children, those born on ships in port, and tribal members of the Indian sovereignties.[88] Congress adopted nearly identical language to that of the Fourteenth Amendment statutorily for citizenship.

Starting with Professor John Eastman of the Claremont Institute, a theory began to emerge that certain types of American-born people could be denied citizenship.[89] As the Trump era progressed, a "strange new respect" for like theories began to emerge from originalist and

---

[84] Trump v. CASA, Inc., 145 S. Ct. 2540 (2025).

[85] *Id.* at 2549.

[86] *Id.*

[87] *Id.*

[88] United States v. Wong Kim Ark, 169 U.S. 649, 681 (1898).

[89] John Eastman, *Birthright Citizenship Is Not Actually in the Constitution*, N.Y. TIMES (Dec. 22, 2015, 11:59 AM), https://www.nytimes.com/roomfordebate/2015/08/24/should-birthright-citizenship-be-abolished/birthright-citizenship-is-not-actually-in-the-constitution.

libertarian academics.[90] A prominent jurist with Supreme Court aspirations began to walk back his previous writings on the subject.[91]

Be that as it may, the judiciary has stood like a stone wall against this new theory, as the proceedings in *Trump v. CASA* demonstrate. We know without doubt that the three dissenters in *CASA*, Sotomayor, Kagan, and Jackson, will rule against the administration when the issue next emerges. That means only two other Justices are needed to thwart this executive action. I cannot imagine that Chief Justice Roberts, Justice Kavanaugh, or Justice Barrett will have any different views. Justices Thomas and Alito may harbor the belief that Congress could change the law on these categories of Americans under its authority over the Fourteenth Amendment, but they are not likely to hold that the President can do so through an EO.

Given that there appears no way to get a circuit split under current law and circumstances, or even a dissent, the Court does not have to take the case.[92] This is a high priority for the administration and, like tariffs, the S.G.'s hand may be forced to petition for *certiorari*. If this case is taken by the Court, it will be to rebuke the administration for breaking with all American jurisprudence on the issue since *Dred Scott*. If they do not take it, they will be doing the administration a favor.

VI. "Money, Money, Money": The Spending Clause and Budgeting.

In addition to *McMahon v. Doe*, which had the added issue of employee termination of civil service protected individuals, there are a host of cases running through the pipeline on whether and under

---

[90] Randy E. Barnett & Ilan Wurman, *Birthright Citizenship*, VOLOKH CONSPIRACY (Feb. 18, 2025, 11:21 AM), https://reason.com/volokh/2025/02/18/birthright-citizenship/.

[91] *Cf.* James C. Ho, *Defining "American": Birthright Citizenship and the Original Understanding of the 14th Amendment*, 9 THE GREEN BAG 367, 367 (Summer 2006), https://www.gibsondunn.com/wp-content/uploads/documents/publications/Ho-DefiningAmerican.pdf; Josh Blackman, *An Interview with Judge James C. Ho*, VOLOKH CONSPIRACY (Nov. 11, 2024, 8:00 AM), https://reason.com/volokh/2024/11/11/an-interview-with-judge-james-c-ho/.

[92] A week after U.S. District Judge Sorokin declined to narrow a nationwide injunction blocking Trump's birthright citizenship Executive Order, the First Circuit appears poised to rule against the President. *See* Chris Villani, *1st Circ. Doubtful Of Trump's Stance On Birthright Citizenship*, LAW360 (Aug. 1, 2025, 7:26 PM), https://www.law360.com/articles/2372304/1st-circ-doubtful-of-trump-s-stance-on-birthright-citizenship.

what circumstances the executive can cut off spending to recipients of grant or other spending programs. The administration has hinted at taking a run at the impoundment cases and the Impoundment Control Act of 1974, passed during the Nixon presidency. There has been severe criticism of the various efforts of the executive's attempts not to spend money in the face of congressional direction to do so.[93] It is not clear, however, how it will get to the Supreme Court at this time. The President has actually used the Impoundment Control Act to rescind nine billion dollars of spending with congressional approval. This eliminates some USAID and PBS related cases issues. Currently Judge Royce Lamberth in the D.C. District Court has restored funds to Voice of America by injunction.[94] As discussed, the Supreme Court has allowed cuts to the Department of Education thus far.[95]

In *Department of Education v. California,* the Court stayed the lower court's grant of an injunction to plaintiffs against cutting off millions of dollars for Diversity, Equity, and Inclusion (D.E.I.) programs.[96] At issue in the case are two grant programs intended to address a nationwide shortage of teachers. The Department of Education canceled all but five of the 109 grants after reviews found "objectionable" diversity and equity training material in the recipient programs. Eight states, led by California, filed a lawsuit in federal court in Massachusetts in early March. They contended that universities and nonprofits in their states had received grants through the programs, and that the Department of Education had violated the federal law governing administrative agencies when it ended those grants. A federal district judge issued a temporary order that required the government to reinstate the grants that it had terminated in the states bringing the lawsuit. U.S. District Judge Myong Joun also prohibited the government from implementing other terminations in those states. The First Circuit declined to put the district court's order on hold while the government appealed, but it fast-tracked the

---

[93] Ilya Somin, *Trump's Attempt to Usurp Congress's Spending Power,* VOLOKH CONSPIRACY (Jan. 28, 2025, 5:22 PM), https://reason.com/volokh/2025/01/28/trumps-attempt-to-usurp-congresss-spending-power/.

[94] Widakuswara v. Lake, 779 F. Supp. 3d 10 (D.D.C. 2025).

[95] *McMahon,* 145 S. Ct. at 2643

[96] Dep't of Educ. v. California, 145 S. Ct. 966 (2025).

appeal itself.[97] This issue has the added fillip of whether D.E.I. programs violate the law or the Constitution, but the issue of unilateral halts to spending still lurks within the case.

Also somewhat related is the now perennial question of student loans. In *Department of Education v. Career Colleges & Schools of Texas*, the Court has taken the question of "Whether the court of appeals erred in holding that the Education Act does not permit the assessment of borrower defenses to repayment before default, in administrative proceedings, or on a group basis."[98] The Department of Education issued a regulation in 2022 that expanded the "borrower defense" rule, making it easier for student loan borrowers to seek loan discharges if they were misled or harmed by their schools. The rule introduced broader definitions of misconduct, allowed group claims, and created mechanisms for the Department to recoup funds from schools. The Career Colleges and Schools of Texas (CCST), representing for-profit institutions, challenged the rule in federal court, arguing it exceeded the Department's statutory authority and violated due process. The Fifth Circuit held that the plaintiff was likely to succeed on the merits, ordering a nationwide injunction against the rule.[99] This case is somewhat related to the Court's decision in *Biden v. Nebraska*, where it struck down a student loan forgiveness program under the Major Questions doctrine.

VII. Potpourri for $500, Alex: Low Key Cases for Liberty Lovers

There are a few cases that seem relatively minor but may stake out positions important to liberty. In *Landor v. Department of Corrections*, the Court will determine whether the Religious Land Use and Institutionalized Persons Act (RLUIPA) provides for money damages against prison officials who violate it.[100] In this case, Rastafarian inmate Damon Landor alleges that he was handcuffed to a chair and two prison guards shaved his head causing him to break the "Nazarite Vow" not to cut hair commanded by his religion.

---

[97] California v. U.S. Dep't of Educ., 132 F.4th 92 (1st Cir. 2025).

[98] Petition for a Writ of Certiorari at i, Dep't of Educ. v. Career Colls. & Schs. of Tex., No. 24-413 (Oct. 10, 2024), *cert. granted sub nom.*, 145 S. Ct. 1039 (2025).

[99] Career Colls. & Schs. of Tex. v. Dep't of Educ., 98 F.4th 220 (5th Cir. 2024).

[100] Landor v. La. Dep't of Corrs. & Pub. Safety, No. 23-1197, 2025 WL 1727386 (U.S. June 23, 2025).

Noem v. Doe stayed a lower court's order that the Secretary of Homeland Security could not revoke a categorical grant of parole to more than half a million noncitizens from certain countries without a case-by-case adjudication.[101] If this reaches the Supreme Court again this Term it may clarify whether mass amnesties granted by one President can be revoked by another President in like manner, or if that grant created some kind of due process rights in the noncitizens in their status.

In *Villarreal v. Texas*, the Court will address a vexing question of whether prohibitions on counsel discussing a criminal defendant's testimony with him during an overnight recess are constitutional.[102] This prohibition has always struck me as problematic, but it is not clear how it will come out.

In *Case v. Montana*, the Court will determine a Fourth Amendment case.[103] The question is whether law enforcement can make a warrantless search of a home on less than probable cause to believe that an emergency is occurring, or whether the emergency-aid exception requires probable cause. There is concern that the exception may swallow the rule if not cabined by the Supreme Court.

Conclusion

I will conclude with what is unlikely to reach the Court this year. The TikTok ban. Last year the Court (over Cato's spirited objection) upheld the law mandating that TikTok could not be controlled by the Communist Party of China.[104] The President has refused to enforce this bipartisan law upheld 9-0 by the Supreme Court. Non-enforcement of law remains the most difficult problem to attack via appeals to the Supreme Court. As usual, however, the Supreme Court is going to be in the thick of current American social and political affairs. The administration's aggressive agenda on transgender issues, tariffs, and immigration issues, as well as its strong "unitary executive" bent will press the Court all Term and leave us all eagerly anticipating the first Monday in October.

---

[101] *Noem*, 145 S. Ct. at 1524.

[102] Villarreal v. Texas, 145 S. Ct. 1897 (2025).

[103] Case v. Montana, No. 24-624, 2025 WL 1549773 (U.S. June 2, 2025).

[104] TikTok Inc. v. Garland, 145 S. Ct. 57 (2025).

Contributors

Thomas A. Berry directs the Cato Institute's Robert A. Levy Center for Constitutional Studies and edits the *Cato Supreme Court Review*. Before joining Cato, he litigated at the Pacific Legal Foundation and clerked for Judge E. Grady Jolly of the U.S. Court of Appeals for the Fifth Circuit. His research focuses on the separation of powers, executive appointments, and the First Amendment. Berry's academic work has appeared in journals such as *The Georgetown Journal of Law & Public Policy, NYU Journal of Law & Liberty,* and the *Washington & Lee Law Review,* and his op-eds have appeared in such outlets as the *Wall Street Journal, USA Today, CNN.com,* the *National Law Journal,* the *National Review Online, Reason.com,* and *The Hill.* He has testified before Congress on the Appointments Clause and his analysis of the Federal Vacancies Reform Act has been cited by federal courts. Berry earned his J.D. from Stanford Law School, where he was a senior editor of the *Stanford Law & Policy Review* and a Bradley Student Fellow in the Stanford Constitutional Law Center, and a B.A. from St. John's College.

Anya Bidwell is a senior attorney at the Institute for Justice and leads IJ's project on Immunity and Accountability. She works to ensure government officials are held accountable when they violate constitutional rights and serves as an adviser on the American Law Institute's Restatement of Constitutional Torts project. Bidwell recently argued *Gonzalez v. Trevino* before the U.S. Supreme Court and has second-chaired cases such as *Martin v. United States, Brownback v. King,* and *Tennessee Wine & Spirits Retailers Association v. Thomas.* Before joining IJ, Bidwell worked for a top national law firm, handling cases in trial and appellate courts. Bidwell grew up in Ukraine and Kyrgyzstan, came to the United States on a scholarship at age 16, and went on to earn her master's degree in global policy studies and a J.D. with honors from the University of Texas. Her work has been featured in numerous publications, including the *Washington Post,* the *Wall Street Journal*, the *New York Times*, *USA Today*, and the *Guardian*. She is also a host of IJ's *Short Circuit* podcast and a co-producer on IJ's documentary-style podcast *Bound by Oath*.

Charles Brandt is a litigation fellow at the Pacific Legal Foundation, where he works in the Separation of Powers Practice Group. Brandt recently wrapped up his tenure at the Cato Institute's Center for Constitutional Studies, where, as a Legal Associate, he contributed to *amicus* briefs for the Supreme Court's 2024-2025 Term. Brandt is an avid writer who has published legal commentary in the *Wall Street Journal*, the *Washington Examiner*, and *Reason* (among others). His academic work has also appeared in the *Federal Circuit Bar Journal*. In 2020, Brandt received his B.A., cum laude, in economics from the University of Maryland, College Park. In 2024, he received his J.D. with honors from the George Washington University Law School. At GW Law, Brandt sat on the *Federal Circuit Bar Journal*, represented clients in the school's FOIA clinic, and served as a Shapiro Public Interest Fellow. He was also active in the Federalist Society—serving as the GW chapter's Executive Vice President from 2023 to 2024.

Matthew P. Cavedon is the director of the Cato Institute's Project on Criminal Justice, where he focuses on reforming plea-driven mass adjudication, ensuring police accountability, and defending constitutional criminal originalism. Cavedon's scholarship has been published (or is forthcoming) in such publications as the *Arizona State Law Journal*, *Seattle University Law Review*, and *Georgetown Journal of Law & Public Policy*, and he has taught courses on criminal law and procedure at law schools. Cavedon previously served as a Georgia public defender and a fellow at the Institute for Justice, and he clerked for both a U.S. district court judge and the Supreme Court of Georgia. He joined Cato following a fellowship at the Emory University Center for the Study of Law and Religion. Cavedon received his A.B., cum laude, from Harvard College and a J.D. and M.T.S. from Emory University.

Cynthia Crawford is senior policy counsel at the Americans for Prosperity Foundation, where she focuses on regulatory issues, freedom of expression, and educational freedom. Crawford previously worked as senior litigation counsel with the Cause of Action Institute, where she focused on defending clients against government overreach, with an emphasis on constitutionally protected individual rights. She also worked in private practice, doing complex business litigation with Nixon Peabody LLP and LeClairRyan. Crawford holds a J.D. and an M.A. in American government from Georgetown University, an M.B.A. from Cornell University's Johnson School of Management, and a B.A. in applied mathematics from the University of California, Berkeley.

Vera Eidelman is a senior staff attorney with the American Civil Liberties Union's Speech, Privacy, and Technology Project. Her practice focuses on protecting free speech and privacy rights in the digital age, including the rights of protesters and young people, online speech, and genetic privacy. Eidelman has litigated a constitutional challenge to anti-protest laws in *Dakota Rural Action v. Noem*, the right to write, publish, and distribute books in *In re Gender Queer and A Court of Mist and Fury*, and a challenge to nonconsensual faceprinting in *ACLU v. Clearview AI*. Eidelman has briefed cases before the U.S. Supreme Court, including *Mckesson v. Doe* and *Mahanoy Area School District v. B.L.* Previously, Eidelman was a William J. Brennan fellow at the ACLU, and she holds degrees from Stanford University and Yale Law School. Before joining the ACLU, she clerked for Judge Beth Labson Freeman of the U.S. District Court for the Northern District of California.

Patrick Jaicomo is a senior attorney at the Institute for Justice and one of the leaders of IJ's Project on Immunity and Accountability, where he works to dismantle judicially created immunity doctrines and ensure that individual rights are enforceable. Jaicomo has litigated immunity and accountability issues, including qualified immunity, judicial immunity, *Bivens*, and the Federal Tort Claims Act. Four of his cases have reached the U.S. Supreme Court, including the police brutality case *Brownback v. King*, the First Amendment retaliatory arrest case *Gonzalez v. Trevino*, and the similar retaliation case of *Murphy v. Schmitt*. Most recently, Jaicomo argued the FBI wrong-house raid case *Martin v. United States* and secured a unanimous victory from the U.S. Supreme Court in June of 2025. Prior to joining IJ, Jaicomo was a litigator at a private firm in Grand Rapids, Michigan. He earned his J.D. from the University of Chicago and an undergraduate degree from the University of Notre Dame. Jaicomo's work has been featured in numerous publications, including the *New York Times*, the *Wall Street Journal*, the *Washington Post*, and *USA Today*.

Eli Nachmany is an associate in the Washington, D.C., office of Covington & Burling LLP, where he advises clients on antitrust issues, administrative law, and complex civil litigation, with particular expertise in appellate matters. He works across industries, focusing primarily on sports and gaming. Prior to joining Covington, he clerked for Judge Steven J. Menashi of the U.S. Court of Appeals for the Second Circuit and taught an undergraduate sports-management course at New York University. Nachmany has published articles in numerous law reviews and served as editor-in-chief of the *Harvard Journal of Law & Public Policy* and co-editor-in-chief of the *Harvard Journal of Sports & Entertainment Law* while in law school. He earned his J.D., magna cum laude, from Harvard Law School and a B.S. in sports management from New York University.

Hon. Neomi Rao was appointed to the United States Court of Appeals for the District of Columbia Circuit in March 2019. She graduated from Yale College in 1995 and the University of Chicago Law School in 1999. Following graduation, she served as a law clerk to Judge J. Harvie Wilkinson III of the U.S. Court of Appeals for the Fourth Circuit and, in the 2001 October Term, as law clerk to Justice Clarence Thomas of the U.S. Supreme Court. Between her clerkships, Judge Rao served as counsel for nominations and constitutional law to the U.S. Senate Committee on the Judiciary. In 2002, she joined the international arbitration group of Clifford Chance LLP in London, England. From 2005-2006, she served as Special Assistant and Associate White House Counsel to President George W. Bush. From 2006 to 2017, Judge Rao was a professor at the Antonin Scalia Law School at George Mason University, where she taught constitutional law, legislation and statutory interpretation, and the history and foundations of the administrative state. In 2014, she founded the Center for the Study of the Administrative State, a non-profit center that promoted academic scholarship and public policy debates about administrative law. In July 2017, she was appointed to serve as the Administrator of the Office of Information and Regulatory Affairs in the Office of Management and Budget. She served in this position until her appointment to the D.C. Circuit.

Damien M. Schiff is a senior attorney at the Pacific Legal Foundation, where he leads the organization's Environment & Natural Resources practice. He represents landowners and property-rights advocates in high-profile environmental disputes and has argued landmark cases such as *Sackett v. United States Environmental Protection Agency* before the U.S. Supreme Court. Schiff's scholarship, which focuses on the Endangered Species Act and Clean Water Act, has been published in law reviews and newspapers, and he frequently comments on environmental law issues in the national media. He earned his J.D. from the University of San Diego School of Law, graduating magna cum laude, and his undergraduate degree from Georgetown University. Schiff clerked for Judge Victor Wolski of the U.S. Court of Federal Claims.

John J. Vecchione is senior litigation counsel at the New Civil Liberties Alliance, where he represents clients challenging the administrative state. He previously served as president and CEO of Cause of Action Institute and has practiced at several Washington, D.C., law firms, including his own, John J. Vecchione Law PLLC. An experienced trial and appellate advocate, Vecchione focuses on strategic litigation in federal district and appellate courts, including the U.S. Supreme Court. Vecchione was Counsel of Record for the Relentless Petitioners in the landmark case *Loper Bright Enterprises, Inc. v. Raimondo* and in *Relentless, Inc. v. Department of Commerce*. Vecchione's commentary has appeared in outlets such as *The Wall Street Journal* and *The Washington Times*.

Larissa M. Whittingham is a litigator with in-house, law firm, and trade association experience. In the last two years, Whittingham has been involved in over 35 amicus briefs filed at all levels of the federal court system and multiple state supreme courts. She has written about constitutional reforms in the United States from 2022-2024 and the role of lawyers in responding to moments of constitutional crisis.

Charles T. Yates is an attorney in the Pacific Legal Foundation's Environment & Natural Resources practice group, where he primarily litigates cases on the Endangered Species Act and the Clean Water Act. Yates was a member of the litigation team for *Sackett v. EPA* at the U.S. Supreme Court. Yates has represented landowners, farmers, ranchers, timber operators, and oil and gas producers as lead counsel before numerous federal trial and appellate courts. In addition to his work as a litigator, he has appeared on a variety of national television and radio programs, has addressed numerous professional and industry gatherings, and has been quoted in numerous media outlets, including the *Associated Press, Reuters, Reason,* the *San Francisco Chronicle,* and *E&E News.* Yates holds a B.A. in political science and international relations from the University of Western Australia and a J.D., magna cum laude, from the University of Baltimore School of Law, where he served as president of his school's chapter of the Federalist Society and was an editor of the *University of Baltimore Law Review.*

Ezra Young is a nationally recognized scholar and attorney based in New York. He maintains a boutique private practice and previously served as a visiting assistant professor at Cornell Law School, where he taught constitutional law, critical race theory, and transgender people and the law. Young's scholarship explores transgender rights and equitable remedies; his work has been widely published and cited by bodies such as the Administrative Conference of the United States and the Congressional Research Service. Young's academic writing has appeared (or is forthcoming) in books and articles published by Routledge, Oxford University Press, the New Press, *American Psychologist, California Law Review Online, Cleveland State Law Review, Jotwell, JURIST,* and *Plastic and Reconstructive Surgery.* He maintains a broad litigation practice representing individuals, nonprofits and governments, including co-litigating landmark transgender rights cases with the U.S. Department of Justice and Equal Employment Opportunity Commission. Young currently serves as board secretary of the African American Policy Forum and is a founding board member and past co-chair of the National Trans Bar Association. Young previously served as legal director of the African American Policy Forum, research director of the Columbia Center for Intersectionality and Social Policy Studies, and director of impact litigation of the Transgender Legal Defense and Education Fund, Inc. Young holds a B.A. in philosophy from Cornell University and a J.D. from Columbia Law School, and he completed postdoctoral studies on trans rights and critical theory at Columbia under Kimberlé Crenshaw.